The

Mystical

Teachings

of

Jesus

From the Heart of Jesus, vol 1

The Mystical Teachings *of* Jesus

KIM MICHAELS

Copyright © 2013 Kim Michaels. All rights reserved. No part of this book may be used, reproduced, translated, electronically stored or transmitted by any means except by written permission from the publisher. A reviewer may quote brief passages in a review.

MORE TO LIFE PUBLISHING

www.morepublish.com

For foreign and translation rights,

contact info@ morepublish.com

ISBN: 978-9949-518-22-7

Series ISBN: 978-9949-518-21-0

The information and insights in this book should not be considered as a form of therapy, advice, direction, diagnosis, and/or treatment of any kind. This information is not a substitute for medical, psychological, or other professional advice, counseling and care. All matters pertaining to your individual health should be supervised by a physician or appropriate health-care practitioner. No guarantee is made by the author or the publisher that the practices described in this book will yield successful results for anyone at any time. They are presented for informational purposes only, as the practice and proof rests with the individual.

For more information: *www.askrealjesus.com*.

CONTENTS

Introduction 3

PART 1 THE INNER MESSAGE

1 | You Know My Voice 13
2 | Progressive Revelation 29
3 | Attaining Christ Consciousness 37
4 | Why Is There Religion in the World? 49
5 | The True Key to Salvation 67
6 | The Problem on Planet earth 81
7 | Understanding Christ Consciousness 97

PART 2 LIBERATING QUESTIONS

8 | Was Jesus Christ the Only Son of God? 121
9 | What Kind of Person Is Jesus? 137
10 | Which Religion Did Jesus Follow? 145
11 | Is There only One True Religion? 151
12 | Is Jesus all Alone in Heaven? 157
13 | Jesus and Reincarnation 163
14 | Did Jesus Remove the Sins of the World? 179
15 | Is the Bible the Word of God? 185
16 | Is God an Angry and Judgmental God? 195
17 | The Question of Evil 211
18 | What about Modern Christianity? 231

PART 3 PERSONAL CHRISTHOOD

19 | How to Attain Christhood 243
20 | Going Within 247
21 | Healing Yourself 261
22 | Techniques for Attaining Christhood 287
23 | The Second Coming of Christ 323
24 | What You Can Do for Jesus 331

INTRODUCTION

Let me briefly explain how this book came about. My parents were not religious people and I was never given what some would call a Christian upbringing. I always had an intuitive sense that Jesus was and is indeed a very significant spiritual figure. The only problem was that I could not reconcile my inner sense of Jesus' importance with the outer teachings and actions of Christianity.

During elementary school I learned about "Bible History," which was focused on the Old Testament. I intuitively sensed that there was a discrepancy between the angry and judgmental God of the Jews and the God I knew in my heart. Later, I learned in history class about the Crusades, the Inquisition and the witch hunts. I knew that such violent actions simply could not be in accordance with the true teachings of Christ, and it left me with a desire to understand how a religion that was based on the teachings of Jesus could turn so violent.

I received no answers to these questions until I was 18 and experienced a process that dramatically changed my view of both Jesus and Christianity. It started when I read that in the year 553 the concept of reincarnation had been removed from Christianity for political reasons. I felt a sense of indignation over the fact that a concept that might have been familiar to

Jesus himself was later removed from the religion that claims to represent him. This started me on a quest that helped me see that many of Jesus' original teachings and intentions have indeed been changed, removed, misinterpreted or even replaced by doctrines that are in almost direct opposition to what Jesus taught.

During the following 20 years I continued to increase my understanding of a shocking fact, namely that there is a very large discrepancy between what Jesus originally taught and the image of Jesus and his teachings that has been handed down by official Christianity for almost 2,000 years. Obviously, this process took me a long time, and I am not expecting anyone to accept my conclusion just because I state it here. However, for those who are open, there are numerous books and websites that talk about this, and I think those who study this material will eventually reach the conclusion that our modern image of Jesus is out of touch with the original.

It was very important for me to realize that there was a difference between my intuitive sense of what Jesus taught and the official image. This opened up a very healing perspective, namely that when the official image contradicted my inner feeling, it might indeed be the official image that was out of touch with reality. To me, this is the difference between those who might benefit from this book and those who will reject it without giving it a closer look.

In today's world, many people have a strong intuitive sense of spiritual principles and many have indeed been disappointed by official Christianity. Many spiritually minded people have rejected Christianity and have consequently rejected Jesus as well—for how do you separate Christ from Christianity? What dawned on me was that Jesus is too significant of a figure in the spiritual life of earth for me to reject him based on a man-made religion. I realized that I could not let the doctrines and actions of Christian churches stand between me and Jesus. I wanted to know Jesus as he really is, not as he has been portrayed by an organization that was too often guided by political motives and expediency.

As Jesus himself said: "ask, and ye shall receive." When I started asking for answers, I found material that helped me gain a deeper understanding of and appreciation for the timeless teachings of Christ. This helped me answer what was for me the greatest question about Jesus, namely why he had suddenly disappeared from the earth 2,000 years ago. I had no problem accepting that Jesus had ascended to the spiritual realm and was still alive there as a spiritual being. Yet why wouldn't he seek to guide us from that position, especially given that he himself had made the promise that he would be with us always? I simply couldn't see Jesus being with us in the official churches so how did he intend to fulfill this promise?

I gradually came to understand that Jesus is indeed with us today and that he has attempted to give us guidance many times over the past 2,000 years. I also saw that because Jesus is now an ascended being, this guidance must be given according to the overall law that determines life on earth, namely the Law of Free Will. The earth is a kind of experience machine in which we human beings are allowed to have certain experiences until we tire of them and decide that we want more. One of the experiences that earth is designed to give us is that we live in a material universe where we are separated from God or where there is no God.

This means that it is completely unrealistic, as some Christians believe, to think that Jesus will soon appear in a second coming that will give undeniable proof. In reality, no undeniable proof can ever be given, as demonstrated by the fact that there were people who rejected Jesus when he walked among them in a physical body. The over-arching law for earth is that plausible deniability must be maintained so that it is always possible for people to deny the existence of the spiritual realm or any guidance or messages coming from that realm.

Jesus has indeed been giving us guidance over the past 2,000 years but it has happened either as a personal inner guidance or it has happened through individual people who served as messengers or "open doors" for his teachings. Jesus will never appear in the sky and give undeniable proof, but he does indeed continually appear through individual people who are open to serving as a bridge for bringing forth teachings in some form or another. The beauty of this scheme is that Jesus can give teachings from his present level of awareness, but because they come through a human being, it is easy for people to find fault with the messenger and use that as an excuse for rejecting the message.

I gradually found various teachings that according to my intuitive discernment seemed to have come directly from a higher realm. By studying such teachings, I continued to expand my understanding of Jesus' inner, mystical teachings, but it never occurred to me that I might become one of these messengers.

That changed in 2002 when I went through a life-changing process. I discovered the spiritual side to life when I was 18 and from then on my life had revolved around the quest for raising my consciousness. A big part of this had been my desire to help transform this planet and bring it closer to a state where some of the atrocities we see have been left behind. I was deeply affected by learning about the Holocaust, war and other shocking forms of evil and I felt a strong desire to help raise the earth to the point where these phenomena could no longer take place here.

Over many years, I had attempted to help raise the collective consciousness by performing spiritual exercises and by raising my own consciousness. In 2002 I came to a point where I recognized that I was not making a difference and I felt a growing sense of frustration. One day I intuitively saw that my frustration was caused by the fact that my spiritual quest had in large part been driven by an ego-based desire to make a difference and do something significant.

After meditating on this for some time, I came to a point where I saw the futility of this. I spontaneously fell to my knees and said out loud: "God, you can take me home right now." At that moment, I felt like I literally gave up all of my human ambitions, expectations and desires and I had nothing left. I was empty. I felt that if I had died at that moment, I could leave behind planet earth with complete peace. There was nothing I wanted to do and nothing I had to do on this planet. I could leave it behind for good, even if it meant I had never done anything of any significance.

I felt as if a giant weight had been lifted from me, and I sensed I was ready to move on. I then felt that a spiritual being approached me, and I became aware that this was the Presence of the ascended being we call Jesus. He sent me an impulse that in my mind became translated to the words: "If you don't have anything you personally want to do on this planet, would you be willing to do something for me?" I felt that from the very core of my being came forth the word: "YES!"

During the following months, Jesus was guiding me through a very intense inner process of looking at and transcending many of the illusions I still had about him, about myself and about how I might serve him here on earth. I was gradually given the vision that Jesus wanted me to create a website where people could submit questions and then he would answer them by dictating the answers through me. This eventually became the *www.askrealjesus.com* website and it has now been up and running since December 24th, 2002. It has had millions of visits and hundreds of questions have been answered by both Jesus and other ascended beings. Recently, the questions and answers have been moved to another website, *www.ascendedmasteranswers.com* and the Jesus website has been focused on helping people claim their highest spiritual potential, namely personal Christhood. The deeper reality about Jesus' mission on earth is that he came to serve as an example that all of us can follow.

During the process of receiving my training to do the website, I one day received the impulse that Jesus wanted to dictate a book through me. I then sat down at my computer, turned on my voice recognition software and started talking, having absolutely no idea what would be said. Over the following nine days I received all of the material in this book. It literally started with chapter one and went all the way through and I hardly had to make any changes. This book contains all of that original material, but in the section on spiritual exercises certain changes have been made because I have now received a very large amount of spiritual exercises.

This book is part of a process called "progressive revelation" in which our spiritual teachers seek to give us teachings adapted to our growth in consciousness. Humankind as a whole has grown in consciousness since the time of Jesus, and many people are ready for a more advanced teaching than he could give 2,000 years ago. In fact, many people are now ready for the teachings that Jesus could only give to his disciples back then, whereas he taught the multitudes in parables.

Again, this teaching is given in accordance with the Law of Free Will, which means it must be easy to deny the teachings. Since the book was first published in 2003, with the title *The Christ Is Born in You*, many people have denounced it and used various arguments for why this could not possibly be the

Introduction

real Jesus. This is as it should be. Yet many more have found the book inspirational and first of all healing.

Many spiritually inclined people have found that the book helped them overcome the wounds they had received as a result of being exposed to official Christianity and its self-assured claim that its doctrines and dogmas should always override our intuitive knowing. May this book also help you make peace with Jesus and discover how much more there is to Jesus as a spiritual teacher than what you might have been told in Sunday school.

PART I
THE INNER MESSAGE

1 | YOU KNOW MY VOICE

My spiritual brothers and sisters know my voice, even when I am speaking through one of their brothers. I am indeed your Jesus, and when I walked the earth, I made a promise that applies to every human being on this planet: "I am with you always, even unto the end of the world."

I am Jesus Christ.

I am offering these teachings because I desire you to know that I have kept that promise and that I intend to keep it in the future. I have been with you always, I am with you now and I will be with you always.

You might wonder why you do not realize or experience that I am with you. The reason is that you have allowed yourself to create a sense of separation from me. If you will read and absorb these teachings, you might realize that the sense of separation exists only in your own mind. I am an unlimited cosmic being, and there are no barriers I cannot cross. Only one thing can separate me from you, and that is your decision to see yourself as separated from me.

I understand that you are concerned about the authenticity of this work. How is it possible that I, the real Jesus Christ, can speak to you through a book?

I am asking you to please consider the situation from my perspective. I know that the human mind is able to question and doubt absolutely anything. Therefore, how could I possibly give you an outer proof of the authenticity of this book? I think an objective evaluation would show you that nothing I could possibly say would constitute such a proof. However, I do not need to give you an outer proof because you have the ability to find an inner proof.

Science has told you that everything in this universe is made of energy. Energy is vibration. Your physical senses are simply instruments that are designed to detect vibrations in the material world. You also have an inner sense which you can use to detect vibrations that are beyond the material world.

The Living Truth that I bring, the Living Truth that I am, is a form of spiritual energy or vibration. If you will silence your analytical mind and go deeply within your heart, you can activate the inner sense that allows you to detect the vibration of spiritual light, spiritual energy. Through this inner sense, you can feel the vibration of the words I am speaking to you through this book. Through your inner sense, you can know that it is, indeed, my voice. You can know that I am the real Jesus Christ and that I am here to call my own.

As you continue to read this book, use your inner sense of the heart. Read this book with your mind, but absorb it with your heart. Your heart will tell you the truth; the Living Truth that I am.

Accept my love

Our Father has given you free will. He has made it a law in Heaven that no one is allowed to violate the free will of a human being. I love my Father, I respect his will, and I respect your will.

1 | You Know My Voice

I love you, and I desire you to experience the fullness of my love for you. Yet if you choose to reject me, to reject my love then I must simply wait until you make a better decision.

However, I do not have to wait in silence. I have the option of speaking through those who have chosen not to reject me. I am the open door, which no human can shut. No human being can turn off the still small voice that speaks in the heart. No one can completely silence my voice. Therefore, if someone decides to listen to his or her inner voice and to acknowledge where that voice comes from, I can speak through that person and describe another facet of the unlimited Being of God. That is how this book was brought into the material universe.

Some people choose to ignore the inner voice, to deny that voice or to make themselves so busy with the things of this world that they have no attention left over for me. Some people have ignored their inner voice for so long that they think they can no longer hear me. Therefore, I must speak to these people through an outer voice that they can hear and read. As you will see later, this is not the way I desire it to be. I want to speak to you directly in your heart, and I want you to be able to hear my voice. I want to have a direct, personal communion with you that no human being or institution can limit or distort.

Therefore, you must not allow these teachings to replace your inner voice. You must use this book only as an inspiration, not as a doctrine. You must let these teachings help you realize that by tuning in to your inner voice, you can hear me directly.

You can commune with me

So many people have allowed themselves to believe that they cannot know or experience me directly, that they must go through some outer organization or doctrine. I am not here to condemn or find fault with any organization or doctrine. Yet I must point out to you that you have the ability to commune with me in your heart.

An outer organization or teaching has one purpose and one purpose only, namely to help you rise to a level of consciousness where you can commune directly with me, your Jesus. If the organization fulfills that purpose, all is well. If it does not then it has shut me out, and therefore it can have no part with me.

Human beings have fallen into a lower state of consciousness, and they need help to get back on their spiritual feet. A person who has fallen and broken a leg might need a set of crutches to learn how to walk again. Before you have learned to walk on your own, you can gain great help and support from using crutches. Yet when you have grown strong and learned to hold your balance, you must decide to take that first step without the crutches. If you insist on holding on to the crutches, you will limit your ability to walk in the Light of my Presence.

There is a way that seems right unto a human, but the ends thereof are the ways of death. The false way is the belief that you can reach me only through someone or something outside yourself.

There is also a straight and narrow way that leads to eternal life. The true way is an inner walk with me. These teachings (as any other teachings about me) are not the way. They are meant to point you towards the inner path of the heart. Open your mind and heart to me, and I will show you the true path.

Follow that path, and you will make it back home to our Father's kingdom, where I am waiting for you with open arms and a heart that overflows with a very personal love for you.

The key to salvation

So many people think that salvation is a process over which they have little or no influence. They think it can happen only through grace or some kind of miracle. I am not saying that salvation does not involve grace. Yet you must understand that, because of the Law of Free Will, no human being can be saved against his or her will. If you are to be saved, you must decide that you are willing to be saved. You must decide that you are worthy to be saved.

Neither God nor I can, or will, make that decision for you. However, I can attempt to inspire you to make that decision, and that is precisely why I am bringing forth these teachings.

William Shakespeare (one of my many messengers) wrote a timeless play about the Prince of Denmark. Hamlet's most famous remark is: "To be, or not to be: that is the question." The inner meaning of that question is that you must choose whether to be who you are or not to be who you are. I hope you will absorb the following teachings and allow them to help you discover who you truly are. I also hope that in the end you will choose more wisely than Prince Hamlet. After all, what is the death of a fictional prince compared to the death of a real being?

In his image and likeness

Many people have read the statement in Scripture that human beings were created in the image and likeness of God. Few people have the courage to consider what this statement truly means.

The barrier to a deeper understanding of this statement is that people tend to reason backwards. They have become self-centered instead of God-centered. They imagine that if God created them in his image then God must be like the human beings they presently know. Most people fail to realize that this is not so.

You were originally created in the image and likeness of God but you are not presently expressing that image. You have, by using your free will in a way that was not intended by God, created a human being that is different from the spiritual being that God created.

What does it truly mean that you were originally created in the image and likeness of God? God is the Creator. To create, you must have two qualities:

- You must have the ability to envision or imagine what you can create. You must be able to imagine your options.

- You must have the ability to choose which one of the options you want to manifest.

God creates by taking his own formless Being and giving it form. God can envision many different forms but, to create anything, God must choose one particular option. God can create a universe in which planets are flat and God can create a universe in which planets are round. However, even God cannot create a universe in which planets are flat and round at the same time because one form excludes the other.

When God created you in his image and likeness, He gave you his own qualities. He gave you imagination and free will. After endowing you with these qualities, God sent you into this particular universe as an extension of himself/herself.

It is extremely important for you to understand that you are not sent here against your free will. You are here because you chose to come here. You are here because your lifestream desired to be a part of God's creation and to express the qualities of God here on this planet.

Unfortunately, many people have forgotten that original desire, that original decision, of their lifestreams. That loss of memory is the only real problem on planet earth!

If you want to escape the prison represented by the limitations of this world then you must restore your original memory of who you are. When you regain that memory, you must decide to express your true identity. However, you cannot express something that you do not know because no one, not God and not a son or daughter of God, can create that which they cannot envision.

I am a spiritual teacher, and I have chosen to remain with this planet out of love for you and your brothers and sisters in Spirit. It is my deepest desire to see you recognize the fullness of who you are as a spiritual being instead of the limited, mortal being that you currently think you are.

Rise above mortality!

How can I possibly help you escape the limited, mortal state of consciousness that is presently entrapping your mind? I must somehow inspire you to look beyond that state of consciousness. Perhaps it might help you to understand why you find yourself in that state of consciousness. Let us consider how a spiritual being, created in the image and likeness of God, could possibly descend into the state of consciousness that is currently dominating life on planet earth.

To understand this mystery of mysteries, you need only recognize that God gave you imagination and free will and that

God did not limit his gifts. God gave you the ability to imagine anything, even things that are different from or in opposition to God's original vision for this universe. God also gave you the ability to choose to believe and create anything you want, even things that are different from or in opposition to God's original vision or will for this universe. In other words, God gave you the ability to create your own reality, even a reality that is different from what God originally envisioned for you.

Many devoutly religious people, be they Christians or non-Christians, look at the atrocities happening all over this planet and find it difficult to understand how God could possibly have created a world like the one they live in. Yet because they are afraid to look beyond a particular outer doctrine, their only option is to reason that God must have willed it so. Some people accept the will of God while others reject God and anything related to God. My beloved hearts, both of these reactions are based on an incomplete understanding of reality. This is another example of human beings using their present state of consciousness to reason backwards and thereby project human qualities upon God.

I am an unlimited cosmic being. I reside in my Father's kingdom. I know my Father and I know his original vision for this creation. God did not desire to have you experience a life dominated by misery, limitations and suffering. When God created planet earth, God envisioned a perfect planet on which lifestreams could grow in understanding of their individuality and in which they could express their creative abilities without limiting themselves or harming others.

Yet you must understand that God respects his own laws. He gave you unlimited imagination and unlimited free will. You have the capacity to imagine that which is limited, that which is not based on love, even that which is dark or evil. You have the ability to choose to focus your attention on imperfection.

1 | You Know My Voice

Yet it is a Law of God that you will create what you allow your attention to dwell upon. If you focus your attention on imperfect forms then you will inevitably begin to create those imperfect forms. The reason being that you create through the power of your imagination and attention.

When God created this universe, the first act of creation was the statement: "Let there be Light!" Light is the basic substance from which everything in this universe is created. God's light is like a lump of clay. God creates by shaping the formless clay into a particular form. God creates by envisioning a particular image and then allowing his light to flow into that image until the light manifests as a material form. You are created in the image and likeness of God. You do not yet have the full creative abilities of God, yet you create the same way God does.

You create by allowing your attention to focus on a particular image. God's light is constantly flowing through your consciousness (or you would not be alive). God's light obediently takes on the form of whatever image your mind is focused upon. If you hold your attention on a particular form for a sufficient period of time, you will manifest that form in your outer world. Hold your image on mortality, limitation and suffering, and you will experience those things in your life. Hold your attention on any imperfect image, and you will manifest imperfection in your life.

The dilemma expressed by Hamlet is meant to illustrate the basic fact that you can never stop creating. Hamlet did not want to act, yet by not acting, he brought about his own death. In their present state of consciousness, many people do not want to create. Yet whether you create consciously or unconsciously, you are still creating. God gave you free will, and you cannot turn off that gift; you cannot stop making choices. If you ignore or deny your ability to create perfection, you are still making a choice. Therefore, choose life! Choose the perfection of God over the imperfection of the lower consciousness. You cannot stop creating, but you can choose what you create.

God did not create imperfection

The basic fact about life on planet earth is that God has not created evil and God has not created imperfection, limitations and suffering. These things were created by human beings. These things manifested in the material world because human beings made the choice to focus their attention on imperfection. For many people this statement might seem brutal, but it seems so only to those who are not willing to take responsibility for their own lives. Throughout history, so many people have desired to blame someone else for their misery. So many people seek to blame other people, be it their parents or the leaders of society, for their situation. The tendency to blame others for your personal situation is simply an attempt to escape personal responsibility and accountability. It is an attempt to justify an unwillingness to change your attitude towards, and your understanding of, life.

What is the ultimate escape from accountability? It is to place blame upon someone that you believe to be beyond your influence. It is to blame an authority figure that you believe is far above yourself. If the authority figure has created your present situation, and if you have no influence over that authority figure then you cannot possibly have any personal responsibility for your situation, can you? So what is the ultimate authority figure upon which human beings can place blame? It is, naturally, God himself.

If God was the one who created your misery then you have no personal accountability and there is nothing you can personally do to change the situation. Therefore, you do not have to change your beliefs or your attitude towards life. You can simply continue to live in the illusion that there is nothing you could possibly do to change yourself, your personal situation or your world.

So many people prefer to think that God has created their misery. They do not want to admit that their situation is self-created and that only they can uncreate it. They do not want to admit this because they do not want to change themselves. It is a fundamental law that you cannot change your world without changing yourself. If you are serious about improving your outer situation, you must begin by changing your inner situation. You must change your understanding of life, your beliefs about life and your attitude towards life.

It is my sincere and loving hope that these teachings will inspire you to go through that personal transformation. If you will allow me to help you, it will be my supreme joy to do so. However, I can help you only if you are willing to let go of ideas and beliefs that are out of touch with reality.

Tough love

I am fully aware that some people have accepted an image of me that will cause them to feel that the real Jesus could not possibly be this direct and outspoken. They have accepted a touchy-feely image of me that has little to do with the real Jesus. I have several comments on this false image.

Over 2,000 years ago, I gave my life to bring forth the same teachings that I have just given you. Those teachings have systematically been distorted and destroyed. If even a small number of people had heeded my original teachings, this planet would have been a very different place today. After having waited for 2,000 years, I simply don't have time for niceties. I do not have time to beat around the bush. This is the time to face reality, and therefore I must give people the truth about their situation.

I am indeed a Master of Love. I have mastered all qualities of love, even tough love. Would it be truly loving to allow people to remain in ignorance and thereby lose their souls?

I think not! I might remind you that 2,000 years ago I said: "I came not to bring peace, but a sword." The sword that I came to bring back then, and that I come to bring again today, is the Sword of Truth which cleaves the real from the unreal. The ultimate lie found on this planet is the belief that human beings have not created their own situation. The ultimate truth is that the limiting conditions found on this planet are entirely the creation of human beings. Therefore, the only way that circumstances could possibly improve is by human beings taking responsibility for their own actions and deciding that they will begin to create perfection instead of continuing to create imperfection.

God never desired to see the misery and suffering found on this planet. God does not desire to see the present conditions continue indefinitely. God desires to see drastic and positive change on this planet. Yet God has given you and everyone else free will, and therefore God cannot bring about positive change unless you decide that you are willing to be the instrument for bringing about that change by focusing your attention on God's perfection instead of continuing to focus your attention on human imperfection.

You cannot serve two masters. You cannot serve God and mammon. You cannot serve God and the Prince of this world. God is perfection and nothing but perfection. Nothing imperfect ever originated from God.

Therefore, the current state of imperfection on earth did not originate from God. God did not create your misery, and therefore you cannot expect that God will somehow whisk it away through some miracle or a mysterious thing called grace. Your personal misery, and all of the imperfections found on this planet, can be removed only by those who created it. It can be removed only when you, and a critical mass of other people, decide to take their attention off imperfection and put it on the perfection of God.

How can you focus on the perfection of God? You must ascend to a level of consciousness higher than the relative, mortal, limited, carnal state of consciousness into which most people have allowed themselves to descend.

I am here to call you up higher. The message I am giving today is the same message I gave 2,000 years ago. The reason I am giving the same message today is that you and most other people have not heeded my original message. This is largely due to the fact that my original message was never made available to the general population. Yet times have changed, and my original message can no longer remain hidden.

What amazes me most about human beings?

If you were to ask me what I find most amazing about human beings, I would have to say that it is their ability to accept a completely false idea and to believe that it represents an infallible truth. Human beings have an ability to believe the unbelievable that surprises even God. As for me, one of the most ridiculous ideas held by human beings is that they could possibly kill the Son of God or destroy his teachings.

Oh yes, they did kill my body 2,000 years ago. Oh yes, they have removed my original teachings from the written account of my life. Yet even the fragmented accounts found in the Bible contain elements of my true teachings and of the true, timeless teachings of God. The Bible states that God has written his law in your inward parts. I too have written my true teachings in the inward parts of your being, and what I am presenting in this book is simply a reminder of what you already know deep within yourself.

I am the open door, which no human can shut. I am the voice of truth that will not forever be silenced or denied.

My truth, my true teaching, has been present in the collective consciousness of humankind for more than 2,000 years. Regardless of the outer appearances, the Living Truth that I brought to this planet has been working behind the scenes. It has been working its way through the many layers of consciousness, and it is now ready to burst forth on the screen of humankind's conscious awareness.

The powers of this world think that they have somehow thwarted my purpose for coming to this planet. In reality, they have simply delayed the widespread acceptance of my true teachings, and they have done so on a very temporary basis (as measured by God's sense of time).

If you are reading this, you belong to a group of people who have the true teachings of Jesus Christ written in their beings. You need only bring those teachings into your outer memory and awareness. This book is nothing but a reminder. This book can tell you nothing which you do not already know at some level of your being. Otherwise, you would not be able to grasp or accept it.

Simply recognize and accept the fact that you have the ability, an inherent God-given ability as old as your lifestream, to know truth. You do not need an outer authority figure or organization to define truth for you. My truth is a Living Truth that cannot be confined to any doctrine or belief system found on this planet. My truth is larger than life, at least larger than the form of life known by most human beings in their present state of consciousness.

Allow yourself to recognize that you have the ability to know truth inside your heart. Allow yourself to recognize and accept that the true teachings of Jesus Christ are written in your being. Make a decision that you will strive to bring that truth into your outer awareness. As you begin to see that forgotten truth, accept it and have the courage to act upon it.

I am Jesus Christ. I desire to see you rise above the limitations you have come to accept. I desire to see you free from mortality and suffering. I desire to see you accept your true identity as an unlimited spiritual being who can as easily create God's perfection as you can create the human imperfection that you currently experience.

Allow me to take you on a journey from your present level of consciousness to a full recognition of your true identity. I promise you that it will be the journey of a lifetime.

2 | PROGRESSIVE REVELATION

The brutal fact about the current state of affairs on planet earth is that human beings have accepted so many lies, so many erroneous concepts, so many unbelievable ideas that even I, Jesus, find it difficult to know where to begin. You have grown up in a culture that is so permeated by erroneous concepts that one might say that your mind is encaged in a labyrinth. The labyrinth has many blind alleys, and it has only one way that leads to the center of being.

I clearly see that human beings are entrapped in a jungle of lies. I also know the truth and reality of God. The problem is that in trying to impart this truth to you, I must begin at your present level of consciousness. I cannot possibly give you truth in its purest form because in your present state of consciousness your imagination simply cannot cope with that truth. Likewise, your free will cannot accept a truth that is so different from the lies and errors that you have come to accept and that you have incorporated into the very fabric of your being—your sense of identity.

Please take a look at the Bible. Please recognize that the Law of Moses was given to a group of people who were trapped in a very low state of consciousness. That is why this law is a set of commandments, saying: "do this" and "don't do that."

It was given to spiritual children who needed a very simple set of rules. It was aimed at changing their outer actions.

Now, compare the Law of Moses to the higher law that I brought forth in the Sermon on the Mount and other teachings. For example, I said that it is not enough to abstain from the outer act of adultery. You must overcome the state of consciousness that makes you desire to commit adultery. In other words, it is not enough that you do not commit an outer act that is wrong. You must rise above the state of consciousness in which you desire to commit such an act. My teachings attempted to transform people's state of consciousness.

For anyone with an open mind, it should be easy to see that the teachings I gave 2,000 years ago represented a progression compared to the Law of Moses. The reason for this progression is that between the time of Moses and my appearance in Israel, humankind had progressed. Humankind had risen to a higher state of consciousness, and therefore people were now ready to receive a higher understanding and a higher teaching; even a higher law.

My teachings were incomplete

It is completely and utterly amazing to me that some people can seriously believe that the teachings I gave forth 2,000 years ago represent the ultimate or highest teachings that God could ever bring forth on this planet.

Let me make this absolutely clear. The teachings that I gave 2,000 years ago were not the highest or ultimate teachings that God can bring forth on this planet. My teachings were nothing more than the highest teachings that could be brought forth at the time, given humankind's state of consciousness.

My teachings were incomplete, and they were limited in many ways. That limitation was not due to a limitation on the part of God or on the part of his mouthpiece, meaning myself. That limitation was due to the fact that humankind was not ready to receive a higher teaching. One might say that my teachings represent a measured response to a crisis. It was not the highest possible response; it was the highest practical response.

Today, humankind has progressed to a higher state of consciousness, and therefore I can now bring forth a higher teaching than I did 2,000 years ago. This book is but one chapter in my teachings for this new age.

Yet despite the fact that humankind has progressed, the people of today are still in a very limited state of consciousness. God is, and always has been, unlimited.

The gap between the limited consciousness of human beings and the unlimited consciousness of God, is, figuratively speaking, almost unlimited. Yet God created human beings in his own image and likeness. A human being has the capacity of consciousness to experience the fullness of God. Yet to experience that fullness a human being must rise above the state of consciousness that is dominated by limitations, relativity and mortality.

The true meaning of the statement that you cannot serve two masters is that you cannot be in two states of consciousness at the same time. The lower consciousness – what my beloved Paul called the "carnal mind" but which I prefer to call the "death consciousness" – simply cannot fathom the reality of God. It will never be able to fathom the reality of God.

Outer knowledge is not enough

If you look at my life in Galilee, you will see that I was in constant conflict with the religious authorities of my time, namely those who represented the orthodox Jewish religion.

I repeatedly rebuked the Pharisees and Sadducees. Why did I run the risk of openly denouncing these authority figures? Because they had taken away the key of knowledge.

Do not misunderstand this statement. These people were not ignorant or stupid. They were very knowledgeable in terms of the outer Law of God. They knew the scriptures, and they could recite long passages from the scriptures. They had a very sophisticated intellectual understanding of the scriptures and of the outer Law of God as it was known at that time. With all of this outer knowledge, how could I claim that they had taken away the key of knowledge?

It is a basic fact that you simply cannot know God and God's truth through outer knowledge. You can know God only through a direct, inner experience whereby God reveals himself to you. The key to receiving this experience is to reach beyond the death consciousness. You must seek union with a higher part of your being, a higher part of your mind.

What do you think Paul meant when he said: "Let this mind be in you, which was also in Christ Jesus?"

The orthodox people were approaching life and God from the death consciousness. They had come to believe the lie that the death consciousness was capable of understanding and experiencing the truth of God. They thought that knowing God was simply a matter of raising up and perfecting the human mind until that mind was somehow magically able to fathom the reality of God.

My beloved hearts, please make a sincere effort to understand that this is nothing but a lie and an illusion. The key of knowledge is not the perfection of the human mind. The key of knowledge is to rise above the death consciousness and unite with a higher part of your mind. The key of knowledge is to follow the admonishment of my beloved Paul: "Let this mind be in you, which was also in Christ Jesus."

You must realize that Paul had never been my disciple while I was physically present on earth. Paul knew me only through a direct inner experience that started on the road to Damascus, but which was repeated on many occasions. Paul never knew me through outer knowledge. Paul never communicated with me through outer means of communication. Paul heard me speak to him only in the silence of his own heart (although I had to speak very loudly at first).

I chose Paul because even though he was persecuting my followers, he was, at inner levels of his being, willing to come up higher. He was willing, in a blinding flash of recognition and honesty, to admit that he had been entrapped by erroneous beliefs. He was willing, in the blink of an eye, to completely surrender and let go of those erroneous beliefs. He was willing to admit that he had been wrong and to move on without self-condemnation. He was willing to instantly turn away from the darkness of his former ways and face the bright Light of my Presence.

Oh if only people would realize that my beloved Paul was not unique. He had nothing that you do not have. You too have the capacity to reach beyond the death consciousness. You too have the capacity to receive an inner revelation of truth. You too have the capacity to choose to let go of your present beliefs and to see them as unreal. You too have the capacity to admit your mistake, to ask for forgiveness, to accept God's forgiveness and to forgive yourself. You too have the capacity to turn away from the death consciousness and to face my shining Presence of love and truth. You too can be transformed by the truth that I am, the truth that I am willing to bring into your life and consciousness, if you will but open the door of your heart a little bit.

If you will reach for my truth with an open heart, you too can be chosen as Paul was chosen. He was not chosen because he was somehow better than you. He was chosen because he was open to my truth.

Please let me into your heart.

I will be gentle.

I will not require you to leave your nets of incorrect beliefs all at once. I will give you time to absorb the truth and reality that I am. Yet it is a Law of God that I cannot give you forever.

All things must come to an end, even your opportunity to come up higher. Take some time to absorb my teachings, but do not procrastinate forever. Work while you have the light, for the night will come when you can no longer work.

Receiving true knowledge

When you look at my life, you will see that I often rebuked those who promoted a doctrine filled with dead men's bones. I did this because I knew that no doctrine could ever capture the fullness of God. To know that fullness, you must use an outer doctrine only as a ladder. Yet to truly know God, you must reach beyond the ladder itself. You must realize that although you cannot climb without the ladder, the ladder itself cannot take you all the way. No earthly ladder can reach all the way into our Father's kingdom. There will always be a gap.

To cross that gap and receive true knowledge of God, you must reach beyond outer knowledge. You must allow God to reveal himself to you in the secret chamber inside your heart. You must follow outer doctrines as far as they can take you, and then you must listen to the inner voice that calls you to come up higher.

That voice is my voice. My sheep know my voice, and you will hear my voice, if you will but listen for it in the stillness of your heart. In today's world, many people know the inner voice as intuition. Much teaching has been given about intuition and the value of intuition. You can gain much inspiration from studying such teachings and from applying a systematic technique for increasing your intuition. Yet do not forget that the very essence of intuition is that it is a form of communication between your conscious mind and a higher part of your being. Intuition, in its highest form, is nothing less than my attempt to speak to you and give you true knowledge of our Father's kingdom.

The key of knowledge is that you can gain true knowledge only through a direct, inner experience of truth. It is what the ancient Greeks and many of my disciples called "gnosis." When you have gnosis, you have closed the gap between the knower and the known. You have gone beyond outer knowledge. You have allowed the truth that is written in your inward parts to shine through all layers of your consciousness until it reaches your conscious mind. You have allowed that truth to transform your consciousness so that you are no longer a mortal, but a spiritual being. As I will show you later, the key to understanding my true teachings is to understand how a spiritual being can descend into mortal form and yet acknowledge that it is a spiritual being who is the Word made flesh.

Paul admonished people to not only hear the Word, but to do the Word. I now say: "Do not simply do the Word—be the Word."

3 | ATTAINING CHRIST CONSCIOUSNESS

I have been with this planet for a very long time. I have seen everything there is to see. I have seen every aspect of the lower state of consciousness that I call the death consciousness. If you desire to be my true disciple, you must realize that the central, in a way the only, key to discipleship under me is that you must overcome the death consciousness.

This is a twofold process. You must overcome the lower consciousness and at the same time you must unite with the higher consciousness. My beloved Paul said: "I die daily!" He meant that a part of his human mind, his death consciousness, died every day. Paul also said that you must put off the old human and put on the new human. He meant that you must put off the death consciousness and put on the Christ consciousness.

This is a process that will take time, and it must happen gradually. If you were to be stripped of the death consciousness all at once, your soul would be thrown into an identity crises. You would no longer know who you were; you would lose all sense of continuity and identity. You would literally go insane. This has in fact happened to people who discovered the spiritual path and attempted to force the process of spiritual growth. They attempted to take Heaven by force and in so doing they invoked so much light from Above that they were not able to hold that light. Instead of raising them up, the light damaged their sense of identity.

The very essence of my message is to point out to you that there is an alternative to the way of life practiced by most people on this planet. Some religious people claim that everything is subject to the will of God, and therefore there is nothing you can do to change who you are. God created you, and that is it. Some scientific authorities claim that your personality, your identity, is the product of environmental and hereditary factors over which you have no control. Both of these belief systems are incomplete.

Obviously, some of the characteristics of this universe are the products of the will of God. Therefore, your personality and individuality are to some degree affected by the will of God. Your personality and individuality are also affected by your heritage and the environment in which you grew up. However, the essential point that I am trying to get across is that you do not have to live the rest of your life as a slave of circumstances beyond your control. You have the potential to take control over your destiny and rebuild your identity. You have the potential, and it is a potential given to you by God himself, to reshape your destiny, to change your psychology and to remake your sense of identity in the image and likeness of God.

In the beginning, God created you in his own image and likeness. In the time between that beginning, which took place a very long time ago, and the present hour, you have created a human being that no longer resembles the image and likeness of God. Yet you have the potential to begin a gradual process whereby you can remake yourself in the image and likeness of your God. In the process of so doing, you can shape your identity in ways that God never imagined but that are, nevertheless, in perfect accord with the will of God.

This process of spiritual growth has always been available to human beings. Throughout the ages, it has been known in every culture and civilization. It has been presented in many different versions in an attempt to appeal to various groups of people. A universal name for this process is the "spiritual path."

Let nothing come between you and God

It is completely and utterly amazing to me that someone can study my teachings, even the incomplete teachings found in the New Testament, and conclude that the only road to salvation goes through an outer organization and an outer doctrine. How can anyone fail to see that I did not come to create a totalitarian organization or to bring forth a closed and closed-minded outer doctrine?

Why do you think I repeatedly rebuked the religious authorities of my time? Why do you think these religious authorities considered me to be such a grave threat that they repeatedly plotted to kill my body and eventually succeeded? The authorities of the Jewish religion wanted to get rid of me because I was the ultimate threat to their power structure.

I rebuked those who set themselves up as the only doorway between human beings and God. They created a belief system which stated that no human being could get to God without going through the orthodox religion and its hierarchy of human beings. They created a belief system which stated that unless a person believed in the outer doctrines, that person would not be saved.

I came to overthrow that closed system. I came to denounce the people who had set themselves up as the link between God and the people. I came to overthrow the power structures and to expose the power plays. I came to restore the key of knowledge which these people had taken away in an attempt to control the population.

The only doorway to God

I did not come to bring peace to Israel. I came to bring a sword that would cut through the veils of illusion that surrounded the minds of the people. I came to cut the people free from the chains by which they had been bound by the representatives of the religion that was originally meant to set people free from all oppression. I, Jesus, was the ultimate spiritual revolutionary, and today I am still the ultimate spiritual revolutionary. I am here right now, and through these teachings I am telling you that you do not need to accept any human organization or person as the doorway to God.

There is only one doorway to God, and it is a state of consciousness which I came to exemplify and demonstrate, namely the Christ consciousness. When I said: "I am the open door, which no human can shut," I did not refer to a person named Jesus. I referred to a universal state of consciousness, the universal Christ mind, which I had united with to such a degree that I could truly say: "I and my Father are one." Yet I also said: "I can of my own self can do nothing; it is the Father within me who is doing the work." What I meant was that it is the universal Christ consciousness within me that is the only true doer.

Many people thought that I was the new king of Israel and that I would lead the Israelites in a violent revolt against the Roman oppression. I did not take up arms against the Romans; yet I declared many times that I came to set the people free. If I did not come to set the people of Israel free from the Romans, who do you think I considered to be the real oppressors of the people? I wanted to deliver them from the very people, the serpents in their midst, who had occupied the place between the people and their God.

The saying: "Let no man take thy Crown" refers to the fact that you must never let any human being or organization take away the crown of your personal, direct, inner contact with God. You were created in the image and likeness of God. You have the capacity of consciousness to commune directly with God inside your heart. When God said: "You shall have no other gods before me," what do you think He truly meant?

Yes, He did mean that you shouldn't worship an outer idol. Yet why shouldn't you worship an outer idol? Because if you identify an outer form as God then you will never get to know the true God who is beyond all form.

God is beyond all form and all concepts created by human beings. You simply cannot experience God with your physical senses, and you cannot fathom God from the state of mind that I have called the death consciousness. However, you can experience God directly by opening your heart to a mystical experience through which God can reveal his Being, his essence, to you. This ability to commune directly with God is the most precious gift that any human being has ever received. That gift is also your supreme personal responsibility. You must never allow anything or anyone in this world to take that gift away from you. You must never allow anything in this world to stand between you and your direct inner communion with God.

Your spiritual potential

So many people think that I was so far above them that they could not possibly learn from my example or follow in my footsteps. Such an intense cult of idolatry has been built around Jesus Christ that it has almost obliterated my true message.

I fully understand why I came to earth 2,000 years ago. I came to demonstrate that it is possible for any human being to attain direct, inner contact with God; to attain true gnosis. That was the essence of my mission. One might even say that it was the only message that I came to get across. I came to demonstrate that the road to God does not go through anything outside yourself. The road to God is an inner path whereby you contact God directly in your heart.

Consider what has happened to that message over these past 2,000 years. Where in the current scriptures can you find that message? Do you think I did not preach my message clearly and openly? Do you think that I somehow wanted to hide that message from humankind or from posterity?

Not so. I, Jesus, wanted that message to be shouted from the housetops, and that is what I told my disciples to do.

What has happened to that message over these past 2,000 years? It has been replaced by a false message!

The essence of the false message is that Jesus Christ because he was the Son of God, nay because he was the *only* Son of God, was so far above and beyond normal human beings that no one could possibly follow in his footsteps. The cult of idolatry built around me is so intense that most of the people who call themselves Christians would not even dare to consider the true meaning of my words: "He that believes on me, the works that I do shall he do also." So many people think that following in my footsteps and attaining a higher state of consciousness – yes, a state of Christ consciousness – is blasphemy.

3 | Attaining Christ Consciousness

The greatest tragedy

I must tell you very directly and openly that from my personal viewpoint this is such a tragedy that I can hardly find words to describe it. The message that I gave my life to bring forth, through both word and example, has been completely eclipsed by a false message.

Instead of being the living example for all to follow, I have been elevated to an idol that no one dare follow, lest they be accused of blasphemy. Over these past 2,000 years, so many Christians have danced around this golden calf, this false image of me.

I came to set people free. The false image of me as the exception rather than the example helps imprison people even more than they were before I came. Therefore, from an outer point of view, one might say that my coming has had the opposite effect of what was intended. Instead of being an instrument for setting people free, I have become a tool for imprisoning them in a mental prison that is more secure than any physical prison could be.

After all, if you truly want to enslave people, chains of iron are not the most efficient way because people will know that they are enslaved and they will long for freedom. It is far more efficient to enslave people by subtle means so that they do not even realize that they are trapped.

I am an unlimited cosmic being. I am called the Prince of Peace, and I am indeed at peace in the unconditional love of God. Yet even I find it difficult to understand how human beings can continue to accept such incredible lies about me.

How can it be that after 2,000 years so few people have dared to look beyond this false image? How can it be that not even the little children have looked at the Emperor's new clothes and said: "But the Emperor has nothing on!"

When will those who call themselves Christians, and who sincerely believe that they are following me, realize that they must look beyond this false image? When will you, my beloved heart, realize that you personally must dare to look beyond that image, go deeply within your heart and ask me to reveal to you the true Being of Jesus Christ?

Ask and you shall receive. Seek and you shall find. Have the courage to look beyond an outer doctrine full of dead men's bones. Have the courage to look for the real Jesus Christ. I promise you that if you will open your mind and look for me in the stillness of your heart, you will indeed find me. I have been with you always, and I am with you today. I am simply waiting for you to make the choice to recognize my Presence within you.

The seed of my word

If you still doubt that it is truly I, Jesus, who is speaking to you through this book then take a look at the Bible itself. The Bible states very clearly that I taught the masses in parables, but when we were alone, I expounded all things to my disciples. This simple statement, which those who have falsified my teachings overlooked and forgot to take out of the Bible, is enough to tell those with an open mind that I taught on two different levels. I had outer teachings designed for the level of consciousness shared by the majority of the population. Then, I had inner teachings designed for the consciousness of those who were further along on the spiritual path and who were therefore open to higher and more direct teachings.

When I appeared 2,000 years ago, only a few people were able to grasp my inner teachings in their purest form. That is why I used parables to explain those teachings to the masses, yet my parables, many of which are not found in today's scriptures, still communicated my message.

Today, the situation has changed dramatically. Even though my outer teachings have been distorted, the Living Word that I brought to this planet was planted as a seed in the collective consciousness of humankind. Oh yes, the powers that be stomped that seed deep underground so that it could no longer be seen. Yet that very act drove the seed of my Word deep into the fertile ground where it could sprout in peace.

The seed of my Living Word has been sprouting for 2,000 years. It is now strong, and it is ready to burst through the soil and blossom in your consciousness. Today, millions of people are prepared, at inner levels, to openly understand and accept my true teachings.

If you read the New Testament, you will see that I repeatedly said: "Let those who have ears, hear." Well, today many more people have ears to hear my true teachings.

Learn from Paul's example

I am fully aware that some people will reject the teachings I am bringing forth in this book. They will come up with numerous sophisticated reasons why these teachings could not possibly be true and why they could not possibly come from the real Jesus Christ.

Yet I must tell you that if you have read this book up until this point, you belong to the large group of people who are ready to accept my inner teachings. If you were not open to my true teachings, you simply would not be able to read this book. You might feel a number of mixed emotions about the teachings I am bringing forth in this book. You might even feel the hostility that Paul expressed towards my followers. Yet like Paul, you are one of my flock. Therefore, you have the potential to go through the same turnaround that Paul experienced.

Some people think that I chose Paul, and in some ways I did because I knew that Paul was ready at inner levels. Nevertheless, I could do nothing against Paul's free will. Yes, I appeared to him, but he still had to choose how he would react to my appearance. He could easily have rejected my appearance as an illusion or even as the work of the devil. To turn away from his former ways and to face the reality of my Presence, Paul had to make a choice. Therefore, in reality I did not choose Paul—Paul chose me.

In a sense, I have chosen you because I know that you are ready at inner levels. Yet you must still come to a conscious recognition of that readiness, and you must still make your own decision as to how you will respond to my call. Therefore, I cannot choose you; you must choose me.

I love my Father in Heaven, and I respect his Law of Free Will. I cannot and I will not make the choice for you. However, I am making known to you that I, Jesus Christ, have appeared to you through the teachings in this book. I am saying to you: "Why are you persecuting me. It is hard for you to kick against the pricks!"

You must choose whom you will serve. The real, living Jesus or the idol, the golden calf, that was created by human beings in an attempt to prevent you from entering our Father's kingdom.

Choose wisely.

Choose to be, and do not, like Hamlet, choose not to be.

Hamlet chose not to be and paid with his life. If you choose not to be, you might pay with your soul.

I am calling you home

I am the Good Shepherd, and I am calling my flock to come home to my true teachings and to follow my example into our Father's kingdom. I have left the 99 sheep to look for the sheep that has gone astray. Amazingly, I am finding many sheep who are lost yet who do not see that they are lost. The reason is that they think they belong to the only true church of Jesus Christ and that they follow the only true doctrine of Jesus Christ.

There is a way that seems right to a human, yet the end thereof is the way of death.

I am the Way, the Truth and the Life.

To get to our Father's kingdom, you must follow the only possible way, and that way goes through the Christ consciousness that I am. The mortal human being, the person caught in a lower state of consciousness, can never inherit our Father's kingdom, no matter what outer church you belong to or what outer doctrine you follow.

You can inherit our Father's kingdom only by rising above the mortal state of consciousness and putting on the new human, drinking the new wine, of my Christ consciousness.

This is my blood; drink all of it.

I am here to show you the way home.

Allow me to take you by the hand, and in the following discourses I will show you how to rise above the many false concepts about me, and about God, that human beings have created out of ignorance, unbelief and impure intentions.

I am the Good Shepherd, and I know the way home.

I am the open door that leads to our Father's kingdom.

I have demonstrated the path that all must follow.

Dare to walk in my footsteps.

4 | WHY IS THERE RELIGION IN THE WORLD?

I would like you to consider why there is religion in this world. Do you think that God needs religion? Do you think that the Being who created an incredibly vast and complex universe has some kind of need to be worshiped by human beings living on a planet that is like a speck of dust in infinity? I am not hereby saying that human beings are not important to God. I am simply saying that God is an unlimited, infinite Being, and God does not have human needs. The idea that God needs to be worshiped is yet another example of backwards reasoning.

The simple fact is that God has no need to be worshiped by human beings. Religion was not created for God's sake. It was created for your sake.

The simple fact is that God does not need religion. Human beings need religion, and it is very important that you understand why. God created you in his image and likeness. You have the capacity of consciousness to experience the fullness of God's infinite Being. Yet as your lifestream decided to descend into the material universe, you faced a challenge that is quite severe.

You must understand that my Father's house has many mansions. By that I mean that there many different levels of

God's creation. Modern scientists have found that the entire material universe is made from energy. Energy is vibration.

You know that your eyes can detect only the types of energy which you call visible light. You also know that there are many forms of light, and many other forms of energy, that your eyes cannot detect. Therefore, there are many different layers or levels of vibration. In fact, one might consider that the totality of God's creation is a vast, but not unlimited, continuum of vibrations.

Visible light is simply part of a continuum of vibrations. Your eyes can see only one pocket of that continuum. Likewise, the material universe is simply one pocket in a larger continuum of vibrations. Your senses, and the lower consciousness of the human mind, can perceive and fathom only a small pocket of the continuum of vibrations that comprise God's creation. That small pocket is what you call the material universe.

The only difference between visible light and invisible light is a difference in vibration. The only difference between the material universe and higher levels of God's creation is a difference in vibration. The only difference between Heaven and earth is a difference in vibration.

There are no impenetrable barriers in God's continuum of vibrations. There is a dividing line between the vibrations of the material universe and the vibrations of the lowest level of the spiritual universe, the level that is right above the material universe in vibration. That dividing line is not an impenetrable barrier. However, your physical senses and the death consciousness will never be able to cross that dividing line. Therefore, to the physical senses and the death consciousness, there seems to be a barrier between the material world and the spiritual world.

The dial of consciousness

You are much more than the physical body and the outer mind. You might think of your consciousness as the dial on a radio receiver. You can turn the dial on the radio and tune in to different stations. What you experience as different stations are simply radio waves broadcast at different frequencies.

Your consciousness has the capacity to tune in to both the material universe and the higher universes in the spiritual world. Throughout the ages, numerous people have had mystical visions of higher worlds. Such visions have been the basis for virtually every religion or spiritual philosophy known to humankind.

Every human being is created in the image and likeness of God. Therefore, every human being has the capacity of consciousness to tune in to the spiritual worlds and have a direct, inner experience of those worlds and the reality of those worlds.

The only reason you do not have direct perception of the spiritual world is that you have not yet learned to turn the dial of consciousness. In a later discourse, I will teach you how to turn the dial of consciousness. For now, I want you to consider why it is so important to turn that dial and attain a direct experience of the spiritual reality.

Imagine that you meet someone in the marketplace who starts telling you about a wonderful new fruit that has recently been discovered. After hearing the description of the amazing properties and delicious taste, your first reaction is a question: "Where can I find this new fruit?"

It is a natural tendency of the human mind that when you hear about something desirable, you want to experience it for yourself. You are simply not satisfied by an image or description provided by a source outside yourself.

I am aware that as children many people were indoctrinated with the saying that curiosity killed the cat. I want you to understand that there is absolutely nothing wrong with the desire to experience something directly instead of relying on a mere description. God would not have it any other way. In fact, God himself embedded in your lifestream the curiosity and sense of longing that can never be satisfied by anything on this earth.

God created you in his image and likeness. God is the ultimate joy, love and bliss. God desired you to venture into the world of form that He has created. He desired you to experience and appreciate that world of form, but He never desired for you to become lost in that world of form. Therefore, your lifestream has a longing for something ultimate, something beyond. That longing is a longing for your Father in Heaven. It is a longing to experience the totality of God's Being, the memory of which you have embedded deep within your lifestream (God has written his law in your inward parts). You will never be fully satisfied, you will never be fully at peace, until you have the direct experience of God's unlimited Being. Nothing else will do.

Because God is the ultimate joy and love, why would God want his children to settle for anything less than the fullness of his Being? Therefore, why would God create you in such a way that you could be satisfied by the things of this world? If your lifestream was satisfied by the conditions found on planet earth, you would never long for anything more. Therefore, you might become stuck at any level of the world of form. Obviously, a God of unlimited love and bliss would not want to see this happen. It is the Father's good pleasure to give you the kingdom. Therefore, your lifestream can never be satisfied until you have a direct experience of God's Being.

Seeing is more than believing

Back in the days of my mission on earth, I often rebuked my followers for showing a lack of faith. I even said: "Blessed are those who see not and yet believe." The reason was that back then the energies of planet earth were more dense than they are today. Therefore, it was far more difficult for people to turn the dial of consciousness and tune in to the spiritual world.

Another limiting factor was the lower state of consciousness of humankind. In other words, I was limited by the conditions found 2,000 years ago, and therefore I could not easily give people a direct inner experience of the spiritual side of life. I had to encourage them to start by believing in the reality of God so that they could gradually raise their consciousness and eventually go beyond belief and have the direct experience.

Today, the equation has changed. Even though there are intense pockets of darkness on this planet, the planet as a whole has progressed to a higher and purer vibration. At the same time, humankind's state of consciousness has been raised, in large part due to the seed of the Living Word that I planted 2,000 years ago, but also due to the striving of many sincere seekers found in all religions and cultures.

Therefore, my hands are no longer tied. I have more options than I had back then. Today, I can more easily take you beyond the consciousness in which you believe in me and believe in God. I want you to reach beyond the consciousness of belief and attain a higher state of consciousness based on direct knowledge. That state of consciousness is the state of inner knowing; the state of *gnosis*.

The consciousness of knowing is beyond faith because it is beyond doubt. Let us return to the example of you meeting a person who tells you about a new fruit. When you ask the person: "Where is it?," the person says that it can be found only on a remote continent. In other words, you simply cannot go there and see the fruit for yourself. You can choose to believe in the existence of the fruit, or you can choose not to believe. Even if you choose to believe, there will always be an element of doubt in your consciousness. After all, how can you really know that the fruit exists? The simple fact of life is that you cannot know for sure until you experience it for yourself.

Time to go beyond faith

Both God and myself are clearly aware that there are many devout seekers on planet earth who are sincerely seeking God. Neither my Father nor I desire to see your efforts be in vain. We desire to see your efforts produce good fruit, the fruit of certainty, the fruit of knowledge. We desire to see you escape the consciousness in which your faith in God can be challenged by the arrows of doubt.

How could you possibly escape the state of consciousness that is vulnerable to doubt? You can do so only through a direct experience whereby you see the reality of God.

I am not in any way denouncing the value of faith. I am very well aware that for these past 2,000 years many sincere and wonderful lifestreams have had a very strong faith in me and my Father. I truly want you to recognize that the faith held by so many devout Christians has been one of the major factors in raising the consciousness of humankind.

I commend you for your faith. Yet I must tell you that it is now time to go beyond faith. Faith was simply a tool for raising the consciousness of humankind to the next level. Planet earth is entering a new age in which people need to move beyond faith. You need to move into a state of consciousness in which your relationship to God, and your relationship to me, is no longer based on faith but on a direct inner experience; a direct personal communion.

Today, it is far easier for you to turn the dial of consciousness and tune in to the spiritual worlds in my Father's kingdom. If you want an outer proof of this, consider the millions of people who have had a spiritual vision as part of a near-death experience. Consider also the fact that many more people claim to have direct communion with the spiritual beings that inhabit my Father's kingdom. In fact, the book you are holding in your hand is another proof of the fact that I can now bring forth a more direct teaching than in the past.

Seek and you shall find

Once again, I am aware that some people will choose to cling to orthodox ideas and use them as an excuse for rejecting what I have stated here. Therefore, let us take another look at the scriptures and my life as Jesus of Galilee.

I stated earlier that I am amazed that so many people believe certain ideas about me. At the same time, I am amazed that there are so many logical questions that are not being asked by sincere Christians. After all, the fragmented account of my life found in the scriptures raises more questions than it answers.

Did I not say: "Seek and you shall find?" Then why are so many Christians afraid to seek? Did I not say: "Ask and you shall receive," meaning that if you ask for knowledge and certainty, you shall indeed receive it.

Then, why are so many Christians afraid to ask? Why are so many Christians holding on to beliefs and doctrines when

I and my Father are quite willing to give you knowledge and proof? Are you afraid of knowing? Do you fear that if you attain direct knowledge, you might have to let go of beliefs that make you feel comfortable? Fear not, little flock; it is the Father's good pleasure to give you direct knowledge of his kingdom.

Why didn't Jesus write down his teachings?

Let us look at one of the questions that I would like all sincere Christians to consider. Some people claim that the historical Jesus was illiterate. Let me assure you that I was in fact literate. Nevertheless, even if you doubt my personal literacy, many of the people around me were literate. With that in mind, consider the following question: "Why didn't Jesus himself write down his true teachings?"

If you take an objective look at modern Christianity, you will see that there are numerous sects and churches that cling to different interpretations of my teachings. Many of them even claim that their particular interpretation is the only true interpretation. Why didn't I simply avoid this confusion by writing down the true account of my life so that there was no room for interpretation?

Let me begin by making one thing clear. No interpretation of my teachings could possibly be true to my teachings. There is simply no way to know the true teachings of Christ through any interpretation that has been affected by the death consciousness. Flesh and blood cannot inherit the kingdom of Heaven. The death consciousness cannot fathom the true spiritual teachings that I brought to this planet. Therefore, no human being could possibly provide an accurate and true interpretation of my teachings. There is no such thing as a true interpretation of my teachings.

4 | Why Is There Religion in the World?

There is only one way to know my true teachings, and that is to receive a portion of those teachings directly from me. No one else could possibly impart my true teachings to you. However, it is possible that a person could serve as a mouthpiece, or messenger, and deliver a morsel of my true teachings. It is possible that a person can raise his or her consciousness and receive elements of my true teachings through a direct inner experience. By having such a direct experience of the Living Word that I am, this person can serve as a messenger who brings forth a cup of my teachings, a cup of cold water in Christ's name. By doing so, the person can impart a portion of my true teachings without interpreting (and thereby distorting) those teachings.

In other words, if a person will make a sincere effort to raise his or her consciousness to the level of the Christ consciousness (even if the person has not yet permanently attained Christ consciousness), that person can serve as my mouthpiece; as my messenger.

Why didn't I write down my true teachings? Because I knew that any written account would be misused, misquoted, misrepresented, misunderstood, misinterpreted and any other kind of mis- that you could possibly imagine. If you will take an objective look at the historical facts of how the written account of my life has been butchered by Church authorities who thought they had the power to decide what people should know about me, you will agree that history does indeed prove me right.

Receive my teachings directly

The real reason I did not write down my teachings is that I intended to provide a way whereby people could receive those teachings directly from me.

Look at the early church that I established. I sent people out to preach my word. I did not send them out with a written account so that they could read aloud from a predefined doctrine. Instead, I told them to take no thought for what they should say because it would be given to them what to say. My early apostles and disciples did not give sermons by reading from a book and interpreting the words in that book. My early disciples and apostles preached by the power of the Holy Spirit. They did not deliver a fixed outer doctrine. They delivered the Living Word of Jesus Christ which I spoke to them directly in their hearts.

The reason I created an organization without an official doctrine is very profound. I stated earlier that the door to our Father's kingdom is not the person of Jesus. The door to our Father's kingdom is a state of consciousness, namely the universal Christ consciousness.

Flesh and blood cannot inherit the kingdom of Heaven. There are people on this planet, even some who consider themselves spiritual teachers, who subscribe to the false belief that it is somehow possible to raise or perfect the human mind, the death consciousness. This is not so. The death consciousness must die before the lifestream can live forever in the Light of Christ.

There is no possibility of a compromise. You cannot take the death consciousness with you into my Father's kingdom. You must use your free will and make a conscious choice to surrender that lower mind and all of the erroneous beliefs that are propping up the tyrant of the human ego.

The only problem

The only problem on planet earth today is that most people have descended or fallen into a state of consciousness in which they no longer have a direct perception of the spiritual side of life. In fact, many people have descended into a state of consciousness in which they no longer have any memory of their spiritual origins or their identity as spiritual beings. They literally believe that they are mortal, limited human beings who are confined to this material universe and that there is nothing beyond the material universe.

There is absolutely no way that a person can rise above the lower consciousness by using the energies found in the material universe. The lower consciousness is made from the vibrations of this universe. You simply cannot use those energies to build a stairway that will take you to Heaven. The ladder that Jacob saw was not a ladder made from material energies. It was a ladder made from spiritual energies, namely the Christ consciousness.

What I am trying to help you see here is that once you have descended into the death consciousness, your lifestream has no way to free itself from that state of consciousness. You cannot pull yourself up by your own bootstraps. You cannot use the energies of the material universe to escape the death consciousness. That is why virtually every religion known to humankind contains the concept of an outer savior.

When a person has descended into the death consciousness, that person can escape only if a savior from the spiritual world comes into this world and imparts to the lifestream a cup containing the higher energies of the universal Christ consciousness.

The real Savior is the universal Christ consciousness. That universal Christ consciousness was created by God at the very moment that God created the world of form. What I am saying here is that the universal Christ consciousness has existed since the beginning of time. In other words, it has existed for more than 2,000 years.

I came to bring forth teachings about the universal Christ consciousness and to provide an example of a human being, in a physical body, who had united with that Christ consciousness.

I did not invent the Christ consciousness.

God did not create the Christ consciousness at my birth. The universal Christ consciousness has always existed, and it has always been available to human beings because it truly is the open door which no human can shut.

The only way to salvation is that the lifestream must receive a portion of the universal Christ consciousness. That Christ consciousness then becomes the leaven that raises the entire loaf of the person's consciousness.

Without the Christ consciousness, no human can be saved. That is why I created the ritual of breaking the Bread of Life. The Bread of Life is meant to represent the Christ consciousness. I broke that Bread of Life for my disciples, and I taught them to raise their consciousness so that they could break the Bread of Life for others.

This is the chain of discipleship that leads from my heart to your heart. I never intended for this chain to be broken. It was my intention that my disciples would impart the Bread of Life to others. That Bread of Life would then raise these people's consciousness until they attained a sufficient level of oneness with the Christ consciousness so that they in turn could impart the Bread of Life to others.

If this chain had never been broken, the Living Word that I brought would have continued to spread as rings on the surface of the ocean. If the chain had not been broken, the Bread of Life would long ago have been imparted to, or at least offered to, every human being on this planet. If my original vision had come to pass, I would not have been speaking to you through this book. I would have spoken to you directly in your heart.

You would have been able to hear me, and you would have known that it was I, your Jesus, who was speaking to you.

The living Word of God

The Bread of Life that I came to bring was the Word of God; the living Word of God. In reality, the Word of God is the soundless sound, and therefore it can never be spoken by the human tongue. You cannot hear the Word of God with your ears, and you cannot understand it with the death consciousness. However, you can hear the Word of God in the stillness of your heart.

I did not come to bring an outer word that could be interpreted and misinterpreted by human beings in the death consciousness. I did not come to bring an outer word that could be turned into a doctrine and used as a weapon to enslave the very people that I came to free. I did not come to create an outer institution, an outer church, that could be used as a weapon in the ongoing human power struggle. I did not come to create an institution through which a small elite of power-hungry people could exercise physical control and mind control over my brothers and sisters in Spirit.

Because human beings have free will, and because some people chose to reject the Bread of Life, the Living Word, my original vision did not come to pass. Therefore, I am sad to say that for the past 2,000 years planet earth has not had a living church that imparted the Living Word in an unbroken chain. However, time is nothing but an illusion created by the lower mind. Therefore, it is never too late to bring forth the Living Word or the Living Church. I do not desire to create a new church which will compete with the many existing churches who claim to be the only true church of Jesus Christ.

Instead, I desire to bring forth a new type of church, a type of church which is the only kind of church that could possibly be the true church of Jesus Christ. That type of a church is an inner church. It is a church built from the lively stones of the Christ flame that burns within your heart. It is a church made up of those who have the courage to reach beyond the death consciousness. Those who have dared to consider what so many call blasphemy, namely that they too could embody the Living Word, as I did.

The word made flesh

So many people have wondered about the mystery of the Word of God that became flesh. In reality, there is no mystery. The Bible itself records how God created the world. God said: "Let there be Light."

God created by uttering a sound, a word. Therefore, the entire universe is created from the Word of God. Even this dense material world is the Word of God made flesh. Without Him was not anything made that was made. Without his word was not anything made that was made.

The problem on planet earth is not a real problem. In the mind of God, in the shining reality of God, the problem on planet earth simply does not exist. Why? Because God knows that no matter what the outer appearances might be, everything is made from God's own substance. Everything that exists is simply God who has taken on a disguise. The entire universe is God smiling to you behind a mask. Some masks look like Heaven and some look like hell, but they are all temporary disguises for the only reality there is: the Living Word of God.

The only reason there is a problem on planet earth is that when a person falls into the death consciousness, that person can no longer see that the material universe is an expression of

God. What I am saying here is that you are not separated from God or from me. There are no real barriers between us.

The sense of separation is nothing but an illusion, a veil created by the denser energies of the material world which your physical senses and the death consciousness cannot see beyond. You are not separated from God; you only think you are separated from God.

The sense of separation exists only inside your mind. It can continue to exist only because you continue to give it power. It will cease to exist only after you come to a conscious realization that it is not real and that there truly is something beyond the material universe.

You can come to that realization only by having a direct perception of the spiritual world. You can have that direct perception only by raising your consciousness, by turning the dial of your conscious mind so that you can tune in to the higher vibrations of the Christ mind. You can perceive the spiritual world only by looking through the open door of the Christ consciousness.

I am Jesus Christ, and I came to set you free. There is only one possible way by which I can set you free from the death consciousness. I must impart to you a portion of the universal Christ consciousness with which I have united.

Your true identity

I want to make it clear that I am an individual, just as you are an individual. I am a Son of God, but I am not the only son or daughter of God. If God created you in his image and likeness then you too must be a son or daughter of God. Without Him was not anything made that was made, including you.

The only real difference between you and I is that I have realized and fully accepted my identity as a spiritual being who is created by God. I have come to this realization by letting go of the death consciousness and by embracing the higher state of consciousness of the universal Christ mind. I have completely united with that Christ consciousness, and therefore I am an individualization of the universal Christ. That is why I can truly say: "I am the open door, which no human can shut."

Yet the very essence of my true teachings is that I was not created by God in the fullness of that Christ consciousness. I had to go through the exact same process, I had to follow the exact same spiritual path, that you are now in the process of following. I came to show you the way that you too can walk, and that you *must* walk if you want to go home to your Father's kingdom.

I know this concept is very difficult to accept for many Christians who have grown up with the current beliefs about me being the only Son of God. Therefore, let us reason together. Consider the question: "Do you believe God is evil?" If you consider yourself a Christian, I am sure your answer is a "No!" Then, think a little bit further and consider if the following scenario makes sense to you:

God created you as a sinner and sent you to an imperfect planet, called earth. As you are wallowing in misery and suffering, God sends you a person, called Jesus Christ, who is the embodiment of God's perfection. This Jesus is the only Son of God, and God sent him into this world so that by seeing the perfection of Jesus, you could come to fully realize your own miserable state of imperfection, a state which God created. The coming of Jesus could be designed only to make you feel like a miserable sinner who could never possibly attain the perfection you saw in Jesus Christ.

If you follow this line of reasoning, you will see that there is only one logical conclusion. If indeed I was the only Son of God then God must be a very strange, and almost evil, God.

Sending me into the world to show you something that you could not possibly attain would be an evil act. Why would God want you to feel like a miserable sinner who could never possibly deserve to sit at the right hand of God?

If God created you in his image and likeness, and if God is a benevolent God then God's only desire for you is to see you escape the temporary prison of mortality and limitation. God wants you to come home to your home of light in his own kingdom.

Therefore, isn't it logical that a true God would provide a way for you to climb back into his kingdom? Isn't it logical that God would send me not as an exception, but as an example of the path that all other sons and daughters of God can follow on their way home to their Father's kingdom?

I desire you to go deep within your heart and, with an open mind, consider these ideas. If you will dare to look beyond the doctrines and dogmas that are full of dead men's bones, I, Jesus, promise you that I will reveal to you the truth about these matters.

I will reveal this truth in your heart. If you will ask me with an open heart that truly desires to know the truth, I will prove to you, through a direct inner experience, that it is the universal Christ Consciousness, and not the outer person of Jesus, who is the Truth, the Way and the Life.

5 | THE TRUE KEY TO SALVATION

Beloved hearts, in the previous discourses I have laid a solid foundation, and we must now begin to build upon that foundation. Therefore, let us consider the question: "What does it take to be saved?"

If you accept that life has a spiritual side then you probably also realize that there is a difference between this world and the spiritual world. People from every religion share an almost universal belief that there is a difference between the spiritual world and the material world. They also share the belief that earth is not the permanent home for human beings. The goal of life is to ascend beyond the material world and enter the spiritual world. Most people also realize that before you can enter the spiritual world, you must fulfill certain requirements.

Take a look at planet earth as you see it today. I think everyone would agree that the atrocities happening on this planet simply could not be tolerated in the spiritual world. Most people realize that the beings who inhabit the spiritual world do not treat each other the way human beings treat each other.

I have tried to help you understand that there is no fundamental difference between the spiritual world and the material world. The only difference is a difference in vibration. Therefore, you do have the capacity to ascend to the spiritual world.

However, before you can enter our Father's kingdom, you must meet certain requirements.

The key requirement is that you must rise above the death consciousness. The atrocities you see taking place on this planet, and many other actions that people do not necessarily consider to be wrong, are the results of the death consciousness.

Flesh and blood, the flesh and blood of the death consciousness, simply cannot inherit the kingdom. Therefore, the only way that you could possibly ascend into our Father's kingdom is by leaving behind the death consciousness.

Let me make it clear that there is absolutely no possibility of a compromise. The vibrations of the death consciousness can never cross the threshold and enter the straight and narrow gate that leads to our Father's kingdom. Even if these vibrations are disguised as what one might call human goodness, they still cannot enter our Father's kingdom. You cannot enter the kingdom by becoming a good human being. In the eyes of God, there is no such thing as a good, or perfect, human being.

You can enter the kingdom only by overcoming the sense of identity that causes you to believe that you are a mortal human being who is separated from God. You can enter the kingdom only by putting off the old human of mortality and putting on the new human, the spiritual being, the spiritual sense of identity. You can enter only by putting on the Christ consciousness and by fully uniting with that Christ consciousness so that you see yourself as a spiritual being. Your sense of identity must be built upon the Rock of Christ instead of the shifting sands of the death consciousness. It is absolutely vital that you come to a conscious, inner realization of the truth behind these words. You must realize and accept that you cannot put the round peg of the death consciousness into the square hole that leads to the City Foursquare.

The goal of life

When you come to an inner realization of this essential truth, you can quickly develop an entirely new perspective on life as a human being. You now see that the very goal of life is your salvation, your ascension into the spiritual world. You also see that the key to realizing this goal is that you must go through a gradual process, which I have called the spiritual path. You must gradually put off the death consciousness and put on the new state of mind, the Christ consciousness.

For centuries, nay, for thousands upon thousands of years, human beings have believed that salvation is an outer process over which they have no control. I am telling you that this is not so. Salvation is not a matter of passively waiting for an outer savior who will suddenly arrive and do the work for you.

I stated earlier that you do indeed need an outer savior. However, that outer savior serves only as the open door through which God can give you a morsel of the universal Christ consciousness. This morsel then acts as a leaven to raise the whole loaf of your consciousness. The passing on of the Living Word, the Bread of Life, is only one side of the coin. The other side of the coin is that you have free will and that the Law of Free Will is the ultimate law of the material universe. You know my parable about the sower whose seeds fall on barren ground. A savior can appear and give you a morsel of the Christ consciousness. Yet if you do not make the free-will choice to accept that Christ consciousness, your salvation simply cannot happen. I can offer you the Bread of Life, but I cannot force you to accept that Bread of Life.

I can lead you to the living waters, but I cannot make you drink. I can impart to you my Christ consciousness, as I am doing in the lines of this book, but I cannot force you to allow that Christ consciousness to raise your consciousness to a higher level.

The raising of your consciousness can take place only if you make the decision to let it happen. In fact, you need to make many decisions. You need to make daily decisions to put off the old human and put on the new, spiritual "human."

The death consciousness has a very deep belief that there is an easy way out, that there is some kind of quick fix or a form of automatic salvation. This belief has given rise to the idea that I am the only Son of God and that by simply believing on me and declaring that I am your Lord and Savior, you will automatically be saved.

I am Jesus Christ, and I am telling you that there is no such thing as an automatic salvation. Salvation is offered to every human being as a gift from God. Yet the key to salvation is not the offering of the gift because it truly rains upon the just and the unjust. The key to salvation is the acceptance of the gift. Without that acceptance, God cannot save you. God must simply wait until you make a decision to accept his grace.

The path to salvation

Salvation is a process, not an instantaneous miracle. The process of salvation has several stages.

I earlier stated that the Law of Moses was given to people in a very low and immature state of consciousness. These people needed a set of rules that could not easily be misinterpreted. They also needed an incentive to follow those rules and because of their state of consciousness, the only practical incentive was the fear of punishment.

God is not an angry God. In reality, God does not punish human beings; human beings punish themselves, as I will explain later. Yet at a certain level of consciousness the fear of punishment is the only way to make people abstain from self-destructive actions. Therefore, the Law of Moses was focused on changing people's actions; their outer behavior.

When the time came for my Galilean mission, things had changed. Humankind had ascended to a higher level of consciousness. Therefore, I was able to give forth a higher law, namely the Sermon on the Mount and some of my other teachings. This law was still focused on getting people to abstain from self-destructive actions, but it went one step further. My new law identified the source of self-destructive actions as a state of consciousness. One might say that whereas the Law of Moses was focused on changing people's *outer* behavior, my teachings were focused on changing people's *inner* behavior.

My teachings were aimed at helping people realize that the most effective way to change outer behavior is to change the state of consciousness that is the cause of that behavior. My teachings were adapted to the level of consciousness that people had 2,000 years ago. Therefore, I described a direct relationship between an outer act and a particular state of consciousness. In other words, I stated that it was wrong to sleep with another man's wife. Yet to avoid committing that act, one had to escape the inner desire for the other man's wife.

For the past 2,000 years, many devout Christians have made great spiritual progress by contemplating and absorbing my teachings, even the fragmented and incomplete teachings found in the scriptures.

Because of this progress, the consciousness of humankind has now risen to a new level. At this new level, you must attain a deeper understanding of the relationship between outer actions and your state of consciousness. It is not enough to say that killing is wrong, and that to avoid killing you must overcome the desire to kill. You must realize that the desire to kill is only one small facet of a larger whole, a larger state of mind.

That state of mind is what I have called the death consciousness. In other words, the desire to kill is simply the effect, and the underlying cause is the death consciousness.

It is not enough to overcome the desire to kill, the desire for fornication, the desire to steal, the desire for mammon and an almost unlimited number of other behaviors or attitudes. Overcoming such imperfect attitudes and beliefs is a step in the right direction, but it is only a step. To go all the way, you must go to the root of the problem which is the death consciousness. You must rise above the very consciousness that causes you to commit acts, think thoughts and feel feelings that are impure, meaning that they are not the acceptable offering.

In the Garden of Eden

To begin the process of overcoming the death consciousness, you must come to a conscious realization of what this state of mind is and how it affects you. To explain the death consciousness, let us take a mental journey back to the Garden of Eden.

I desire you to understand that the Biblical account of the Garden of Eden is based on a very old oral tradition. This tradition was passed from generation to generation for so many thousands of years that most people, be they followers of orthodox Christianity or the religion called scientific materialism, would scarcely be able to accept the true time frame. Because of this long process, some of the original meaning has been lost. I will later give you a more detailed account of what truly happened in the Garden of Eden. However, for now I desire to focus on the fact that the cause of the Fall of human beings was that they partook of the forbidden fruit. The forbidden fruit is said to be the fruit of the knowledge of good and evil. In reality, it was the fruit of the knowledge of *relative* good and evil. The concept of a fruit is simply an illustration of a deeper reality. That deeper reality is a state of consciousness. Human beings fell into a lower state of consciousness, a state of consciousness that was dominated by the concepts of relative good and evil.

I have told you that everything in God's creation is created from God's light and that the only difference between various levels of creation is a difference in vibration. In the higher realms of the spiritual world, everything is made from light of a very high vibration. Therefore, the beings living in one of the spiritual realms, even the lower spiritual realm, find it easy to see that everything is an expression of a deeper reality, namely God. When you are in the spiritual realm, you directly perceive that everything is made from God's light. Therefore, you realize that there is something beyond the realm in which you live; there is a deeper reality. You cannot fail to see that your world is not an isolated world, but simply one part of a larger continuum of vibrations.

Because you clearly see that everything in your world is the expression of a deeper reality, you could never fall prey to an illusion that makes you think you are separated from the rest of God's creation or separated from God himself. You know that you, like everything and everyone around you, is simply an expression of the deeper reality of God. You know and accept that you are a son or daughter of God, and you could never lose this sense of identity.

When you are in the spiritual world, you have an absolute guiding rod which clearly tells you what is constructive and destructive behavior. It is easy for you to see what is of God (what is in accordance with God's law and vision) and what is not of God (what is outside of God's law and vision). Therefore, you clearly see what is in your own best interest, what is enlightened self-interest. Obviously, if you know that a particular act is harmful to yourself, you will naturally chose not to commit such an act.

The cosmic schoolroom

The material universe is made from energy of a lower vibration than the energies in the spiritual realm. In fact, the energies of the material realm are so dense that it is not immediately obvious that the things of this world are a manifestation of a deeper reality. It is not immediately obvious that this world is simply one pocket in a continuum of vibrations.

When a lifestream desires to descend into the material world, it is necessary that the lifestream go through a process of preparation and learning. The lifestream must learn how to operate a physical body and how to perceive the material world through the senses of that body. The physical senses are not able to perceive the higher vibrations of the spiritual realm; they can perceive only the vibrations of the material universe. Therefore, when a lifestream descends into a physical body, it no longer has the direct perception that the energies around it are simply an expression of a deeper reality. The lifestream cannot see that there are spiritual realms beyond the material universe.

To further complicate matters, the physical body is a very complex creation. If a lifestream had to make conscious decisions to maintain the vital functions of the physical body, such as breathing and the beating of the heart, the lifestream would quickly be overwhelmed. It would have no attention left over to actually do something with the physical body or even enjoy life in the material world. Obviously, this would defeat the very purpose for the lifestream's descent into the material world.

Therefore, the human body was originally designed with a mind of its own. We might compare this mind to a computer and say that this carnal mind is simply a computer that runs the physical body.

The physical body is created from the energies of the material universe. That is why the physical senses cannot see beyond those energies. Likewise, the body computer is created from the energies of the material world. Therefore, the body computer cannot fathom the concept of spiritual worlds or a deeper spiritual reality. It can fathom only what I have called the death consciousness, meaning a state of mind that sees itself as separated from God.

The death consciousness simply cannot fathom the idea of God and God's law. Therefore, to the death consciousness there is no such thing as an absolute truth. There is no such thing as an absolute law. In other words, the death consciousness itself has no concept of absolute right and wrong; it has no concept of enlightened self-interest. It sees only its immediate self-interest, and it defines this self-interest based on a relative standard.

The death consciousness is a state of mind that is dominated by relativity and separation. The death consciousness does not see itself as an extension of a deeper spiritual reality. Although it is created from God's energy, it does not see itself as a son or daughter of God (and it is not a son or daughter; as is the lifestream). The death consciousness cannot make the distinction between ideas that are of God and ideas that are not of God. It cannot fathom that something could be outside of God's law and God's vision because it cannot fathom God's law and vision.

To the death consciousness, everything is relative. Good is a concept that has meaning only as the opposite of evil. Right has meaning only as the opposite of wrong. In reality, God is good. The goodness of God has no opposite. Evil, as it is perceived by human beings, has no ultimate reality. Evil is not the opposite of God. Evil is simply the opposite of relative good, a concept of good that exists only in the material world.

The Fall

The Garden of Eden was a cosmic schoolroom. It was designed to teach your lifestream how to operate the physical body without losing your sense of identity as a spiritual being. As all schools, the Garden of Eden had graded lessons. The younger students took the easy lessons, and only the graduate students, those who were almost ready to descend into the material world, were allowed to take the most difficult lessons. The most difficult lesson of all was to learn how to operate the body computer without losing your sense of identity as a spiritual being. Therefore, to the younger students this lesson was forbidden. The reason being that if an unprepared student was to partake of this lesson, the student would almost certainly be overwhelmed by the density of the physical body and the relativity of the death consciousness. In other words, an unprepared student would almost certainly lose its sense of identity as a spiritual being.

This is exactly what happened. A group of students decided to partake of the forbidden fruit before they were ready to deal with this initiation. Thereby, they fell into the death consciousness in which their lifestreams began to identify themselves with the physical body and the carnal mind. Instead of seeing themselves as sons and daughters of God, they saw themselves as mortal beings who were separated from God.

In reality, the students who had fallen into the death consciousness were not forcefully cast out of the Garden of Eden. The Garden of Eden existed in the spiritual realm that is right above the material world. In fact, this realm is almost congruent with the material world. Therefore, when the students fell

5 | The True Key to Salvation

into the lower state of consciousness, they could no longer see the Garden of Eden; they could see only the material world.

In the beginning, most lifestreams still had some memory of their spiritual origin. Yet over time this memory was gradually lost. Therefore, you now have a situation on planet earth in which billions of people have lost the conscious memory of their spiritual origin and their true identity as sons and daughters of God. Instead of seeing themselves as immortal spiritual beings, they identify themselves as mortal human beings.

You must understand that you are not here on earth because God decided to punish you for your sins. You were never forced to come here. God did not create you as a sinner, and God did not send you here as an act of punishment.

You are here because you made two choices. The first choice was to partake of the forbidden fruit, to experiment with the death consciousness of relativity and duality. The second choice was to hide from your spiritual teacher.

You might recall from the Bible that after Adam and Eve (who represent the masculine and feminine aspects of every lifestream, not man and woman) had partaken of the forbidden fruit, they hid from God. The "God" of the Garden was actually a spiritual teacher, a representative of God. There were many lifestreams in the garden of Eden who partook of the forbidden fruit. Some of them went back to the teacher, confessed their mistake and asked for forgiveness. They received that forgiveness, and they received further training in how to overcome the relativity of the death consciousness. Now consider what happened to those who did not go back and ask for forgiveness. God has given everyone free will. If you decide to hide from your spiritual teacher, the teacher cannot confront you without violating your free will. God does not violate his own laws. If you decide to turn your back upon the teacher and decide that you either do not want to go back to God or that you are not worthy to go back to God then the teacher can only wait until you make a better decision.

The essential point that I am trying to communicate here is that you are here because you made the decision to turn away from God, or rather your spiritual teacher. The only way that you could possibly be saved is by undoing that original decision. How do you undo a bad decision? You simply make a better decision!

Decide to be saved

I have said that salvation is a process that takes time. However, until you make a fully conscious decision that you are willing to come back to God, you cannot even begin to walk the path to salvation. As long as you are upholding your original decision to turn away from God, you cannot begin the spiritual path. How could you possibly begin the process of climbing back to God's kingdom if you are still running away from that kingdom? It should be obvious that this simply isn't possible.

You cannot serve two masters. You cannot enter a house as long as you are running away from that house. You cannot move forward by walking backwards. You cannot follow me as long as you are kicking against the pricks. What I am trying to help you see here is that many human beings presently find themselves at an impasse. They have maneuvered themselves into a blind alley, a dead end or what one might call a spiritual catch-22. So many people are unhappy with their present situation and feel that life is just a continuous stream of suffering. Yet they are not willing to make the one decision that will get them started on the path whereby they can escape the misery and suffering of the death consciousness.

The situation is simple. If you truly want to improve your life, you must make a decision. You must choose which master you will serve. Will you serve the master, the tyrant, of the death consciousness? Or will you serve the true Master of the Christ consciousness? Will you choose the death consciousness or the life of the Christ mind?

I, Jesus, say as did Moses before me: "Choose Life!" Choose the true life of the Christ consciousness. Choose to focus your attention on me and accept the Bread of Life that I give to you, the bread of the Christ consciousness that I am. Take, eat—this is my body (the body of the Christ mind) which is broken for you.

6 | THE PROBLEM ON PLANET EARTH

Let us take these considerations to a world scale. The most amazing phenomenon on planet earth today is no doubt the inhumane behavior of human beings. However, when you understand the characteristics of the death consciousness, you gain a new perspective on human inhumanity.

The main characteristic of the death consciousness is relativity. To the death consciousness, nothing is absolute. Therefore, for a person caught in the death consciousness, there is no such thing as absolute right or wrong, and there is no such thing as too much.

When people are caught in the death consciousness, they can never be fully satisfied. That is why you see people engage in a lifelong quest to gain more wealth, more human love, more power, more sex, more possessions, more recognition, etcetera, etcetera, etcetera.

You can see people today who have achieved astonishing wealth or power, yet these people are still not satisfied. The simple fact is that as long as people are caught in the death consciousness, nothing will satisfy them.

I mentioned earlier that the lifestream has a built-in memory of its spiritual origin. Nothing can satisfy you except direct contact with the infinite and unconditional love of God. Therefore, no amount of wealth, power, recognition or human love can fully satisfy the lifestream.

What I am saying here is that your lifestream has a longing for something that is final, ultimate and absolute. When you combine this with the relativity of the death consciousness, you get a very dangerous cocktail. You see, to the death consciousness there is nothing absolute, and therefore there are no limits. To the death consciousness, everything is relative. Therefore, the death consciousness simply cannot stop itself. The death consciousness does not have the ability to say: "I have gone too far." The death consciousness cannot fathom the idea that it could somehow violate an absolute law because the death consciousness cannot recognize any absolute laws.

Therefore, you now have a lifestream who is on a quest for the ultimate experience yet is seeking that ultimate experience through the relativity of the death consciousness. If a soul is completely identified with the death consciousness, it is prepared to do anything in order to satisfy this quest for an ultimate experience. The death consciousness does not understand what the lifestream wants, but it is prepared to do anything to satisfy the soul's longing. The soul is like the crime boss who wants the money, and the human ego is the hired killer who will do anything to get that money. This unholy alliance is a recipe for disaster.

The death consciousness can justify anything

The problem is that by using the relativity of the death consciousness, the ego can always justify its actions. If you were to objectively examine some of the worst atrocities that have been committed on this planet, you would discover something truly amazing. It is easy to think that atrocities, such as the Holocaust, where caused by evil beings.

Yet contrary to outer appearances, there are no evil lifestreams. In reality, all lifestreams were created by God, and they were created in the image and likeness of God. God never created anything imperfect because God simply does not have the ability to envision anything imperfect. His eyes cannot behold iniquity.

You can point to any number of historical figures who committed atrocities that can easily be characterized as evil. Yet if you could go inside these people's minds (as I can), you would realize that they did not see themselves as evil people committing evil acts. In fact, they believed that their acts where necessary, reasonable and that they could be justified according to some ultimate standard.

I know this idea will seem shocking to many people, but I am here to tell you that no evil act was ever committed on planet earth. All seemingly evil acts were the result of one thing, and one thing only: ignorance. In reality, evil is a concept created by the death consciousness; it is not a concept created by God or accepted by God. His eyes cannot behold iniquity. To God, there is no such thing as evil; it simply does not exist.

What I am saying here is that even the people committing the most evil acts did not believe they did something evil. They believed that their acts were justified. How can a human being possibly justify the killing of millions of people? When you are operating from the relative standard of the death consciousness, you can justify anything. How can you possibly say that something is absolutely wrong or absolutely right? To the death consciousness, there is nothing that is absolutely wrong or absolutely right. In fact, one might say that to the human ego there is no such thing as right or wrong.

The ego has only one concern: Will this achieve my goal, or will it not achieve my goal? The ego is prepared to do anything to achieve its goal. It has no standard for saying that even the most noble goal cannot justify certain acts. Once the ego is set on achieving a certain goal, any means become acceptable. The ego does not ask: "Is it right?" It asks only: "Is it effective?" The motto of the ego is: "If it works, do it!"

The relative standard of the death consciousness is what one might call a self-centered standard. It defines this standard based on what it sees as being in its own best interest. Therefore, one person can feel completely justified in committing an act that another person thinks is completely wrong. In fact, one person might define its actions as being absolutely right. You might notice I just said that to the death consciousness nothing is absolute. The meaning is that the death consciousness cannot fathom the absolute, undivided reality of Christ. The death consciousness defines its own relative standard and then it elevates it to the status of being absolute. Thus, it is not truly absolute, but it seems absolute in the mind of the person who is blinded by the death consciousness.

When people are caught in this relative frame of mind, there is literally no limit to how far they will go. If you feel completely justified in pursuing the goal of purifying the human race, killing six million people in concentration camps is not wrong. It is a justifiable act. If you feel completely justified in spreading the ideology of communism to the entire world, killing 21 million of your own people is perfectly justified. The reason being that to the human ego the end justifies the means.

The ego does not have the ability to say: "Even though I believe my goal is just, I cannot use certain means to achieve that goal." To the ego, this evaluation is meaningless. To the ego, anything goes.

The Christ standard

You now begin to see how human beings can justify the most atrocious acts. The human ego does not consider right and wrong, but the lifestream might. Yet when the lifestream identifies itself with the ego, it can only evaluate right and wrong based on a relative standard. The ego sees right and wrong as relative concepts. In other words, right is in opposition to wrong and good is in opposition to evil. When you create a scale that has two extremes, everything on that scale is relative to one of these extremes. If something is good, it is good only in relation to evil. This is not an absolute standard. This is not a standard that comes from God.

God's standard is completely different from the relative standard of the death consciousness. In reality, there is only one relevant question: "Is it of God or is it not of God?" Is it within the framework defined by the laws that God used to create this universe, or is it outside the framework of those laws?

The relative standard of the human ego is self-centered. It defines its standard based on what, at the moment, seems to be in its own best interest. Therefore, the standard of the ego can shift faster than the sands of the desert. The standard of God is not self-centered; it is God-centered. Therefore, it never changes. It is absolute and invariable.

Human beings often misunderstand the concept of God's law. Because of the culture of fear promoted by many religions (which we will talk more about later), many people look upon God's law as a restriction of their freedom. In reality, it is quite the opposite. God's law is what gives you the opportunity to express your individuality.

God's law ensures that the material universe (as a whole, not necessarily planet earth at the present time) evolves in a way that is sustainable. In other words, because of God's law, the universe will not suddenly self-destruct, and as a result your lifestream can count on having a stable platform upon which you can build your individuality. The dangers found on planet earth are not the result of God's law. They exist only because humankind, in its ignorance, has departed from God's law and therefore created a self-destructive spiral.

When a lifestream identifies itself with the ego, it dwells in ignorance. The lifestream is ignorant of the laws of God, and therefore it cannot see what is in its own best interest. How can a lifestream escape from ignorance? It must come to know God's laws so that the lifestream can see what is best for itself.

I have said that there are no evil lifestreams. If a lifestream truly understands what is in its own best interest, it will not do something to harm or destroy itself. The lifestream has free will, and therefore it has the potential to destroy itself. Yet because the lifestream is created in the image and likeness of God (it is designed after the divine blueprint) it will not knowingly choose to destroy itself. A lifestream can commit self-destructive acts only as a result of ignorance.

How can a lifestream know the laws of God? It can do so only through a direct, inner experience. The lifestream cannot attain this experience from the death consciousness or the physical senses. The lifestream can know the laws of God only through the Christ consciousness. The only possible way that a lifestream can escape ignorance is by attaining Christ consciousness.

You already have discernment

You might think: "But how could I, a human being in a mortal body, possibly know the absolute standard of God?" In reality, this is not nearly as difficult as you think.

Take a look at human history. Numerous atrocities have been committed by human beings. These atrocities often attract undue attention. In reality, many more good and unselfish acts have been committed by human beings.

It is a fact that all human beings on planet earth have descended into a lower state of consciousness than what was originally intended by God. Yet not everyone has become completely lost in the death consciousness. If you look at humankind today, you will see that people can be put on a scale. At one extreme of this scale you find people who are completely absorbed in, and identified with, the death consciousness. These people believe that the end can justify the means, and there is no limit to how far they will go in pursuing the goals that they feel are justified. As you move towards the other end of the scale, you find people who are affected by the death consciousness, yet they still cannot accept the idea that the end can justify the means. Why are there people who are not completely absorbed in the selfishness and relativity of the death consciousness? What is it that gives these people the ability to say: "This simply isn't right."

The ability to stop yourself from doing a selfish, and self-destructive, act simply cannot come from the death consciousness. The ego could never make this determination.

The flesh and blood of the death consciousness simply cannot reveal to the lifestream what is right according to a higher standard. Therefore, there is only one possible explanation for the fact that so many people have the ability to say: "Enough is enough; this is not right!"

The explanation is that every human being has a built-in ability to reach beyond the relativity of the death consciousness. This inner ability is the open door which no human can shut. It is often called the "still small voice within" or simply intuition. In reality, it is much more than what most people perceive.

In reality, the ability to reach beyond the lower vibrations of the death consciousness can come from only one source—the universal Christ consciousness.

The outer and the inner savior

I have told you that there is a difference in vibration between the material universe and the spiritual world. When human beings fell, they fell into the death consciousness. When the lifestream is trapped in this lower state of consciousness, it simply cannot reach beyond the vibrations of that consciousness. That is why the lifestream needs a savior from outside itself. That Savior is the Christ consciousness. The Christ consciousness is the mediator between a human being blinded by the death consciousness and the higher consciousness of God. The Christ consciousness is the only begotten Son of God, and it is meant to serve as the mediator between God and the offspring of God, including, but not limited to, human beings.

The Christ consciousness was not something that was created by accident. It was not something that God created because certain lifestreams fell into a lower state of consciousness. The Christ consciousness was created by God at the foundation of the world. The Christ consciousness was built into the system from the very beginning.

No lifestream could become completely lost in this world. Within the lifestream is the open door which no human can shut. That open door is the individual lifestream's potential to develop Christ consciousness.

To fully understand the function of the Christ consciousness, you need to understand that God has created a very complex world. The world created by God has numerous levels. My Father's house has many mansions.

If you begin at the highest level, you find a spiritual realm that is made from extremely high vibrations. The highest spiritual world vibrates within a certain frequency spectrum. Below that world, you have another world which vibrates within a spectrum of slightly lower frequencies. In other words, the highest spiritual world has the highest vibrations and the succeeding levels of God's creation were created by stepping down the vibration of the pure Light of God. This stepping down of vibration continues all the way to the material universe. The material universe is made of vibrations that are quite low compared to the highest spiritual octave.

In the highest spiritual world, it is easy to see that everything is created from God's essence, God's light. As you move into the lower spiritual worlds, it becomes more difficult to see the formless God beyond the outer form. In the material universe, it is not immediately obvious that everything is created from the spiritual energies of God. Therefore, a lifestream can potentially become lost in this world.

I told you earlier, that the Garden of Eden was a schoolroom in which lifestreams were prepared for life in the material world. Before a lifestream can safely descend into the material universe, it needs to develop a certain level of Christ consciousness. The lifestream needs something to bridge the gap between the higher vibrations of the spiritual world and the lower vibrations of the material world. Therefore, the true purpose of the Garden of Eden was to train your lifestream to achieve Christ consciousness. Christ consciousness can be achieved in stages, but in the end it becomes a permanent state of consciousness in which you can live in this material world, yet never for a moment lose sight of the fact that you are a son or daughter of God. You are truly *in* this world, but not *of* this world.

A lifestream was not allowed to leave the Garden of Eden until it had attained a certain level of Christ consciousness. Unfortunately, a number of lifestreams decided to violate this law. They did partake of the fruit of the knowledge of relative good and evil, and therefore they became lost in the death consciousness.

Your potential for Christhood

What I am trying to help you see here is that every lifestream has the potential to develop Christ consciousness. It is a built-in ability that is a gift from God. This ability was not lost when lifestreams fell. This ability can never be lost; it is the open door which no human can shut.

Any lifestream that entered the Garden of Eden was in the process of developing Christ consciousness. Even lifestreams on planet earth are in the process of doing so, although few are consciously aware of this fact. Because of the density of this world, developing Christ consciousness is more difficult than it was in the protected environment of the Garden of Eden. Yet it is by no means impossible. In fact, billions of human beings have already attained some measure of Christ consciousness. That is what gives you the ability to say: "This simply isn't right; the end cannot justify the means."

The essence of my message is that Christ consciousness is not something that is above and beyond you. You can attain full Christ consciousness. You can walk the earth as a Christed being while you are still inhabiting your physical body. The proof of this is that you have already attained some measure of Christ consciousness. If you had not attained this measure, you would be a completely selfish and self-centered person, and you most certainly would not be reading this book. Therefore, if you have even the slightest recognition of the spiritual side of life, this recognition is a direct proof that you have already attained some measure of Christ consciousness. The flesh and blood of the human ego could not possible recognize the spiritual side of life. Only the Christ consciousness could give you this recognition.

My message to you is: Please, make the conscious decision to accept the fact that you have the potential to attain Christ consciousness! Please recognize that you have the potential to follow in the footsteps of Jesus Christ and do the works that I did. Please accept that you have the potential to follow the admonishment of Paul: "Let this mind be in you, which was, and is, also in Christ Jesus."

Attaining Christ consciousness is not some alien, far-flung goal that is above and beyond you. You already have a measure of that Christ consciousness, you simply need to develop it further. You need to allow the seed of Christ consciousness that I have already planted in your being to blossom and grow. You need to let that seed become the leaven that raises the vibration of your entire consciousness.

When I came to earth 2,000 years ago, most people had descended into such a low state of consciousness that they were virtually consumed by the death consciousness. Everyone still had the open door deep within their lifestreams. Yet that open door was covered over by so many layers of the death consciousness that it was virtually impossible for people to discover that door on their own.

People were so dense that they needed something to raise them out of the density of their consciousness. They needed a quickening of their consciousness so that they would be able to see beyond the lower mind and grasp the very idea of Christ consciousness and the potential for developing Christ consciousness. My beloved hearts, it was my great privilege to be the herald of the Christ consciousness. My assignment from God was to go into this world and give people an awareness of their own potential to become the Christ. I was in no way, shape or form meant to appear as an exception. I was meant to be the example.

My plea to you

I am Jesus Christ. At this very moment, as you are reading these words, I am kneeling before your lifestream at inner levels.

I am pleading with you.

I am imploring you to please, please make the conscious free-will decision to listen to my inner message. Please dare to look beyond the cult of idolatry that has been built around the outer person of Jesus Christ. Please listen for my inner message and decide that you are willing to follow in my footsteps.

When I came to earth, I withheld nothing from God. I sacrificed everything for the purpose of saving your lifestream. To this day, my mission and my sacrifice has not borne the fruit that it was intended to bear. The reason for the lack of harvest is not any fault of my own. I truly imparted my individual Christ consciousness to every lifestream on this planet. I planted the seed of that Christ consciousness within your lifestream. The reason my seed has not borne fruit is that you have not yet made the conscious free-will decision to water

6 | The Problem on Planet Earth

that seed and allow it to grow until it bears the fruit of Christ consciousness. You have not dared to let my individual Christ consciousness, which was broken for you, blossom into the fullness of your Christ consciousness.

My beloved hearts, I do not need you to be Christians—I need you to be Christs! I do not need you to be Christs after you depart from this planet. I need you to be Christed ones in embodiment here on earth, right now, in this age. I need you to be the Christ here below as I am the Christ here Above.

In this way, we can become one—as Above, so below. Through that oneness, we can bring our Father's kingdom into full physical manifestation on this planet. It is the Father's good pleasure to give you the kingdom.

So many people, no matter what religion they belong to, subscribe to the fallacy that God's kingdom can be attained only in the spiritual world. In reality, God desires to see his kingdom manifest at every level of his creation. Why would God possibly want to create a world in which his kingdom was not manifest? Does this idea really make sense to you?

God's kingdom is not presently manifest on planet earth because people's state of consciousness is simply too low for God's kingdom to manifest. God desires to change that situation. I desire to change that situation. However, neither God nor I can change the situation against your free will. It is not necessary that every human being on earth agrees to having God's kingdom physically manifest. But it is necessary that a certain number of people, a critical mass of people, make the conscious free-will decision that they do indeed want God's kingdom to be manifest on this planet. And then they must make the decision that they are willing to be the instruments for bringing that kingdom to earth. They must be willing to be the Christed ones in embodiment and thereby provide the open door through which God can bring forth his kingdom.

There is only one way to bring God's kingdom to earth, and that is through the Christ consciousness. There is only one way to solve the almost infinite variety of problems found on this planet. The only possible solution to the problems created by the death consciousness is to bring the higher consciousness of the Christ mind.

I am Jesus Christ, and I desire to see God's kingdom manifest on earth. Yet I am not in embodiment on planet earth. Therefore, my hands are tied.

Even if I were in embodiment, it is not enough that one person decides to bring forth God's kingdom. God wants a certain number of people to reach the conscious awareness and make the conscious decision that they are willing to reach for the Christ consciousness and to reach for God's kingdom. It is only through this conscious decision that God will bring forth his kingdom in this world.

God has given you free will. God respects his own law. If you decide to ignore, deny or explain away the message I have just given you, God will respect your choice. God will simply allow humankind to continue to descend into the self-destructive spiral they have created. God will allow civilization to self-destruct through the relativity of the death consciousness. What else can God do without violating your free will?

However, if a certain number of people will make the conscious decision that they will not allow civilization to self-destruct then these people will give God the authority to create change on planet earth.

Please do not sit here and think that this message applies to someone else. Please do not make the decision that even though you think my message is true, someone else will have to carry it out. If everyone makes that decision, nothing will happen.

Therefore, the key to bringing about change on this planet, the key to bringing about change in your personal life, is you and your decision to reach for your individual Christhood. Do not be concerned about other people. Right now, the only thing that matters is you.

How will you respond to my message? Will you choose to be the Christ that you truly are, or will you choose not to be that Christ? Will you continue to be the mortal human being instead of the immortal spiritual being? Or will you decide that it is time to drink the new wine of the Christ consciousness? I, Jesus, can only wait until you make your decision.

7 | UNDERSTANDING CHRIST CONSCIOUSNESS

I am sure you are beginning to realize that the main point of these discourses is to encourage you to begin the process of attaining Christ consciousness. Because this is a very important goal, and because most people have been indoctrinated with various beliefs that are in direct opposition to that goal, I desire to give you a more detailed understanding of Christ consciousness. To give you this understanding, we need to step back and consider how God created the world of form.

To a lifestream who is fully or partially engulfed by the death consciousness, God will inevitably seem like a mystery. Yet as you begin to put on Christ consciousness, the mystery starts fading until it is replaced by knowledge.

I am aware that it might be difficult for you to understand the following ideas. Therefore, I am asking you to please avoid making an outer judgment about the validity of these ideas. Do not allow your human ego to cause you to reject these ideas because they somehow go beyond or contradict an outer doctrine that you have come to accept as infallible. Instead, I am asking you to contemplate these ideas with an open mind and heart. Allow me to reveal the truth of these ideas directly in your heart.

To a human being, it is often difficult to accept that God has both an impersonal and a personal aspect. Most people see God as a Being who is far removed from them. Therefore, they tend to think that God has no personality or individuality. This idea is both correct and incorrect at the same time.

What is God?

Let us consider the question: "What is God?" In the ultimate sense, God is a state of pure Being. This state of pure Being has no form, no expression, no individuality or personality. It is virtually impossible to describe this pure Being through the words and concepts found in the material universe. Many spiritual teachings have described this state of God as the "void" in an attempt to indicate that you cannot project material images upon God. God is beyond any words or images found in this world. That is one reason why the death consciousness, which thinks in the words and images of this world, cannot fathom God.

One might say that the pure Being of God simply is. And that is all that can be said about it.

The state of pure Being is formless. You live in a world in which everything has some kind of form, and I call it the "world of form." The state of pure Being did not create the world of form. This world was created by another aspect of God which one might call the "Creator."

The Creator is a being who is conscious of its own existence and of its ability to create. I have already said that in order to create you must be able to make choices. God has unlimited imagination, and before creating the world of form, God could imagine an infinite variety of options. Why did God choose to create this world and not one of the many other options? Why is this world designed the way it is and not some other way? The answer is that the Creator designed the world the way it is because God simply expressed its individuality. The God who acts as the Creator is different from the impersonal aspect of pure Being. The Creator is an individualization of the state of pure Being. This does not mean that God has a personality that resembles the personality of a human being. It is important that you do not try to reason backwards and project human qualities upon God. Yet it does mean that God has individuality, and it is this individuality that you see expressed in the world of form in which you live.

When God started the creative process, God said: "Let there be Light." During this process, the Creator extracted from the state of pure Being a substance, namely light, that could be molded into any conceivable form. This light was not fundamentally different from pure Being. Pure Being is a form of consciousness. The Creator is a form of consciousness. Therefore, the Light of God is also a form of consciousness, a state of being.

What we now see is that the entire world of form is the result of an interaction between two beings or two expressions of the consciousness of God. You might notice that up until this point I have not attached a gender to God. The state of pure Being is beyond all divisions or classifications. Therefore, it is meaningless to say that the state of pure Being has gender. The Creator is an active state of consciousness and it acts upon the passive element which I have called light.

The most simple, yet beautiful, illustration of this polarity between an active and a passive element is a symbol found in the religion of Taoism. This symbol is called the Tai-Chi. It depicts two elements, the yang, active or male element and the yin, passive or feminine element. It is the interaction between these two elements that gives rise to the entire world of form. In the Judeo-Christian tradition, people have traditionally attached the male gender to God. In reality, God is both male and female. One might say that the Creator is the Father and that light is the Mother. Therefore, the world is created by the Father-Mother God.

God has individuality

The Creator set the basic matrix for the world, and this matrix is a hierarchical structure with numerous levels. I have earlier described this as a continuum of vibrations. The continuum can be divided into a series of octaves or spheres. You might visualize this as a series of concentric spheres that radiate from the very center of Being. I am not saying this visualization is entirely accurate, but no material image can accurately describe God's creation.

At the center of creation is a sphere in which reside the highest representatives of God in the world of form. These two beings are called Alpha and Omega. They are not the only spiritual beings in that sphere. One might say that the Father-Mother God created sons and daughters of God.

Beyond the central sphere is a number of other spheres that stretch all the way from the center of God's Being to the material universe in which you live. The central sphere is created from light of a very high vibration. As you travel away from the center, you travel into spheres that are created from light of successively lower vibrations.

Each sphere is inhabited by a number of spiritual beings. Each spiritual being is created in the image and likeness of God. In other words, each of the spiritual beings in God's creation has consciousness, individuality and the ability to create. Each lifestream has a unique individuality, and one might say that the very purpose of life is to express that individuality by creating part of God's creation.

The image I am trying to communicate is that the entire world of form was not created by one being. The beings at each level act as co-creators and help create their particular world. In the process of helping to create their world, these beings also help create or build their individuality.

On earth, children might have many similarities with their parents, but they are still unique individuals. Therefore, children might decide to travel away from their childhood home. This is also the case in the spiritual worlds. The beings at each level produce spiritual children. Some of these lifestreams choose to leave their native world and travel into other spheres. A lifestream can travel in both directions. It can choose to ascend to a higher sphere, or it might descend to a lower sphere to experience life at that level of God's creation.

The spiritual hierarchy

What I am trying to help you understand here is that the world of form is created by a hierarchy of spiritual beings who are conscious of their own existence and of their ability to create. How does this relate to you?

You might look at yourself as a mortal human being who is somehow separated from God. In reality, you are a spiritual being who is part of the hierarchy of spiritual beings that leads all the way back to the highest spiritual beings, namely Alpha and Omega. Your lifestream was created as part of this hierarchical chain. In one sense, you are the offspring of the Creator. Yet your lifestream was not necessarily created directly by the Creator or by Alpha and Omega. Many lifestreams on earth were created by spiritual beings at one of the other levels of the spiritual world.

A newly created lifestream can be compared to a child who does not fully know itself or its creative potential. Therefore, when your lifestream was created, you saw yourself as the offspring of your spiritual parents, but you did not see that your spiritual parents were the offspring of Alpha and Omega. In other words, you did not realize that you are part of a chain that goes all the way back to God. You did not realize that you are a son or daughter of God.

It is not God's intention, nor is it the intention of your spiritual parents, that your lifestream should forever remain in ignorance of your true identity. It is God's intention that your lifestream should gradually build a sense of identity as being an individualization of God. How can a lifestream build this sense of identity? It can do so only by perceiving a direct connection between itself and God.

How can a lifestream see a direct connection between itself and the highest expression of God? It can do so only by looking beyond the level of the world of form at which it is created. What gives the lifestream the ability to look beyond any aspect of the world of form and see that, regardless of outer appearances, everything is created from the essence of God? The lifestream can do this only through the Christ consciousness.

The only begotten Son

The universal Christ consciousness is the only begotten Son of the Father-Mother God. It is called the only begotten Son because it alone knows its heritage. In other words, the Christ consciousness can see that all manifestations in the world of form are simply the expressions of the deeper reality of God. The Christ consciousness can see beyond any outer appearance. It can even see beyond the world of form and perceive the state of pure Being. The Christ consciousness is a universal state of consciousness. By that I mean that it is not individualized. It is individualized only when a spiritual being (a son or daughter of God) makes a free-will decision to unite with that Christ mind and thereby come to a full recognition of its spiritual identity and origin.

Alpha and Omega personally created a number of spiritual beings. Even these spiritual beings were not created in the fullness of the Christ consciousness. They had to go through a gradual process of putting on that Christ consciousness. Yet for a spiritual being created by the highest individualizations of God, putting on Christ consciousness is not a difficult process. Still, such a spiritual being must make a choice to put on the Christ consciousness.

Obviously, as you move to the lower levels of the spiritual world, the lifestreams created at those levels have to go through a more difficult process to put on their individual Christ consciousness. Yet any lifestream created at any level has the capacity to put on the full measure of its personal Christ consciousness.

In the image and likeness of God

Any lifestream, any spiritual being, is created in the image and likeness of God, meaning that it is given free will and the ability to imagine and create. Obviously, a new and inexperienced lifestream does not have the full creative abilities of Alpha and Omega. If it did, it could literally destroy the entire universe by thinking one wrong thought. Therefore, a new lifestream must go through a process whereby it gradually grows in understanding and maturity. The lifestream learns to express its individuality in a way that is not destructive to itself or other beings in God's creation. As a lifestream goes through this process, its creative abilities will be increased. As a lifestream shows itself to be faithful over a few things, God will make it ruler over many things.

This process is a path whereby the lifestream puts on the Christ consciousness and eventually comes to the full realization that it is a son or daughter of the most high God. When that state of consciousness is achieved, the universal Christ consciousness has become individualized through that lifestream's union with the universal Christ mind.

The point of telling you this long story is to help you realize that the material universe was not created by the highest individualization of God. It was created by certain representatives of God. According to the Hebrew Bible, the earth was created by Elohim. In Hebrew, Elohim is a plural word.

In other words, a number of spiritual beings (seven to be exact), created planet earth. However, the Elohim did not finish the creation of this planet (in God's ever-expanding creation, nothing is ever finished). They created the earth only as a platform. A number of spiritual beings, what you would call human beings, decided to descend to this planet and take on human bodies. Originally, these spiritual beings were meant to be co-creators with Elohim. In other words, they were meant to continue the creation of this planet and to fill in the details of the larger picture created by Elohim. The inhabitants of earth are meant to be part of a hierarchy of spiritual beings leading all the way back to Alpha and Omega.

For a long time, the inhabitants of earth did in fact fill their place in the chain of being. They made a sincere effort to attain Christhood and they used their creative abilities in accordance with the laws of God. Therefore, planet earth was a shining star in the firmament of God's Being. Then came the Fall from grace, and things began to change.

7 | Understanding Christ Consciousness

Knowing your true identity

Through the Christ consciousness, a person will recognize his or her identity. Through the Christ consciousness, a person will gain a direct perception of the laws and principles that God used to create a sustainable universe that will not self-destruct. Therefore, that person can co-create with God in such a way that he or she will not self-destruct. If enough people strive for Christ consciousness, humankind will not self-destruct.

When you know your spiritual origin and when you know the laws of God, you have the perfect foundation for expressing your individuality in a safe environment in which you will not destroy yourself or your spiritual brothers and sisters. Likewise, you will not destroy the material platform created by your spiritual parents.

It is essential for you to realize that knowing and following the laws of God is not a restriction of your individuality or of your creative expression. Knowing your true identity is the very key to expressing your individuality. Right now, you might identify yourself as a being with many human characteristics. In reality, you are far more than both the physical body and the outer personality.

Behind this outer facade is an incredibly beautiful spiritual being. Your lifestream was created by two spiritual parents who imagined nothing but beauty and perfection. Your spiritual parents gave you a unique individuality. You are different from any other lifestream in the world of form. And I can tell you that there are numberless numbers of lifestreams inhabiting the world of form.

Yet in this myriad of lifestreams you have a unique individuality. You can bring forth a facet of God that no other lifestream could possibly bring forth. You can bring a gift to planet earth that no one else could possibly bring.

I sincerely hope that these words will inspire you to look beyond the outer disguise of the physical body and the human personality. I hope I can inspire you to look beyond even the death consciousness itself. I hope I can inspire you to start putting on your individual Christ consciousness so that you can see the divine individuality that you truly are.

Please understand that your true individuality is not something that is set in stone. Your spiritual parents created you, but they did not complete the creative process. It is up to you to finish the process (although the process might never be finished) of building your individuality. Your spiritual parents simply gave you a starting point. It is up to you to decide how you will continue to form your individuality as a spiritual being with the potential to become all of God.

I am aware that to some Christians these ideas will seem like blasphemy. When I walked the earth 2,000 years ago, the Jewish religion imposed capital punishment upon anyone who dared to compare himself to God or to say that he was the offspring of God. Yet the Bible itself contains the statement: "Ye are gods." I repeated that statement on several occasions. The Bible itself also contains the statement: "Without Him was not anything made that was made."

Simply consider the question: "How could God possibly create something that was different from itself?" In the ultimate sense, God is what I called the state of pure Being. This state of Being is all there is. The state of pure Being does not have form. Therefore, it does not have any limitations in time or space. It is meaningless to talk about time, space or any other form of limitation when you are talking about the state of pure Being. It isn't this or that; it simply is. In other words, there is nothing that is outside of, or different from, the state of pure Being. Even if the original Creator wanted to create something that was different from itself, it simply could not do so. It is not possible to create something that is not made from God's substance.

It is possible to create something that is different from God's original vision and intention for this particular universe. It is possible to create something that is not in accord with the laws of God. Therefore, that something might appear to be different from God or separated from God. This is precisely what happened on planet earth. Human beings, or rather spiritual beings, were originally designed to be co-creators with God. When human beings fell into a lower state of consciousness, that original intent was not altered.

You are a co-Creator

How do you co-create? You create because your lifestream is constantly receiving a stream of energy from the spiritual world. You create by qualifying this spiritual energy through the images that you allow your conscious attention to dwell upon. In other words, the pure spiritual energy of God takes on the form of any image that you hold in your mind. Therefore, you are constantly creating.

If you focus your mind on the perfection of God and the laws of God, you will create within the framework of God's laws. Therefore, your creation will be sustainable and it will not self-destruct. It will also be an individualized expression of the perfection of God. If you allow your mind to dwell upon imperfect images then you will begin to create imperfection.

Before the Fall, the earth was a very different place from what you see today. Everything on this earth was an expression of the perfection of God. Everything was pure, and everything was beautiful. There was no such thing as poverty, disease, starvation, suffering or any of the other limitations you see today. The beings that inhabited planet earth before the Fall did not treat each other the way human beings treat each other. There were no wars and there was no crime. There was only beauty and perfection.

After the Fall, a large number of lifestreams lost the direct perception of God's laws. Because these beings could not stop co-creating, they inevitably began to create in a way that was not in accordance with God's laws. Therefore, they brought forth imperfect forms.

I earlier stated that God did not create the misery and suffering found on earth. Human beings created it all. They did so because they lost their sense of identity.

The only way to know God's laws, the only way to start creating perfection instead of imperfection, is to attain Christ consciousness. Christ consciousness is literally the only solution to the problems found on planet earth.

When I appeared 2,000 years ago, I came to bring the very message that I have just given you. I was somewhat limited by the state of consciousness found on the planet in those dark days. Yet I did bring forth essentially the same message that I am giving you today. It was expressed in different words, and I used parables and stories adapted to the culture in which I appeared. Nevertheless, it was the same message.

Let those who have ears, hear. Let those who have eyes, see. Let those who have a measure of Christ consciousness recognize the truth in my inner teachings that have now become, for the first time in human history, the outer teachings. Let those who have a love for me absorb my teachings as the Bread of Life broken for you. Let them water the seed, the Christ consciousness, that I have personally planted in their lifestreams.

When I walked the earth, it was dangerous to express the teachings found in this book. It was dangerous for people to follow those teachings. You could be nailed to a wooden cross or burned at the stake for daring to say that you were a son or daughter of God.

In the past 2,000 years, there have been periods when it was still dangerous to openly strive for Christ consciousness. Ironically, the very Church that claims to be the Church of Jesus Christ has at times persecuted those who dared to follow my true teachings. Fortunately, times have changed. You will no longer be nailed to a wooden cross or burned at the stake for being a true follower of the true teachings of the true Jesus Christ.

Dare to follow my teachings. Some people might persecute you in various ways. They might rail against you and accuse you falsely for my sake. Nevertheless, what is that to thee; follow thou me into the Christ consciousness.

I am the Good Shepherd, and I am here to call my flock home. My sheep know my voice. Dare to recognize my voice and dare to recognize yourself as one of my flock. If you love me, keep my commandments. The only commandment I ever gave was to be who you truly are; to be a Christed one in embodiment.

Dare to be all that I am. Dare to follow my example and put on your individual Christhood. I am Jesus Christ, and I am an individualization of the most high God. You are an individualization of the most high God. I recognize and acknowledge who I am. You do not yet recognize and acknowledge who you are.

Yet the only difference between you and me is a decision. I have made that decision; you have not yet made that decision. Will you make that decision now, or will you continue to procrastinate? Will you choose to be, or will you choose not to be?

The solution to human problems

Beloved hearts, to explain why I am pleading with you to make the decision to seek Christ consciousness, let me summarize what we have looked at so far.

We have seen that God has not created the state of suffering, limitation and misery found on planet earth. Instead, human beings have created their own situation. We have seen that there is only one possible solution to the problems found on this planet. That solution is the Christ consciousness.

I have told you about the universal Christ consciousness. Yet the solution to the problems on earth is not the universal Christ consciousness. The reason being that the universal Christ consciousness simply cannot enter this world. God has created the Law of Free Will, and no being in Heaven will ever violate the free will of human beings. Therefore, the cosmic Christ consciousness itself cannot act in this world.

As a result, the key to changing the current situation on planet earth is not the universal Christ consciousness, but the individualized Christ consciousness. When I walked the earth, I expressed my individualized Christ consciousness in this world. I was, quite literally, the Light of the World. It is true that I was completely united with the universal Christ consciousness. Yet I still was not expressing the universal Christ mind. I was expressing my individualized Christ mind. The essential point is that you cannot expect some spiritual force from Heaven to suddenly descend and solve all of the problems on earth. You cannot expect that God or myself will suddenly appear in the sky and whisk away all of humankind's problems. This simply will not happen.

God can indeed solve all of the problems on earth, but God can do so only through his sons and daughters. God can bring about change only if you decide to be the instrument for bringing about change by putting on your personal Christhood.

When you consider the impact that my short mission has had on this planet, I think you can see the potential impact of thousands of Christed beings walking the earth. I hold a very high and beautiful vision for this planet. I hold the vision of 10,000 Christed beings in physical embodiment. I desire to give you a glimpse of my vision.

I see a large-scale and dramatic change in people's consciousness. I see a large-scale awakening whereby millions upon millions of people will come to a realization and a conscious acceptance of the spiritual side of life, their spiritual identity and their spiritual potential. I see a vision of millions of people recognizing their potential to put on Christ consciousness. I see them making the conscious decision to put on that Christ consciousness and engage in the spiritual path that will lead them to that goal. I see the potential for a golden age of progress, peace and growth that will turn this planet into a bright star, as opposed to the dark star it is today.

However, I also see that for this to happen, people must have examples to follow. My example took place too long ago. Furthermore, the intense cult of idolatry built around the outer person of Jesus Christ makes it very difficult for people to identify with me and to see me as an example. That is why I need you.

The call for 10,000 christed ones

I know that 10,000 lifestreams are prepared at inner levels to attain the full measure of Christ consciousness in this lifetime. Most of these lifestreams volunteered for this mission before they came into embodiment. Most of these people have not yet come to a conscious realization of their mission. However, if those 10,000 people receive this book and accept its teachings, they can quickly rise to a high level of Christ consciousness. Thereby, they can become the shining examples that millions of other people can follow.

Most of these 10,000 lifestreams have already attained a high level of Christ consciousness at inner levels. They simply need to come to a conscious acceptance of their inner attainment. Therefore, many of these people have the potential to go through a very swift and dramatic transformation from their current level of consciousness to a high degree of Christhood. I can assure you that if 10,000 people manifested a high level of Christ consciousness and continued towards the full Christ consciousness, you would begin to see some very dramatic changes on planet earth.

I also know that millions of people are prepared at inner levels to come to a conscious acceptance of their potential to become the Christ. These people have already attained a certain level of Christ consciousness. They still have a ways to go to attain the full measure, but if they will make a sincere effort, it can be attained in this lifetime. I can assure you that if these millions of people were to receive this book and receive my teachings, they would make an immense contribution to the positive change occurring on this planet.

If 10,000 people were to accept their Christhood, and if millions more were to accept the potential for Christhood, planet earth would never be the same. You would literally see so many changes within a few decades that the concept of future shock would take on an entirely new meaning.

As a result of such an awakening, the vast majority of humankind would rise above their current consciousness of materialism, hopelessness and despair. People would recognize the spiritual side of life. People would gain hope from seeing the dramatic changes that would begin to occur. People would gain a new sense of meaning and purpose. They would realize that life is not something that is forced upon them, nor is it some form of punishment from an angry God.

- Life is a miracle.

- Life is a gift.

- Life is an opportunity for growth.

- Life is an opportunity to express your God-given individuality.

- Life is pure joy.

My vision for earth

My beloved hearts, if you will make an effort to still the outer mind and emotions and to go deeply within your heart, I will show you at least a portion of the vision I hold for this planet. Were you to see even a glimpse of this vision, you would be so uplifted that your life would never be the same. You would realize that God has a solution for every problem on earth. You would realize that God is ready to bring forth that solution as soon as some people raise their level of consciousness so that they can be the open door through which that solution can be brought into the material world.

Furthermore, you would realize that you have the potential to become the open door through which God can bring forth one or several solutions to problems that human beings currently consider insoluble. You cannot tell me that this would not make you excited. I know you, I know your lifestream at inner levels, and I know you have a deep inner desire to see positive change on planet earth. My beloved hearts, if you are reading these words, you are one of my flock. You are one of my servants. You are one of my brothers and sisters in Spirit. You are already working with me at inner levels. However, I can do so much more for you and for humankind through you if you will consciously realize your divine origin and your potential to manifest Christhood.

There is almost no limit to what I could do for this planet, if I had 10,000 Christed beings in embodiment and millions of people who were sincerely striving to become Christed beings. However, we must start somewhere. Everything begins with one person who decides to raise his or her consciousness. If you desire to help bring about my vision, you must begin the only place you could possibly begin, namely by changing yourself. Make an effort to turn the dial of consciousness so that you can hear me speak to you in the stillness of your heart. I will show you, measure for measure, your personal path to Christhood.

This is not an empty promise. If you will listen with an open mind and heart, you will hear my voice. You will know that it is indeed I, your Brother of Light, Jesus Christ, who is speaking to you. If you can recognize my voice through this book, you can recognize my voice in your heart.

Dare to listen.

Dare to be.

PART 2

LIBERATING QUESTIONS

DARE TO ASK QUESTIONS

If you are reading these words, I assume that you have made the decision that you are willing to pursue your personal Christhood. I am fully aware that you might have made this decision hesitantly, and this is acceptable. I am especially aware that you might still have many ideas or beliefs that make it difficult for you to fully accept your divine identity and your potential to manifest Christhood. This is also understandable and acceptable, as long as you have an open mind and heart and a willingness to allow me to impart to you the inner truth that will set you free.

The following section is dedicated to bringing forth some of the truth that will set you free. I am aware that many people need to go though a purging process before they can accept their potential to become Christed beings. I do not expect you to go through this process overnight. However, I do expect that it will not take the rest of your life to go through this process.

I am Jesus Christ.

I am a spiritual being.

I am very much alive, and I am willing to commune with my own.

The only thing that separates the material world from the spiritual world is a thin veil of energy. I am on this side of the veil, and you are on the other side. You probably think that I am on the other side. I can commune with you through the veil if you are willing. In fact, the difficult part for you is not hearing my words. The difficult part is actually listening to my words and accepting that they are my words.

I am fully aware that many people find it difficult to accept my true, inner teachings. This difficulty springs from the fact that over these past 2,000 years much has been taken away from and much has been added to the outer teachings.

The world has changed

I have already told you that when I walked the earth, I taught at two different levels. I had general teachings for the multitudes, and I had inner teachings for those who were ready to receive the fullness of my truth. My inner teachings were never written down, and they have not been preserved in an outer form. The reason being that the planet, or rather humankind, was simply not ready to receive those inner teachings. The situation has now changed, and today millions of people are ready to receive my inner teachings.

My outer teachings, of which fragments were indeed written down, contained important keys to discovering my inner teachings. Unfortunately, most of these keys have been taken away from the written account of my life. At the same time, false ideas have been added to that written account. Originally, my outer teachings were meant to be a stepping stone. If people sincerely followed and applied my outer teachings, they would raise their level of consciousness to a point where I could start imparting to them my inner teachings. I would do this directly in their hearts.

Because of what has been taken away from and added to my outer teachings, this original goal has been somewhat subverted. My outer teachings were meant to be a stepping stone for discovering my inner teachings. Yet most people have not been able to do this, simply because the outer teachings no longer contain the necessary keys.

If the outer teachings had been preserved in their original form, you would not be reading this book. I simply would not have needed to bring forth this book because I could have given you my inner teachings directly in your heart. I am bringing forth this book for one reason only, namely that my outer teachings have been distorted to the point that most people cannot use them as a stepping stone for discovering my inner teachings. Therefore, this book is mainly meant to be a reminder. I want to quicken your memory, your inner memory, of your potential to discover, accept and embody my inner teachings.

In the following chapters, I will comment on what has been taken away from and what has been added to my true teachings. In the process of doing so, I will also reveal aspects of my inner teachings. I earlier stated that it is amazing to me that so many Christians do not ask certain questions about me and my teachings. Therefore, each of the following sections will be focused on one of the questions that I think all of my followers, even those of my followers who do not belong to a Christian religion, should be asking.

8 | WAS JESUS CHRIST THE ONLY SON OF GOD?

In a sense, I have already answered this question. Everything in the world of form is created from God's substance. Without Him was not anything made that was made. Therefore, every lifestream is a son or daughter of God.

However, there are many devout Christians who feel very strongly that I was someone special, and there is some validity to this belief. I am not thereby saying that I completely agree with this belief, I am merely saying that it is understandable why so many Christians hold on to this belief. Let me explain.

What does it truly mean to be a son or daughter of God? God has given you free will, and God has given you the ability to create. Originally, your lifestream was created in the image and likeness of God, meaning it had a unique individuality. However, your spiritual parents did not create your individuality as something that was set in stone. You have the free will and the creative potential to build your individuality upon the foundation laid by your spiritual parents. This is indeed what you were meant to do.

Therefore, life can be seen as a process through which your lifestream is constantly building its sense of identity. In an overall sense, you are meant to keep building your sense of identity until you reach a point where you realize that you are an individualization of God and that you have the full creative powers of God itself. That is why I said: "Ye are gods."

However, when a lifestream falls into a lower state of consciousness and forgets its spiritual origin, the lifestream begins to build a false sense of identity, a pseudo identity. From God's viewpoint, that false identity, as a mortal human being, is not real. Yet as long as your lifestream accepts that sense of identity, the pseudo identity becomes the only reality that you know. Therefore, that sense of identity becomes the lifestream's reality. Because the lifestream knows nothing else, it does not realize that the pseudo identity is unreal and temporary. To the lifestream, this is the only sense of identity there is.

The viewpoint of the lifestream

From God's viewpoint, a lost lifestream is still one of his sons or daughters. Yet if you go inside the box of the lifestream, inside its sense of identity, that lifestream does not see itself as a son or daughter of God. Therefore, in the here and now, the lifestream is not acting as a son or daughter of God. If a lifestream does not accept its divine origin, it cannot express its divine potential. If a lifestream does not accept its potential to be the Christ then the lifestream cannot be the Christ in action.

When I appeared on earth 2,000 years ago, only a few people had come to a full realization of their Christhood. Therefore, one might say that I appeared to be the only Son of God on earth. I had realized the fullness of my sonship, and therefore I was and I acted as a Son of God. In other words, when you look at the situation from a specific viewpoint, it is possible to say that Jesus Christ was indeed the only Son of God who appeared in that particular place at that particular time. Therefore, I can understand that some Christians have strong feelings for this idea. I am not saying that I share those feelings. Unfortunately, most people never understood that the statement that I was the only Son of God was correct only from a certain viewpoint. The death consciousness has a tendency to create idols. Therefore, people were quick to turn me into an idol and to start believing that the statement that I was the only Son of God was universally true.

Let me make it clear that every living lifestream is, in reality, a son or daughter of God. If the lifestream does not identify itself as a son or daughter of God then that lifestream cannot express the fullness of its divine potential. Therefore, from an earthly viewpoint, the lifestream is not a son or daughter of God. The lifestream has the potential to act as a son or daughter of God, but that potential is not realized. Yet I want to make it clear that I am not the only person to appear on earth with a full recognition of his or her divine identity and origin. I am not the only person to appear in the fullness of Christhood.

There have been others before me and there will, I sincerely hope, be others after me. In fact, I hope that some of the readers of this book will be counted among them.

The doctrine of exclusivity

Why did the idea that I was the only Son of God ever become an official doctrine of the Christian church? I have already given you part of the answer, namely the death consciousness and its tendency to create idols. Let me explain this in further detail.

To the death consciousness, everything is relative. Nothing is absolute; nothing is final. The consequence is that the death consciousness can never take full responsibility for anything. The human ego simply cannot come to the realization that: "I made a mistake, I was wrong and I am the one who needs to change." The death consciousness is the ultimate master when it comes to creating excuses for why a person doesn't have to change. If you look at the history of humankind, you will see this psychological mechanism at play in numerous circumstances. Human beings have a very deep resistance to change. Take a look at my embodiment on earth, and you will see how often I rebuked those who were not willing to embody my teachings and change their sense of identity. Did I not say: "Woe unto you lawyers, you entered not in yourselves (you were not willing to let the truth of God change you), and those that would enter, you hindered (in an attempt to build the case that if no one else changes, you do not have to either)."

Why are human beings resistant to change? I earlier stated that all human problems spring from ignorance. If people truly understood that their actions were hurting themselves, they would change their behavior. The problem is that as long as a lifestream identifies itself with the human ego, the lifestream will never know, the lifestream will never realize, that an act is hurting itself. The reason being that the relativity of the death consciousness can always come up with an explanation that seems to justify the person's actions and beliefs. If everything is relative, nothing can ever be completely wrong. Therefore, one can always come up with some kind of justification for an act. And if an act can be justified then why would you have to change?

As long as a lifestream identifies itself with the death consciousness, that lifestream will reject the truth of God. The lifestream will reject the truth because if it accepted the truth, the person would have to change. If the lifestream knew better, it would simply have to change accordingly. What happens when a person is confronted with a true statement, such as my outer teachings? Because the ego does not want the lifestream to escape its control, the death consciousness will seek to find some kind of relative justification for why the idea isn't true or doesn't apply to the person. That is why you see so many people, even many people who consider themselves to be devout Christians, who come up with incredibly intricate arguments for why they don't have to follow a particular aspect of my outer teachings. Of course, such people will also find ample reason to reject my inner teachings, and that is why they simply cannot discover those teachings.

The Sword of Christ

I hope you can see what I am trying to explain here. As long as the lifestream identifies itself with the ego, the person does not see any reason to change. That is why I said: "I come not to bring peace, but a sword." The sword that I came to bring is the Sword of Truth that cleaves the real from the unreal. That sword is the Christ consciousness.

To the death consciousness, nothing is really wrong and nothing is really right. Everything is relative. To the Christ mind there is an absolute standard for determining right and wrong.

The Christ mind simply asks: "Is it of God, or is it not of God?" If something is not of God then it is unreal, and it must be changed right now, right here. In the Christ mind, there is no variance or turning, and there is no room for intricate arguments to justify anything. If something is not of God, a Christed being will immediately leave it behind.

When the lifestream begins to unite with the Christ consciousness, the person becomes willing to change. Through the Christ consciousness, the lifestream can gain an ultimate perspective on what needs to change. As soon as the lifestream receives the understanding that a particular act or idea is wrong then that person will instantly leave its old ways behind and embrace the new understanding. You might recall the story of how I gathered my disciples. Imagine yourself being a fisherman at the sea of Galilee. It is an ordinary day, and you are going about your daily business of cleaning your nets. Suddenly, a stranger appears in front of you and says: "Leave your nets, I will make you fishers of men!"

How do you think a person who was identified with the ego would react to that situation? The person would immediately start evaluating, judging, interpreting and explaining away the significance of the situation. The person would come up with all kinds of excuses for why it did not have to follow the Christ, or why it did not have to follow the Christ right now.

I am telling you that there were indeed people who reacted this way when I came to them. I called more than 12 people to be my disciples, yet not all of them answered the call. Those who did answer the call did so because they had already attained a certain measure of Christ consciousness and they were willing to follow their inner understanding. Therefore, when I appeared to them, they recognized me as the Christ in embodiment and they were willing to follow me.

These blessed lifestreams did not argue or interpret anything. They instantly recognized me and upon that recognition they immediately made the free-will decision to leave everything else behind and follow me, the Living (embodied) Christ.

When a lifestream is identified with the ego, it cannot recognize the Christ, and therefore it cannot follow the Christ. The person simply cannot leave its nets of entanglement with the conditions of life. Today, more lifestreams than ever before are ready to leave their nets and follow the Christ. Yet 2,000 years ago that was not the case. Only a precious few had attained that level of consciousness, and the multitudes were still so identified with the death consciousness that they simply didn't want to be bothered by the appearance of the Living

Christ. They wanted to remain in ignorance so that they would not be disturbed and have to change their ways.

Therefore, these people were more than happy to accept the idea that Jesus Christ was the only Son of God. Why is this so? Because this gives them the ultimate excuse for continuing their lifestyle. If I was the only Son of God then they could not possibly follow in my footsteps. Therefore, they could do nothing to work out their own salvation. They simply had to wait for the outer savior, namely myself, to come and save them.

If I was an example to follow then people might have a responsibility to follow me. In other words, if they had the potential to become Christed beings, and if doing so would require them to make an effort, they would have to change their ways. They would have to leave their nets.

Do you see how the idea that I was the only Son of God can become the ultimate excuse that gives people the perfect justification for continuing in their ways?

Human beings are psychological beings. You can look at human history, and you can try to find outer explanations for why people have done what they have done. Many modern scientists and historians have tried to explain human history in terms of such outer factors, be they economic, sociological or political. In reality, the only way to explain human history is to look inside the human psyche.

Everything springs from a process that takes place inside the human psyche. People's outer behavior begins as a process in the psyche. People's outer behavior is simply the effect of what is going on in the psyche. If you want to understand the effect, you must understand the cause. If you want to understand why certain images appear on a movie screen, you cannot confine your investigation to the movie screen itself. Unless you go to the projection room and investigate what is on the film strip, how could you possibly understand what appears on the movie screen?

The ongoing human power struggle

I have given you the inner explanation for why so many people have accepted the idea that I was the only Son of God. Let me now give you the outer explanation.

Why do you think the Jewish authorities wanted me executed? It was because they saw me as the ultimate threat to their power over the people. If you look at human history, you will see that some people have had an insatiable desire for power and control. This desire for power is based on a psychological need, but I will not go into that for now. Let us simply acknowledge the fact that at any time in history there were people who had this desire for power. These people had a desire to attain absolute power over others.

You must understand that to these people religion has always been a threat. What the members of this power elite want is to attain ultimate power here on earth. They want to set themselves up as the ultimate authority, an authority that cannot be questioned or gainsaid.

The biggest problem facing the power elite is that most people stubbornly refuse to let go of the idea that there is an ultimate authority which is above and beyond this earth. As long as people believe in a God who is above and beyond any force on earth, no person could ever attain ultimate power on this planet. No matter what the kings and the emperors do, they will always be second in command. They might be able to exercise great power over the people, but they can never attain ultimate power. The reason most people on earth do not understand the existence and methods of such a power elite is that most people simply do not have an insatiable desire for power. Therefore, they cannot imagine that someone would do absolutely anything to attain power.

I know this is a difficult topic that you would rather not think about. Yet for a moment, try to imagine how this power elite thinks. Their first and foremost desire is to completely wipe out religion on this planet. A planet without religion is their ultimate dream because on such a planet they have the potential to set themselves up as the ultimate authority. Today, they are aggressively pursuing this ideal, and they are using science as their main tool for attaining this goal. Yet the general population stubbornly refuses to let go of the belief in God.

If you cannot make people abandon the belief in God then what are your options? You can follow the motto: "If you can't beat 'em, join 'em." In other words, if you cannot make people abandon their belief in God, seek to use that belief as a tool for attaining power over the people. How can you do that? You can do so by using organized religion. You start by promoting the idea that a particular church is the only true church, meaning that it provides the only road to salvation. Most people have a need to feel better than others so this idea is sure to find widespread support. Then, you set yourself up as the leader of this church. Finally, you promote the belief that the leader of this church is the mediator, the only mediator, between God and human beings and that his word is infallible.

If you can make people accept that your church is the only true path to salvation, and that the leader of that church is the only true mediator between them and their God then you have, in effect, set yourself up as the ultimate authority on earth. Even though people still believe in God, they think they can know God's will only through you, and therefore you have become an authority which cannot be questioned or gainsaid. If you were a person who had an ultimate quest for power, where would you have wanted to be during these past 2,000 years? I will tell you where such as soul would want to embody. It would want to be the Pope of the Catholic Church. Before that, a power hungry soul would have wanted to be one of the temple priests of the Jewish religion because they too had set themselves up as the ultimate authority between the people and their God.

Gods on earth

If you want to understand my true teachings, you must recognize the existence of a power elite consisting of people who want to set themselves up between God and humankind. You must understand that it was this power elite who plotted my death. You must also understand that part of my Galilean mission was to bring forth the judgment of this power elite. That is why I said: "For judgment I am come."

For thousands of years a small group of souls have repeatedly plotted to set themselves up as an authority that stands between the people and their God. I came to judge some among this power elite, and by their act of killing the embodied Christ, they did indeed receive their judgment. These souls are no longer on planet earth, but that does not mean that the entire power elite has been removed from this planet.

Why did the Church create the doctrine that I was the only Son of God? The very essence of the message that I brought forth 2,000 years ago is that the only true mediator between God and human beings is the Christ consciousness. The universal Christ consciousness is the open door that no human can shut. Therefore, each human being has the potential to attain individual Christhood, and through that individual Christhood each human being can commune directly with God.

When people have attained a certain level of Christhood, they do not need an outer hierarchy in the form of an organized church. I am not thereby saying that an organized or outer church becomes unnecessary. What I am saying is that people do not need church leaders who serve as the communications link between them and God. They do not need to have church leaders who deliver to them the Word of God or interpret the Word of God. They can receive the living Word of God directly in their own hearts, and they can understand that word through their individualized Christ consciousness.

This is the true message that I brought to earth. The power elite of the Jewish religion knew this very well, and that is why they killed me at the first possible opportunity. This power elite hoped that by killing my physical body, they had also killed me and my teachings.

This hope was shattered by the fact that I had the ability to commune with my own even though my physical body was no longer walking the earth. Some of the early Christian writings, such as the Pistis Sophia, record that I appeared to my disciples for a number of years after my resurrection. This is the truth. I did indeed appear to them, and therefore my teachings did not die with my physical body.

For many years after my resurrection, the Christian movement did not have a clearly defined and organized church. It was not clearly defined and organized because I had not instructed my followers to create an official church or set forth an official doctrine. Instead, I instructed my followers to put on their individual Christhood and then listen to my voice as I was speaking to them inside their own hearts. For some time, the Christian movement was a loosely-knit network of people who were, in various ways, pursuing the path of individual Christhood. Today, this movement is often referred to as the Gnostic movement. The orthodox Christian churches often look upon this movement as being chaotic and dominated by false teachings and dangerous ideas. The Gnostic movement was indeed somewhat chaotic and disorganized. Yet within that movement were individuals and groups of people who truly followed my inner teachings.

After a surprisingly short period of time, something very peculiar began to happen. An organized church started to form. This church gradually became more powerful, and it began to define and enforce an official doctrine which supposedly set forth the true teachings of Christ. Interestingly, that doctrine did not contain the idea of individual Christhood or an individual path to salvation. Instead, the only path to salvation goes through the sacraments and doctrines controlled by the organized church.

If you want to know my immediate personal reaction to this development, it is this: "Where in hell did that idea come from?" Forgive the bluntness of this expression, but I am using it for a good reason. The reason being that hell is exactly where that idea came from. I can assure you that the idea did not come from Heaven because up here, we all know that the path to salvation is the path of personal Christhood and that it is an inner path. Therefore, this idea could only have originated in a state of consciousness that is based on denial of God, denial of self and denial of self as God.

In reality, this idea came from the very same power elite who for thousands of years have attempted to set themselves up as the ultimate authority on earth. In the beginning, the powers that be aggressively tried to destroy the Christian movement. When they realized that this could not be done, they decided to join the Christian movement and use it as a tool for attaining power.

The oppressive Church

The development of a Christian church that was designed to be a tool for gaining ultimate power took some time. It did not really come to fruition until the Roman emperor Constantine decided to use the Christian church as a tool for uniting his ailing empire under one religion. The Roman Empire was based on a simple idea. This idea stated that the Roman Emperor was the only representative of God on earth. Therefore, the Roman Emperor was the ultimate authority figure, and he could not be questioned or gainsaid, even if he committed acts that were clearly insane.

Does it not seem peculiar to you that after the formation of the Roman Catholic Church the leader of that Church suddenly became the only representative of God on earth? I am aware that the organized Christian church previously contained the concept of a vicar of Christ. Yet it was not until after the formation of the Roman Catholic Church that the Pope attained the status of the ultimate and only representative of God on earth. Likewise, it was not until the formation of the Catholic Church that the Church began enforcing (through excessively militant means) the doctrine that Jesus Christ was the only Son of God.

What I am trying to help you see here is that my true inner teachings have been taken away from the people. At the same time, those inner teachings have been replaced by outer doctrines which are in direct opposition to my inner teachings. My inner teachings state that every human being has the potential to manifest Christhood.

Therefore, Jesus Christ was not the only Son of God. Jesus Christ was the example who was meant to show that all people have the potential to claim their divine inheritance. Each son and daughter has the potential to walk the earth as a Christed being.

If you belong to a power elite who wants ultimate power here on earth, you realize that a Christed being is the ultimate threat to your authority. A Christed being recognizes only the authority of God. A Christed being will follow an earthly authority, but only if that earthly authority is in alignment with the will of God. And because the Christed being knows the will of God, the Christed being can never be fooled by the false claims of an earthly authority.

Now imagine that a Christed being, namely myself, suddenly appears on earth and challenges those who have set themselves up between the people and their God. The power elite attempts to deal with this threat by killing my physical body. Yet even before they have time to congratulate themselves, I begin to speak to my followers and to encourage them to become like me.

The power elite now faces the sobering realization that instead of having to deal with only one Christed being, they could potentially have to deal with thousands of Christed beings. They know that if this were to happen, it would mean the end of their reign on this planet. If other people started to embody the true teachings of Jesus Christ and putting on their individual Christhood, the power elite simply would not be able to stop the rising tide that would eventually wash away their empires of power. Through these Christed beings, God could put down the mighty from their seats and exalt those of low degree.

Therefore, the power elite had to make a determined effort to completely obliterate and distort my true teachings. They had to make sure that no other human being could or would dare to follow in my footsteps.

My beloved hearts, do you see that this is precisely what they have done to my true teachings? So far, they have been largely successful in preventing other people from following in my footsteps. It is my deepest desire, and it is the deepest desire of my Father in Heaven, to change this situation. The key to changing this situation is that you must make the choice to pursue your individual Christhood.

9 | WHAT KIND OF PERSON IS JESUS?

How come so many Christians have never seriously considered what kind of person I was? Why don't they consider what kind of personality and individuality I expressed during my mission?

One obvious reason is that they consider me to be the Son of God. Because of the intense cult of idolatry built around me, people find it difficult to imagine that I had individuality and personality. Yet I was born of a woman, and I grew up as any other child. Why wouldn't I have been born with a certain individuality, and why wouldn't I have developed a distinct personality during my formative years?

What I am trying to help you see here is that most people consider me to be almost a non-person. They think that the Son of God would not have personality or individuality. This simply is not the case.

I earlier said that it is dangerous to reason backwards. The reason being that as long as the lifestream is trapped by the death consciousness, it will project human qualities upon God. Therefore, the lifestream will develop a false image of God. Yet there is nothing wrong with reasoning that the Son of God has individuality.

The reason I am bringing up this point is that every lifestream was originally created with a distinct individuality. The lifestream has a very deep inner desire to preserve and develop that individuality. This inner desire is the driving force behind what people call the survival instinct. Your spiritual survival instinct is a desire to preserve your true individuality so that it is not destroyed by any outside influence.

Because of this survival instinct, no human being will want to put on Christhood if they believe that putting on Christhood means that you have to lose your individuality or personality. Therefore, it is important for me to help you understand that you do not lose your individuality by putting on your Christhood.

By putting on the new human of your Christhood, you will have to put off the old human of the death consciousness and your pseudo identity. Therefore, in one sense you might lose some of the characteristics that you currently consider to be part of your personality. For a lifestream who is very identified with the death consciousness, this might seem like a loss. However, as soon as the lifestream begins to shift its sense of identity towards the Christ consciousness, that sense of loss will quickly disappear.

Imagine that you are walking down the street and meet a man who is dressed in expensive clothing. The man asks if you have a penny, and you show him a coin. The man now tells you that if you will give him the penny, he will give you a million dollars in return. Would you lose anything in that bargain? Yes, you would indeed lose the penny, but would it be a true loss?

When I walked the earth, I was like the man who offered everyone the million-dollar value of the Christ consciousness in return for their pocket change of the human personality. It truly was the deal of a lifetime, yet I am sorry to say that most people rejected my offer.

So many people preferred to hold on to the pseudo personality of the human ego instead of embracing the true personality that was given to them by God.

Please do not hold on to a few pennies and thereby lose the Kingdom of God. You will not lose your true individuality by putting on your Christhood. Instead, you will find your God-given personality, and you will be free from the prison house of the false individuality that is constantly tormenting your soul.

He who is willing to lose his life (the mortal sense of identity) for my sake (for the sake of attaining Christ consciousness) shall find it. He shall find eternal life through his God-given individuality.

I have a distinct personality

I desire you to understand that I do indeed have a distinct personality. I expressed that personality during my mission in Galilee. Therefore, my teachings are to some degree affected by my personality.

The truth of God is beyond this world. That truth is universal, yet when you try to express the truth through words, you can never fully express the universal truth of God. Words are not very well suited for expressing a spiritual truth. Therefore, any expression of truth will, by necessity, be affected by the personality, individuality and knowledge of the person speaking the truth.

This does not mean that there is anything wrong with the truth I was expressing. However, the way that I expressed my version of truth is not the only way that God's truth could possibly be expressed.

What I am trying to help you see here is that from a higher viewpoint there is only one truth. Yet there are many ways that this universal truth can be expressed here on earth. This is important for several reasons:

- Christianity is not the only true teaching or the only true religion found on planet earth. There are many ways to express God's truth. I will later address this question in greater detail, but I desire you to recognize that there is more than one way to express God's universal truth. I earlier said that there is no way that the universal Christ consciousness can be expressed on earth. It can come to expression only when it is individualized. This also applies to expressing God's truth, which is the universal Christ consciousness. Any expression of truth is individualized, and therefore it is not the only possible way to express truth.

- There is no expression of truth that accurately and completely describes God's universal truth. There is no automatic path to salvation. To walk the path to salvation, you must absorb God's truth. However, you cannot absorb that truth by simply memorizing an outer teaching. If you look at my life, you will see that I repeatedly rebuked those who had memorized the outer doctrines, yet had never made an effort to attain an inner understanding of the truth behind those doctrines. Therefore, you must always look beyond the outer teachings. You must use the outer teaching only as a stepping stone for attaining an inner understanding of the universal truth behind that particular expression of truth.

My particular expression of truth was affected by my individuality and personality. You have heard the saying: "Don't shoot the messenger." I would like to paraphrase that saying as follows: "Don't use the personality of the messenger as an excuse for rejecting the teachings."

When I walked the earth, there were indeed people who rejected my teachings because they did not like my personality. Once again, the death consciousness is constantly seeking an excuse for not changing its ways. Well, the truth of God can be expressed in this world only through a person in physical embodiment. Therefore, that person will inevitably have personality and individuality. As a result, the death consciousness can always find some imperfection in the person's personality or behavior and use that as an excuse for rejecting the teachings. Many people found imperfections in my personality and actions. Think about how I was criticized for healing a sick person on the Sabbath. Some people literally used that one instance as an excuse for rejecting the totality of my message.

How sad it is to see a lifestream who is ready to lose its place in God's kingdom because of a perceived imperfection in the personality of a messenger of God. I wish I could have helped the people who rejected my teachings because of my outer personality. I wish I could have helped them see beyond that personality. Yet they had their free will, and I respected that free will. I hope you will not reject my teachings because of my personality or the personality of the messenger who is bringing forth this book.

I desire you to know that my personality is not set in stone. As every other son and daughter of God, I am constantly in the process of learning and growing. I am very happy to see the rise of the self-help movement, which in recent decades has encouraged people to pursue personal growth as never before.

I want you to know that there is much more to our Father's kingdom than sitting on a pink cloud and playing the harp. The world of form is a gigantic schoolroom that offers the student an almost unending opportunity to learn and grow. For the past 2,000 years, I have not been resting on my laurels. I have actively been pursuing the opportunities for growth that exist in the spiritual world.

In some ways, I have become a gentler and more understanding teacher. I am not as quick to confront my students with their imperfections or unbelief. Yet do not let that fool you into thinking that I have gone soft.

I am a very direct Master. I do not beat around the bush. I do not indulge anyone's human ego or the death consciousness. I give you the strong meat of the Christ consciousness that I am. When I walked the earth, many people were offended by my directness. They used it as an excuse for rejecting me and my message.

I am not soft

I am concerned by the fact that so many people have built an image of Jesus Christ as being a touchy-feely Master. I simply do not understand where this image came from. It could not have come from a study of my life, even the fragmented record found in the scriptures.

Take another look at the scriptures and see how many times I was open and direct when confronting people about the folly of their ways. I came to bring the Sword of Truth and to divide the real from the unreal so that my followers could see through the relativity of the death consciousness and embrace the Living Truth of the Christ consciousness. I am here today to bring that same Sword of Truth, and in the past 2,000 years it has only been sharpened.

I hope you will not use my directness as an excuse for rejecting my message. I am Jesus Christ, and I have been around this planet for a very long time. I have heard every conceivable excuse for not pursuing one's Christhood. I have heard these excuses over and over again. Let me make the situation clear. I have ascended into my Father's kingdom, and therefore I have become a permanent resident of that kingdom. God's kingdom lasts forever, and therefore I have all the time in the world. I could sit here for another 2,000 years and listen to your wonderful excuses for why you cannot put on your Christhood. It would make no difference to me personally because I have already been saved.

You have not yet ascended into our Father's kingdom. You have not yet been saved. God is a merciful God, and He will give a lost lifestream a very long time to change its ways and start walking the path of personal Christhood. In fact, my Father is far more patient than I am.

Yet God does not give you forever. Therefore, you simply do not have time to continue thinking up excuses instead of directing all of your energy and attention towards pursuing your Christhood.

I am a direct Master. I want you to get off the couch, turn off the TV and pursue your Christhood instead of wasting your energies in a meaningless pursuit of entertainment and pleasure. Let those who have ears, hear my words.

If you will look in the innermost garments of your lifestream, you will find that you have long since tired of pursuing the things of this world. At the deeper levels of your lifestream, you are ready for something more.

You are ready for personal Christhood, and nothing else will satisfy your lifestream's inner longing. Therefore, recognize that longing and let go of anything that stands in your way as you walk the path to personal Christhood.

I am calling you to come up higher. Simply start walking, and I will show you the way. As long as you are sitting on the fence, I can do nothing for you.

10 | WHICH RELIGION DID JESUS FOLLOW?

Few people think to ask this question because they assume that I grew up as a Jew and then became a Christian. Yet this is not the case.

In reality, I did not see myself as belonging to any formal or outer religion. I was, and I still am, a follower of the universal religion of God, and I belong to the Living Inner Church of God.

I am not thereby saying that there is anything wrong with outer religions or outer churches. Not every human being is ready to follow the inner path. Therefore, many people need an outer organization that can gradually lead them to discover the inner mysteries of God. Yet God's intention behind inspiring an outer religion is that people will use it only as a stepping stone. The outer religion and its doctrines must never become a mental prison that traps your mind. In other words, an outer religion is meant to help you discover the true inner religion.

The true inner religion is a universal religion. To understand this, you must realize that in Heaven there are no divisions. You can ascend to Heaven only when you realize that everything and everyone is created from God's substance. Through this realization, you clearly see that everything originated from the same source. Therefore, individual differences are not seen as the source of division and conflict. In Heaven, we are all one.

The divisions found on earth did not come from God. They came from the death consciousness and its relativity and sense of separation. The death consciousness cannot see unity behind diversity. Therefore, to the human ego differences must inevitably lead to division and conflict. To the death consciousness, differences are also the source of a value judgment. In other words, the death consciousness always seeks to determine that one person is better than another person or that one church is better than another church.

Because of people's identification with the death consciousness, people have a desire to define one church as being the only true church. From God's viewpoint, this is a completely false and unnecessary desire.

In reality, a true church is the church that leads people to discover the inner path of Christhood. In reality, many of the churches found on earth have qualified as true churches. Unfortunately, some of them qualified only in their early stages, and they were later perverted and used in the eternal human power struggle. Nevertheless, it is essential for you to realize that the idea of one true church simply did not come from God.

There are no Catholics, Jews, Protestants, Buddhists, Muslims or Taoists in Heaven. In Heaven, you find only sons and daughters of God because once you are here, it really doesn't matter which path you followed to get here. Once you step through the straight and narrow gate, you leave all the outer human divisions behind. Or perhaps I should say that before you can step through the narrow gate, you must voluntarily leave all human divisions behind.

10 | Which Religion Did Jesus Follow?

I am a Christian mystic

For the past 2,000 years, some people have had the courage to go beyond the doctrines defined by the orthodox Church. These people have often been labeled as the Christian mystics. If I had to put a label on myself, I would use the term "mystic." I was a student of the mysteries of God.

I am still a student of the mysteries of God. I desire you to know that while I was in physical embodiment, I did indeed study and apply several different religions. You might recall that the scriptures do not say anything about what I did between the age of 12 and 30. I disappeared from the scriptures, and the reason is that I disappeared from Galilee. I went on a pilgrimage that took me far away from my birthplace. I went to Egypt and I went to the Far East. In both places I studied and applied the mystical religions found there.

In fact, there are historical records that document my travels to the East. I traveled to Persia, India, Tibet and Kashmir. Wherever I went, I studied and practiced the local religion. However, true to my personality and mission, I did not follow the orthodox religion. I followed and applied the inner mystical version of the outer religion.

In several places I began to preach the same universal truth that I later preached in Galilee. In some places, the orthodox priests would eventually attempt to silence me, and in several cases I had to flee for my life.

India has a very old lineage of spiritual teachers or gurus. During my travels in that country, I did indeed meet a spiritual teacher who briefly served as my personal Guru. He was part of an ancient tradition and lineage that stretches back untold millennia.

This tradition originated with God, and it is meant to be the outpicturing on earth of a process that takes place in Heaven. That process is the Guru-chela relationship.

When a new lifestream is created, it is not simply left to its own devices. It is offered a gradual path that will lead it towards greater spiritual understanding and maturity. As part of that path, a lifestream is offered a personal teacher or Guru. Every lifestream has a personal Guru. Every human being on earth has a personal Guru in the form of a spiritual teacher who resides in the spiritual world. Some people also meet an embodied spiritual teacher who serves as their personal Guru on earth. However, many people do not need an outer Guru; they need to discover their inner, spiritual Guru.

India is one of the few places on earth where the physical extension of the Guru-chela relationship has been preserved. Yet the idea of a spiritual teacher who teaches a number of students is a universal principle that reaches all the way back to God.

I am part of that universal lineage. I serve as a personal Guru for millions of lifestreams on this planet. There are other Gurus, and therefore not every lifestream on this planet is my personal student or chela.

Nevertheless, every human being is my disciple in the sense that they are meant to walk the path of personal Christhood, a path that I came to represent for all people on earth.

I also hold a spiritual office as the representative of the universal Christ for all people on earth. Therefore, all human beings, no matter what outer religion they belong to, must pass through my Sacred Heart in order to enter the kingdom of Heaven.

The point I want to get across is that I see myself as belonging to a universal, inner religion. I have no desire to tell you which outer religion you should or should not follow.

However, I do have a desire to help you recognize the universal inner path behind all outer religions.

I also want you to understand that in order to follow me you do not have to be a member of an outer Christian church. Being my disciple, even being my personal chela, is not an outer thing. I have disciples from every religion on earth. Strange as it may seem, I have many disciples who do not belong to any outer religion. I even have a few disciples who consider themselves to be atheists. Unfortunately, most of these disciples find it difficult to rise above a certain level of spiritual understanding.

I hope you will open your mind and heart to the idea of a universal, inner religion. If you will do so, you will discover the inner path. If you have the courage to follow that path, you will realize that religion is meant to be a personal walk with God. Religion is a path of self-discovery. Ultimately, that path will lead you to the discovery of your true self, the self that is God individualized.

11 | IS THERE ONLY ONE TRUE RELIGION?

I have already commented on this question as part of the answer to the previous question. Yet I desire to give you a deeper understanding. The answer to the question of whether there is only one true religion is: "Yes and no."

There is only one true religion, but that religion is the universal, inner religion of God. On planet earth, there is no such thing as one true religion. There are many true religions because there are many religions that teach elements of the universal path.

I earlier stated that there are many ways to express the truth of God. Therefore, there can be many religions who all teach a particular version of the truth of God and of the universal path to God's kingdom.

No religion could possibly give you a complete understanding of God. This understanding is simply beyond words. If you will think about this, you will realize why. The scriptures state that if everything that I said or did should be written down, the world itself could not contain the books that should be written. This is a slight exaggeration on the part of the author of this particular passage, nevertheless the statement does apply to the truth of God.

God has created the entire world of form, a world so vast that no human being could possibly grasp the grandeur of God's creation. If one were to write down a complete description of all that God is, planet earth simply could not contain the books that should be written. However, it would not be possible to express in human words the totality of God's Being. The inner mysteries of God simply cannot be expressed through words. No religion could possibly give an accurate description of God. The importance of this statement is that the only way to know God is by looking beyond the outer teachings and doctrines found in any religion. The only way to know God is to discover the universal, inner path behind the outer religion.

One truth, many religions

Why are there many religions in the world? I earlier stated that God does not need religion. God is a self-contained spiritual being. God does not need to be worshipped, God does not need to be admired, God does not need to be feared. Therefore, God does not bring forth a particular religion because God needs that religion. God brings forth a particular religion because a particular group of people need that religion.

Take a look at planet earth today, and then look at the history of humankind. If you were to characterize the human experience with one word, that word would have to be "diversity." This small planet has witnessed an incredible diversity in the form of many different groups of people. Based on my personal experience as a spiritual teacher, it is obvious to me that it simply would not be possible to design one religion that would appeal to all people for all time. Therefore, a particular outer religion is given by God in an attempt to appeal to a specific group of people living at a particular time. In some cases, a religion is meant to be short-lived. In other cases, God hopes that the religion will take on a more timeless and longstanding quality. Yet you must understand that God has absolutely no desire to see one religion replace or suppress all other religions.

Religious conflict is meaningless

I have a very deep desire to help you understand that the most meaningless of all human conflicts is a conflict over religion. All true religion, meaning all religion that is inspired from Above, has one purpose and one purpose only. Religion is meant to serve as a stepladder that will help people ascend into our Father's kingdom. In other words, true religion is meant to help you graduate from earth's schoolroom as quickly as possible.

As I have already said, the key to entering the kingdom of Heaven is to recognize the unity behind all diversity and thereby overcome all sense of separation and division. Therefore, nothing is more sad than to see people use religion as a source of division and conflict. When the relativity of the death consciousness is allowed to pervert people's attitude towards religion, religion inevitably becomes the source of conflict. That conflict binds people even more firmly to the death consciousness, and this prevents them from ascending back to Heaven. Therefore, religious conflict is always in direct opposition to the purposes of God. Religious conflict always works against God's reason for bringing forth religion on this planet.

If you consider yourself a religious or spiritual person, you simply must overcome all sense of division and conflict concerning religion. You must have an uncompromising respect for other people's right to follow a religion that is different from your own.

It is perfectly acceptable to share your religious beliefs and experiences with other people in an attempt to inspire them.

However, I do not desire to see my followers try to convert anyone to a particular outer religion, even a Christian religion. You might recall that I told my disciples to go out into the world and make all people my disciples. Yet I did not mean that I wanted all people to become members of a particular outer Christian church.

I am Jesus Christ, and I am a follower of the inner, mystical path to God. I want all people to follow that inner path. I want all people to be my disciples, but only in the sense that they follow the universal path to individual Christhood. That path is an inner path, and you can follow that path no matter which outer religion you belong to, even if it is a non-Christian religion. Because the path is an inner path, it does not require membership of a particular outer religion.

Let me conclude this section by making one thing absolutely clear. The representatives of God are very well aware of the conditions found on earth. We know how the death consciousness can turn a true statement into a relative doctrine. We know about the power elite who will do anything to gain absolute power. Therefore, we are perfectly aware of the risk associated with bringing forth religion on this planet. Because of that risk, we simply do not grant a patent to any human being or any human organization. No religion ever has had a patent on God and no religion will ever be granted such a patent.

The reason so many Christians believe that Christianity must be the only true religion is that they believe I was the only Son of God. If I was the only Son of God then obviously the church that I founded must be the only true church. I hope you have now realized that the idea of me being the only Son of God is false. Therefore, it should be easy to accept that Christianity is not the only true religion found on planet earth.

Let me make one thing clear. Anyone who engages in religious conflict is not one of my true followers. Nothing is more sad than to see a human being who uses religion to justify the killing of one of his brothers or sisters. I hope you realize that there is no such thing as a holy war. The idea that it could possibly be justified to kill someone in the name of God can originate only from the relativity and selfishness of the death consciousness. It has absolutely no reality in God.

If you consider yourself to be one of my true followers then make peace with those of your brothers and sisters who follow a religion that is different from your own. If you cannot or will not make peace with your brothers and sisters, how could you possibly hope to make peace with your God? If you have not made peace with your God, how could you possibly hope to enter his kingdom?

12 | IS JESUS ALL ALONE IN HEAVEN?

This question might seem naive, but I would like you to consider it. The reason being that so many Christians seem to assume that I am all alone up here with God. Because of the cult of idolatry built around my outer person, many people believe in ideas that would seem to indicate that I am on some kind of ego trip. If they think I am the only Son of God, it follows that they think I am the most important being in Heaven and that I want all people to see me as such. This is a completely flawed idea.

The Bible itself contains the statement: "God is no respecter of persons." The meaning of this statement is that God does not respect the high and the mighty on earth, yet it also applies to the beings in Heaven.

In Heaven there are no favorites. No spiritual being is more important than any other spiritual being. God has no favorite son. To God, all of his sons and daughters are favorites. How could there be favoritism and rivalry in Heaven when we all recognize that everyone is an individualization of God? How could one individualization of God possibly be more important than any other individualization of God? This simply does not make sense.

Once again, the problem is that human beings reason backwards and project human qualities, namely the favoritism and the value judgments springing from the death consciousness, upon God. I want to be absolutely certain that you realize that I am not alone in Heaven. I also want you to understand that I am not the only spiritual being who is working with planet earth. I am not the only spiritual teacher ever to come to humankind.

I am a team player

I see myself as being part of a team, and I am not the leader of that team. We are a group of spiritual beings who are constantly working to inspire human beings (what we call unascended spiritual beings) to raise their state of consciousness. This is a spiritual brotherhood and sisterhood. There is no competition or rivalry among us. We are truly one in our desire to serve God and to help bring all of his sons and daughters back home.

You will see this spiritual team referred to in the Bible as the "Heavenly Host." Throughout the ages, our spiritual team has worked with people in many different cultures. Our team has inspired all of the true religions found on this planet, and today we are continuing to inspire anyone who is willing to raise his or her consciousness and listen.

Some spiritual beings on our team have never descended to planet earth and taken on a physical body. However, most of our team members did descend to earth, as I did, and wore the same kind of physical body that you are now wearing. I am telling you this because I want you to understand that we who are your spiritual teachers are no different from yourself.

Human beings are so quick to turn anyone who rises above the crowd into an idol. We have no desire to become human idols, but we do have a desire to be seen as examples for all to follow. When a spiritual being descends to planet earth, that spiritual being takes on the same kind of physical body that you are wearing. That spiritual being faces the same challenges that you are facing.

Many of the spiritual beings that are now with me here in Heaven have gone through the same process that you are going through. They fell into a lower state of consciousness and lost the memory of their divine origin. They followed a systematic path that allowed them to gradually climb back into a state of consciousness in which they could finally ascend back to Heaven.

What one has done, all can do

I am telling you this because I want you to realize that what one human being has done, all human beings have the potential to do. I descended into a physical body, and I had to go through a process before I could qualify for my ascension. Contrary to popular belief, my ascension was not guaranteed. It was subject to my free will, and I did indeed have the potential to fail.

Yes, I want you to realize that the Jesus Christ whom you consider to be above and beyond you did indeed have the potential to fail. I could have refused to walk the spiritual path and attain Christ consciousness. I could have refused to go through the crucifixion, and I actually asked God to take that cup away from me. Yet I also said: "Not my will, but thine be done."

By the grace of God, and my own free-will choices, I did walk the path, I did attain Christ consciousness and I did ascend back to our Father's kingdom. Yet to do that, I had to follow the exact same path that you are now following—even if you do not realize that you are following the spiritual path. I had to take on a physical body, and I had to make choices just like you are now making choices.

I want you to realize that there are many beings in Heaven, and I would like you to consider them to be ascended beings or ascended masters. These beings are not fundamentally different from you. They were once embodied on planet earth, and they faced the same trials and challenges that you are facing. I can assure you that some of these beings made the same, and in many cases even more severe, mistakes that you have made. They faced situations that were fully as difficult as the situations you are facing. Yet the very fact that these lifestreams were able to make it back home demonstrates that you too can make it back home.

Let me mention just a few people from the Bible who are now ascended beings and part of the team of which I too am a part. My beloved mother, Mary, is today an ascended master, who is the feminine counterpart of Archangel Raphael. My beloved father, Joseph, is today an ascended master, and I will later tell you more about him. My beloved Magda is an ascended master, and so is my beloved Paul. The same is true for John the Baptist and John the Beloved. Over the past 2,000 years, a number of people have ascended, and some of them were indeed Christians. The best known is my beloved Francis of Assisi.

There are also many ascended masters who were not Christians. The most well-known is no doubt my beloved Brother of Light, Gautama Buddha. Yes, there is indeed no rivalry between myself and the founder of the beautiful philosophy of Buddhism. Another one of my brothers of light founded the philosophy of Taoism, and yet another the philosophy of Confucianism. I am also a brother of the Lord Krishna, who is my Eastern counterpart. Krishna brought the knowledge of the Christ consciousness to the East, as I brought it to the West.

In Heaven, we are all brothers and sisters. On earth, human beings have allowed the relativity of the death consciousness to divide them. I speak for all of my brothers and sisters when I say that we all desire to see the formation of a universal brotherhood and sisterhood on planet earth.

This does not mean that we desire to see all people join a particular outer religion. On the contrary, we desire to see people from every religion decide to follow the universal inner path that I describe in this book. We desire people from every walk of life to recognize that a person who follows that universal path is one of their brothers and sisters in Spirit. We desire you to love these brothers and sisters as you love yourself.

I am Jesus Christ, and I desire you to love your brothers and sisters as I have loved you and as I still love you. In Heaven, all interactions are based on love. If God's kingdom is to become manifest on earth, someone must begin to embody that divine love. Someone must begin to treat everyone with divine love. That someone must be a person who recognizes the inner path and who dares to follow that inner path.

My beloved heart, that someone could be you.

13 | JESUS AND REINCARNATION

The topic of reincarnation might seem shocking to many Christians, yet I have a good reason for asking you to consider it. Let us begin with historical facts. The concept of reincarnation has been part of religious life on this planet for as far back as we have recorded history (and indeed much longer). When I walked the earth, there were many groups and sects in Israel that believed in reincarnation. Recent archaeological discoveries have shown that I was affiliated with the Essene community at Qumran. The Essenes believed in reincarnation.

I have told you that I traveled to the East and studied and practiced the religions of Hinduism and Buddhism. These religions teach reincarnation. Therefore, I think even the most orthodox Christians should be able to accept the idea that Jesus Christ was indeed familiar with the concept of reincarnation. Now, let us expand our question a bit and consider whether there are any indications of reincarnation in the scriptures. Consider the passage that describes how I healed a man who was blind from birth. After the healing, my disciples asked me: "Who did sin, this man or his parents?"

Consider why my disciples would ask such a question? Obviously, my disciples must have believed that it was possible for this man to have brought his blindness upon himself. Yet the man was born blind. When could he possibly have sinned? I know that some theologians reason that he must have sinned in the womb, but does that honestly make sense to you? How could an unborn child commit a sin so serious that it warranted the punishment of blindness? Would a just and loving God ever impose such a punishment?

If you consider the Old Testament law of an eye for an eye, it would follow that blindness would be a punishment for destroying the sight of another human being. How could an unborn child possibly inflict blindness upon anyone?

A simpler explanation

Instead of such contrived theological arguments, would it not be simpler to say that the man had sinned in a previous lifetime? He was born blind as a result of the actions he committed in that life. I will leave the answer to you.

Now consider another passage from the Bible. I stated that John the Baptist was indeed Elias come again. If John was Elias, how could he have come again? John did not suddenly appear as the result of some kind of miracle. John was conceived and born by a woman like any other child that was ever born on this planet. Therefore, would it not seem logical that John the Baptist was the reincarnation of the prophet Elias?

Obviously, John was closely associated with my mission. Does it seem impossible that the spiritual being who was the prophet Elias could choose to reincarnate in order to support my Galilean mission? Today, John the Baptist is indeed an ascended master, and he is part of our team.

That team has existed for a very long time, and some of the members of that team descended to earth long before my embodiment as Jesus Christ. They came to lay the foundation for my mission. I have given you these thoughts because I know that many Christians have been programmed against the idea of reincarnation.

Did Jesus Teach Reincarnation?

Anyone who cares to dig into the historical records of the early Church will see that between the fourth and the sixth century, the Roman Catholic Church issued a number of decrees that effectively banned the idea of reincarnation as heresy. This knowledge is available for anyone who cares to do a bit of research. In fact, some theologians are aware that the edict to ban reincarnation as heresy did not receive papal approval. Therefore, some argue that this edict is not official Church doctrine. However, I do not desire to go into these arguments about the politics of the Church.

The fact that the Church made a determined effort to ban reincarnation as heresy demonstrates that the concept of reincarnation was part of early Christianity. This is simply a historical fact that no one, at least no one who is willing to face reality, can deny. If reincarnation was indeed part of early Christianity then how could this idea possibly have been brought into the Christian faith? Is it possible that the idea was part of early Christianity because it was introduced by the very person who founded Christianity, namely myself?

Before I answer this question, let us consider why there is such opposition to the idea of reincarnation. As was the case with the idea of me being the only Son of God, there is an inner and an outer reason.

Inner opposition to reincarnation

The inner reason for rejecting reincarnation is the human ego and its complete refusal to take accountability for anything.

As long as a person identifies with the ego, that person is constantly seeking ways to justify his or her actions. This can be a rather difficult proposition.

You live in a universe that is guided by a natural law which modern science refers to as the Law of Cause and Effect. In other words, you live in a universe where all of your actions have some form of consequences. Every religion found on this planet does, in one form or another, describe this universal law. The Bible is no exception because it teaches that as a man sows, so will he reap. I am sure you realize that this biblical statement also applies to women.

It is a fact of life that your actions produce consequences and that those consequences will affect you in some way. Therefore, when the ego seeks to justify a particular action, it has to find a way to deny or explain away the Law of Cause and Effect. If you accept the idea that every act has consequences then you simply cannot justify certain acts because you realize that you cannot escape the consequences.

However, the ego does have a way out of this dilemma. Most people experience that they can indeed commit a wrong act and avoid suffering the consequences. If you commit a wrong act and if no one finds out about it or can prove that the act was committed by you then you can (seemingly) "get away with it." The ego uses this common experience to make the argument that it is possible to commit a wrong act and escape the consequences of that act. In other words, if you are smart enough to avoid detection then you can also avoid the consequences of your actions. The ego thinks this is a perfectly logical and sound line of reasoning. Millions of people have been so consumed by the relativity of the death consciousness that they seriously believed this line of reasoning. How does such a person react when it is confronted with the idea of reincarnation?

The very essence of the idea of reincarnation is that you can never escape the consequences of your actions. You might be able to hide a wrong act from other human beings so that you do not suffer any consequences of that act in this lifetime. However, you can never hide anything from God, and therefore you will inevitably suffer the consequences of your actions. If you do not feel these consequences in this lifetime, you will feel them in a future lifetime.

The concept of reincarnation is a severe blow to the ego's reasoning that it is possible to escape the consequences of your actions. Therefore, a person who has based his or her life on the idea that it is possible to escape punishment is not likely to be positive towards the idea of reincarnation. This idea places all accountability upon the individual, and that can be a scary thing for some people.

What I am trying to help you see here is that many people fall prey to a psychological mechanism that predisposes them to ignore, reject or explain away the concept of reincarnation.

Outer opposition to reincarnation

Now let us look at the outer reason for the rejection of reincarnation. It is a historical fact that one of the persons who was instrumental in having the Church ban the idea of reincarnation was the wife of the Roman emperor Justinian. Her name was Theodora, and she did not like the idea that she could be punished for her actions in a future life. Therefore, she used her considerable influence to move along the process that eventually caused the Roman Catholic Church to remove all traces, or almost all traces, of reincarnation from Christianity. Theodora was a living example of how a power elite responds to the idea of reincarnation. First of all, members of this power elite do not like the idea that they cannot escape punishment. Yet beyond that personal concern, they have another reason why they do not want people to believe in the idea of reincarnation.

The idea of reincarnation states that you can be punished for your actions in a future lifetime. However, the other side of the coin is that you have more than one lifetime to work out your salvation. This idea does not appeal to a power elite who wants to use religion to gain absolute power over the people.

The modus operandi of the power elite is to set up an organized church and claim that it offers the only path to salvation. This idea works best if people believe they have only one lifetime to secure their salvation. If people believe that it is now or never, they are far more likely to follow the edicts of the outer church. If you believe that you have more than one chance to qualify for salvation then some of the immediacy goes away. You are not as likely to follow the outer church to the letter, and you are not as likely to blindly accept the claims made by the church.

Let me illustrate this by asking you to consider a historical example. When Christianity started spreading throughout Europe, Europe had a very old culture centered around the ownership of land. The owner of a piece of land would pass that land on to his children in order to ensure their survival. When the Roman Catholic Church began to spread its influence throughout Europe, the Church did not own much land. Yet after only a few centuries, the Catholic Church had become the largest single landowner in Europe. The Church did not buy land, and it did not, in general, use military power to take that land by force. How did the Church come to be the largest landowner in Europe?

Imagine that you are a landowner who has lived the good life and therefore obviously committed a number of acts that the Church has labeled as sinful. During your youth, you were not particularly concerned about these acts. However, you are now old and you are on your deathbed. In that situation, most people naturally begin to worry about what might happen to them after death. Therefore, you send for the Catholic priest who comes to your side. You have been brought up with the idea of hell and eternal damnation, and you have a natural desire to avoid this. The priest asks you to confess your sins, and after having done so, you clearly realize that things don't look good. However, the priest offers you a way out. If you will donate a portion of your land to the Church, the Church will absolve you of your sins so that you can escape eternal damnation. Suddenly, the immediate need to avoid eternal punishment can outweigh your sense of responsibility towards your children. On the other hand, if you believed that you had many more lifetimes to work out your salvation, you had no need to "buy" that salvation from the Church.

Most people are aware that the medieval Church did indeed sell indulgences. Such letters of absolution allowed a person to buy forgiveness for sins, and some bought absolution for sins they had not yet committed.

I am not saying that this example is the only explanation for the fact that the Catholic Church became the largest landowner in Europe. I am saying it is part of the reason, but what I truly desire to illustrate is that a power elite, who wants absolute control, simply cannot allow people to believe in the concept of reincarnation. This concept places the question of punishment in the hands of God, an authority that is above and beyond human beings. The power elite wants the concept of punishment to be controlled by themselves. In other words, to attain absolute control over the people, the power elite must eradicate the concept of reincarnation. They must make you believe that they hold the key to your salvation and that it is now or never. If you don't do what they say then you will go to hell right now, and there is no possibility of escape.

Why is reincarnation important?

I am bringing up the concept of reincarnation because I want all of my followers to consider this topic. Let me give you the reasons I consider this topic important.

The concept of reincarnation can explain many of the questions that Christians so far have been unable to answer. If you will contemplate this concept and consider how it applies to some of the questions you have about life and God, you will find many answers in your heart.

When I look at modern Christianity, I see so many people who have made a sincere and devout effort to follow my teachings through the outer scriptures and the outer churches. Yet because the outer scriptures do not contain the keys to my inner teachings, people have numerous questions that seemingly have no answers. Because of these unanswered questions, many Christians have a very deep, and often unrecognized, anger and resentment towards me and towards God.

Many people feel that the mission of Jesus Christ was somehow a slap in the face of humanity. The reason being that orthodox Christianity holds up a goal, yet it provides no clearly defined path to reaching that goal. The goal held up by mainstream Christianity is eternal life, yet Christianity does not provide a logical path to attaining that eternal life.

I hope you can now see that the main reason orthodox Christianity does not provide the path to eternal life is that the teachings of individual Christhood have been removed. The only key to attaining eternal life is individual Christhood.

To return to the idea of reincarnation, let me say that this idea can help you answer many of your unanswered questions. For example, many people have seen children who were born with severe handicaps, be they mental, emotional or physical.

If you do not believe in reincarnation, your only option is to reason that God wanted the person to be born that way. You are then left to wonder why God would want a soul to come into the world, into what is supposedly the soul's only lifetime, with such a severe handicap. When you add the concept of punishment, promoted by the orthodox Church, you are left to reason that God must have wanted to punish that soul. Yet why would a just and loving God want to punish a soul who had not even had the opportunity to sin?

When you accept the concept of reincarnation, you see an explanation. Every human being has lived before. Therefore, the conditions you experience in this life are the effects of causes that you personally set in motion in previous lives. In its pure form, the concept of reincarnation does not incorporate the idea of punishment. Let me explain this in greater detail.

When God created the world, God said: "Let there be Light." Light is simply energy. Everything in the entire world of form is made from God's energy. Therefore, everything you do is done with God's energy.

God has given you free will, and you can decide what to do with God's energy. However, it simply would not be just to create a universe in which beings with free will could do anything they wanted regardless of the consequences it had for others. Therefore, God has created the Law of Cause and Effect. This law states that the energy that you send out into the universe will inevitably be returned to you.

The Law of Cause and Effect is a completely impersonal law. It is as impersonal as the law of gravity. If you jump out of an airplane without a parachute, gravity will cause you to fall to the ground and die. Your death is not the punishment of an angry God. Your death is the impersonal consequence of a natural law which causes all objects to fall. The Law of Cause and Effect, or the Law of Karma as it is called in the East, was not created because God has a desire to punish human beings. It was created as a safety mechanism to prevent the misuse of free will. In reality, the Law of Cause and Effect is a substitute teacher.

I have already told you that the Garden of Eden was a schoolroom designed to prepare your lifestream for life in the material universe. The god in the Garden of Eden was not God in the ultimate sense of the word. It was a representative of God, namely a spiritual being who had volunteered to act in the capacity of teacher. I also told you that a number of lifestreams, after eating the forbidden fruit, decided to hide from their teacher.

When God created the universe, God desired that lifestreams should always be part of the chain of hierarchy, the Guru-chela relationship. In other words, no lifestream would be left to its own devices; all lifestreams would have the loving guidance of a spiritual teacher. However, God also gave all lifestreams free will, and therefore God realized that some lifestreams might use that free will to turn away from the spiritual teacher. If a lifestream turns away from the spiritual teacher then there has to be some mechanism that can act as a substitute teacher.

If a lifestream rejects the spiritual teacher, how can the lifestream possibly learn? It can learn through the Law of Cause and Effect. This law states that the material universe is simply a mirror that mirrors back to you whatever you send out.

If you send hatred into the universe, that energy of hatred will be returned to your own doorstep. If you send love into the universe, the universe will send love back to you. The Garden of Eden was the school of loving, spiritual guidance. The Law of Cause and Effect is the School of Hard Knocks. That is why the Old Testament required an eye for an eye and a tooth for a tooth. This law was given to people in such a low state of consciousness that they were not able to understand a higher law.

The Law of Cause and Effect

The Law of Cause and Effect is designed to teach you by making you experience the consequences of your actions. When you commit an act, the act itself starts a chain reaction. Your action sends an energy impulse into the universe, and that energy impulse will inevitably be returned to you. However, because of the mechanics of the material universe, which modern science will someday explain, it takes time before the energy returns to you. Imagine that a person kills another human being, but the person is never identified as the murderer. Therefore, the person does not receive an earthly punishment for his actions. The person dies of old age without experiencing any consequences. If that person had only one lifetime, he would get away with murder.

In other words, if people had only one lifetime on earth, God would have given an unfair advantage to those who were willing to lie and cheat. If you were a liar, you could escape punishment for the most horrendous acts, as long as those acts were not discovered by other human beings. By setting up the Law of Cause and Effect, God has rectified this seeming injustice. God has ensured that no one could ever escape the consequences of their actions. However, in most cases people will not experience those consequences until a future lifetime.

One might reason that the delay of consequences makes it more difficult to learn your lessons. Would it not be better if the universe somehow struck you with a bolt of lightning at the very moment you committed a sin? Yet this line of reasoning is applicable only if you have no knowledge of the Law of Cause and Effect. Such ignorance was never God's intention. God wanted people to know that they can never escape the consequences of their actions. Furthermore, if you had only one lifetime on earth, and if you committed an act that caused the universe to kill you then you would have aborted your opportunity to learn. Therefore, God has created a delayed response, and in reality this is an act of mercy.

You see, the delayed return of your karma opens up the possibility that God, through his mercy and grace, could prevent you from suffering the consequences of your actions. To fully understand this, you must let go of the age-old human idea that God is an angry God who wants to punish you for any transgression of his law. In reality, God is a loving God who only wants to see you grow in Christhood. Therefore, God has only one desire and that is to see you learn your lessons in life.

By delaying the return of the consequences of your actions, God opens up the possibility that if you truly learn your lesson, and abandon the state of consciousness that caused you to commit a wrong act then you do not have to suffer the consequences of that act.

The moment you commit a wrong act, you send an energy impulse into the universe. However, if you fully realize that your act was wrong and therefore rise to a higher level of consciousness in which you would never have committed that act then there is no purpose in you suffering the consequences of that act. God does not want to punish you; God wants you to learn. If you have learned your lesson, there is no purpose in holding back your growth by requiring you to suffer unpleasant consequences.

In other words, if you learn your lesson before the energy impulse is returned to you by the universe, God can, through his grace and mercy, consume that energy impulse before it hits you in a future lifetime. In many cases, God allows one of your spiritual brothers and sisters to bear that burden, to bear that karma, for you. However, if you do not learn your lesson then God will allow the universe to return the energy impulse to you. Therefore you receive a second opportunity to learn (the hard way).

I am aware that many people will say: "Well, how can people learn from a disaster when they have no idea it was the result of their own actions?" This is a valid concern, yet it really has no bearing on God and God's design of the universe. God has created the Law of Cause and Effect, and God has given forth numerous religions that teach people about the Law of Cause and Effect. The fact that some people have chosen to ignore God's teachings on the Law of Cause and Effect really isn't God's responsibility. It is an inevitable consequence of the fact that some people continue to misuse their free will.

God desired everyone to always have the loving guidance of a spiritual teacher. When people turned their backs on the spiritual teacher and descended into the material universe, God did not leave them comfortless. God gave forth spiritual teachings that explained the conditions that people face in this world. If people decide to ignore or distort even these teachings then God has no option left but to let the law be their teacher.

God can only hope that people will someday begin to wonder why certain things are happening to them. Perhaps they will one day consider that it is their own actions that are leading to the conditions they experience. Perhaps humanity will one day realize that they are in the process of destroying themselves and that it is up to them to change this downward spiral. God cannot do anything to change the situation without violating people's free will, and God respects that free will.

The School of Hard Knocks

Another reason the Law of Cause and Effect is an effective teacher is that people, who have lost direct contact with a spiritual teacher, often learn only through experience. For example, imagine a person who is born to be the king of a country in medieval Europe. The king abuses his power and treats his subjects very poorly. He lives in extravagant luxury while his subjects live in abject poverty. The king lives in his beautiful palace and has no idea how his subjects are suffering. Therefore, the lifestream of the king will not learn anything about the consequences of his actions.

Yet the Law of Cause and Effect will require that the soul of this king must, in some future lifetime, experience the situation from the opposite side. In other words, the soul must be born as the subject of another tyrannical king. By going through a direct experience of the consequences of its former actions, the lifestream has an opportunity to learn, and therefore it might choose to abandon the state of consciousness that leads to selfishness.

Obviously, some lifestreams have a hard time learning this simple lesson. Therefore, they keep incarnating in the same outer circumstances over and over before they finally learn the lesson and move on to better circumstances. Yet if such a lifestream is willing to turn to a spiritual teaching and a spiritual teacher, the lifestream can quickly learn the lesson that selfishness never leads to growth. The lifestream might even learn the final lesson that it must abandon the entire death consciousness and embrace the consciousness of the Christ mind.

I am Jesus Christ, and I gave my life to bring forth the teachings about the Christ consciousness. The spiritual teachers who are my brothers and sisters have also attempted to bring forth these same teachings in various contexts. In fact, no human being has ever lived on planet earth without having access to some form of spiritual teaching. I admit that because of the existence of a power elite and because of the relativity of the death consciousness, many people did not have access to a pure spiritual teaching. Yet there was always something that the person could use as a stepping stone to a higher understanding of life. If the lifestream had been willing to use what was available, and then look beyond the outer teachings, the lifestream would indeed have received higher teachings from within.

The essential message that I want to get across in this section is that God has done everything possible to make it easy for you to learn the one lesson that you need to learn in life. Yet the relativity of the death consciousness is endless. The ego can think up an infinite variety of excuses for not accepting or following the true spiritual teachings.

God has given you free will, and it is up to you to choose whether you will follow the true way that originates from the spiritual hierarchy of Light or whether you will follow the false way, the way that seems right to the ego.

Before I leave the topic of reincarnation, let me give you one more reason why I want my followers to consider this concept. I want you to consider reincarnation because reincarnation is reality. When I appeared on earth, I knew my Father's law, and I taught that law to my followers. I never wanted the later Christian churches to take away the keys to knowledge. Therefore, I say to those authorities in the orthodox churches who have taken away the concept of reincarnation: "Woe unto you lawyers, for you have taken away the key of knowledge. You entered not in yourselves, and those that would enter, you hindered. Therefore, I know you not."

14 | DID JESUS REMOVE THE SINS OF THE WORLD?

The question of vicarious atonement has caused much confusion among Christians. I desire to give you a deeper understanding of this concept. The only way to fully understand this concept is to understand the Law of Cause and Effect, including the concepts of reincarnation and karma. When the universe returns your karma to you, you will be burdened by that karma. Returning karma can manifest in many different ways, but all of these ways will be a burden to you. Your karma will often limit your ability to walk the spiritual path and raise your consciousness above the level of the death consciousness.

When I came to earth 2,000 years ago, humankind was severely burdened by returning karma created in past ages. It became clear to me that people would have little chance of following my true teachings while they were so burdened by this karma. Therefore, I petitioned my Father in Heaven to be allowed to bear humankind's returning karma for the next 2,000 years. I was granted that petition, and therefore I have carried the burden of humankind's karma for the past 2,000 years. Bearing the burden of someone's karma is not the same as permanently removing that karma. Therefore, it is not true to say that Jesus Christ has taken upon himself the sins, or the karma, of the world. I have given people a temporary reprieve from the burden of their karma. I have not given them a permanent escape from that karma.

When you consider the idea of vicarious atonement, as it is preached by some Christian churches, it is not difficult to see that there are certain aspects of this idea that simply do not make sense. First of all, we have the idea that I have taken upon myself not only the sins that were committed up until my embodiment as Jesus, but also all of the sins that could possibly be committed after that time. How could I possibly take on sins that have not yet been committed? Because I am not caught up in the death consciousness, I completely fail to see how anyone can make any sense of such an idea. This would be giving people a blank check and allowing them to do whatever they wanted without ever having to face the consequences. How could people possibly learn from this?

I am a spiritual teacher. I desire to help human beings learn their lessons as quickly as possible. However, the very essence of being a teacher is that you cannot learn someone's lessons for him or her. It simply isn't enough that I learn that human actions have consequences. You must learn that lesson for yourself or the lesson will have no impact on your life. People must learn their own lessons, and they must do so by coming to an inner realization of the truth of that lesson. A teacher can help people learn their lessons, the teacher can point the student in the right direction, but the teacher cannot learn the lesson for the student. This is expressed in the saying: "You can lead a man to water, but you cannot make him drink."

If I were to take upon me the sins of the world, and thereby remove those sins, I would also take from people their opportunity to learn their lessons in life. I am a true spiritual teacher and therefore I would never deprive my students of their opportunity to learn.

Paying your debts to life

Let me tell you a little parable to illustrate this point. Two men went to the bank, and each person received a $10,000 loan. Neither person had to make any payments for the next five years, but then the loan had to be paid in full. One man spent the money on riotous living, and when the five years were up he had no money left. He could not pay back the loan, and therefore he was thrown in jail. The other man invested his money in a business venture, and after five years he had made $100,000. Therefore, he paid back the loan in full and hardly even noticed the sum that was taken out of his account.

This is the divine intention for delaying the return of your karma. The idea is that in the time between committing a wrong act and reaping the karma of that act, you can increase your fortune. When you commit a wrong act, you incur a debt to life. At some point in the future, you will have to pay back that debt. Yet when you commit a righteous act, you make good karma and lay up treasures in Heaven. If you use your opportunity wisely, you can become a millionaire before having to pay back your debt. In that case, paying back your debt will be no big deal.

Likewise, when I volunteered to bear the burden of humankind, I intended people to use their time wisely. I intended them to apply my inner teachings and therefore increase the treasures they have laid up in Heaven. When my dispensation was over, people would be required to bear their own karma and to pay back their debts to life. Yet if they had used the opportunity to lay up treasures in Heaven, it would be a simple matter to pay the debts in full.

Unfortunately, my original intention did not come to pass. Because people were deprived of the keys to my inner teachings, most people have not become spiritual millionaires in these past 2,000 years. At the same time, most people have not made a sincere effort to rise above the death consciousness and to put on personal Christhood.

I am now faced with the fact that the 2,000 years are up, and God will not allow me to continue to bear the karma of humankind. Therefore, that karma must inevitably begin to descend, and you already see numerous signs of this on earth. God does provide the possibility that I, or one of my spiritual brothers and sisters, could volunteer to take upon ourselves the karma of a human being who is still in embodiment.

Yet this is allowed only when the person has truly learned his or her lessons in life, has abandoned the death consciousness and has made a sincere effort to attain personal Christhood. In such cases, we of the spiritual hierarchy can be permitted to permanently remove a portion of someone's karma. We have done so for many individuals in the past, and we are still doing so today. However, this can be done only on an individual basis, and it is done only when a person merits this grace.

What I am telling you here is that because of what has happened, or rather what has not happened, over the past 2,000 years, humankind does not merit the permanent removal of its karma. Therefore, I am not allowed to remove the karma of humankind. I am allowed to do this only on an individual basis. The returning karma of humankind is a serious matter that could cause much upheaval on this planet. You might have noticed that in recent decades there has been a dramatic increase in the number of prophecies that have been brought forth from various sources.

Although not all of these prophecies are true, the sheer number of prophesies should demonstrate to you that you are living in unusual times. The reason for the increase in prophecy is the return of humankind's karma.

We of the ascended masters are concerned about this situation, but God's mercy is infinite. God has offered a solution to this problem which I will describe in the last part of this book.

15 | IS THE BIBLE THE WORD OF GOD?

I am addressing this question because so many of my most devout followers have allowed themselves to become so attached to the Bible that they are not open to considering any other spiritual teachings. In fact, many of them are not even open to hearing my Living Word. Obviously, I am not happy with a situation that prevents me from communicating with my own. I am aware that many of these Christians are not likely to read this book. Yet I desire to address the question.

I am Jesus Christ and I am an ascended being. Everything that ever took place on earth has been recorded, and I have full access to those records. When I look at the history of the Bible, I can truly say that the Bible is the most complex literary work on the planet.

The origins of the Bible go so far back that both orthodox Christians and materialistic scientists would be reluctant to accept it. The Old Testament springs from an ancient oral tradition that has been told and retold over countless generations. I am sure you can see the possibility that during such a long process some things might have been lost, some things might have been distorted and some things might have been added.

Parts of the Old Testament did indeed originate as the result of divine inspiration. Many things have been added to the original delivery, and these additions were also the Word of God through divine inspiration. Therefore, parts of the Old Testament are indeed divine inspiration. However, during its long history, the Old Testament has been changed by people who did not respect the Word of God and who had no compunctions about adding, subtracting and distorting to suit their purposes.

Therefore, the best one can say about the Old Testament is that it does indeed contain fragments of the Word of God but that much of it is no longer the pure Word of God. At the same time, one must also recognize that some parts of the Old Testament were never meant to be the Word of God. They were simply historical records telling the story of a certain group of people in an attempt to preserve those records for posterity.

As for the New Testament, I have already told you the reasons I did not personally organize the writing down of my teachings. I did not want to bring forth an outer doctrine because I knew that it would inevitably be distorted. And why would I bring forth an official outer doctrine when I was still delivering the Living Word? Furthermore, I have tried to help you see that it was my intention to keep delivering that Living Word indefinitely.

Therefore, I desire you to recognize that when the original gospel writers wrote down the New Testament, they did not attempt to provide a complete account of my life or my teachings. Their aim was to preserve a historical record of some of the highlights of my life so that the growing Christian movement would not have disputes about what I did or said. This was a noble goal, but once again I must tell you that had people been willing, they could have received that information directly from me.

I must also tell you that the only way to resolve disputes among different groups of Christians is through the Living Word and the Christ consciousness. When you look at the many contemporary Christian sects, who each claim to have the correct interpretation of the scriptures that were delivered 2,000 years ago, I am sure you will agree that no written record could possibly resolve the disputes among Christians. The death consciousness can create conflict where no conflict exists, and you can never resolve that conflict by using the death consciousness itself. Therefore, no written record, regardless of how authoritative it might seem, could ever resolve the disputes and differences between people who are enveloped in the death consciousness.

I want you to understand that the original gospel writers did indeed have a certain measure of Christhood and that much of what they wrote was inspired writing. Obviously, the Book of Revelation was brought forth through direct inspiration. Therefore, it is not incorrect to say that the New Testament, in its original form, was the Word of God. However, you need to understand what is meant by the expression the "Word of God."

What is the Word of God?

It is not impossible for God to speak his words directly in this world. Nothing is impossible to God. A representative of God did indeed speak the words: "This is my beloved Son in whom I am well pleased, hear ye him." However, I must tell you that these are rare occurrences. Most of the time God delivers the Living Word through an individual human being who raises his or her consciousness to the level of the Christ consciousness. Therefore, that person becomes the open door through which the Living Word can enter this world.

I was such an open door, and so were my apostles and many other people both before and after my coming.

You must also understand that when God delivers the Living Word through a person, that word becomes individualized. In its purest sense, the Word of God is the Christ consciousness. I have already told you that the universal Christ consciousness cannot enter this world in its purest form. To enter this world, the universal Christ consciousness must be individualized.

I want you to understand that the individualization of the Christ consciousness, or the Word of God, is not necessarily a degradation of that Word. However, the individualization of the Word will inevitably be affected by the mind of the individual who serves as the open door. I have already told you that my teachings are in many ways affected by my personality.

I desire you to understand that the Word of God can be delivered in many different ways that are all valid and that all pay homage to the universal truth from which they came. Therefore, when I say that my teachings were the Word of God, I want you to understand that it was one version of the Word of God and not the only possible version of the Word of God. I want you to avoid any kind of fanaticism concerning the scriptures.

I also want you to recognize that throughout history there have been instances in which a person was selected to deliver the Word of God, but that person was not able to be a completely pure instrument. Therefore, you can find spiritual teachings on this planet that were inspired by the ascended masters yet still contain some false ideas or concepts. I will not point the finger at any particular teaching, I simply desire you to understand that even though a teaching is inspired from Above, it is possible that some of the original message can be lost in the process of bringing it into the material world. In all fairness, I must tell you that being the instrument for the delivery of the Word of God is not an easy process.

Addition and subtraction

I hope you will see that the New Testament in its original form was to a large degree inspired by God, and therefore it is not incorrect to say that it is the Word of God, as long as one understands what I have stated above. We now need to consider what has happened to the original Gospels in the almost 2,000 years that have passed since they were brought into this world.

Once again, I have access to the full historical records and nothing is hidden to me. As much as it might pain you, I must tell you that the Gospels you have today are but fragments of what was originally brought forth. Therefore, they simply do not contain the fullness of what I want you to know about me, about my life and about my teachings.

I know many Christians will be reluctant to accept this fact, but you ought to read the scriptures that you claim are the Word of God. The scriptures themselves say that if all I did and said should be written down, the world itself could not contain the books that should be written. Is that not a clear indication that even the original scriptures did not contain the fullness of my message?

I must tell you that I completely fail to understand how so many Christians can ignore this obvious truth. How could they possibly reason that I, Jesus Christ, do not have any more to tell them about my Father's kingdom than what is recorded in the present-day Gospels? To me, this is astonishing.

What is even harder for me to understand is that so many Christians cling to the written scriptures, and cling to a particular interpretation of those scriptures, completely closing their minds and hearts to my Living Word, which I have been delivering almost continually for these past 2,000 years through many different sources.

I must tell you that progressive, ongoing revelation is my true desire. What do you think I meant when I said: "I will be with you always?" Why do you think I appeared to my disciples after my resurrection? I never intended to leave you alone in a dark world where all you had as a guiding rod was a set of written scriptures that provided a fragmentary account of my life and teachings. I desired to continue to give you comfort and understanding through the living Word of God which I am. That is why I said: "I have yet many things to say unto you, but you cannot bear them now." Why do those who consider themselves to be my followers reject my Living Word?

The delivery of the Living Word

For these past 2,000 years, I have delivered my Living Word through various people who had the courage to open their hearts and minds to me. Some of them did indeed work within the context of the orthodox Christian churches. Yet in many cases the fanaticism of the orthodox Church forced me to go outside of that Church in order to bring forth another piece of my ongoing revelation. This tendency has continued until the present day, and the book you are holding in your hand is only one in a long series of these deliveries from me.

The New Testament does not represent the be-all and end-all of the delivery of my Word. You will find that Word in many other sources. Likewise, this book is not meant to be seen as the be-all and end-all of the delivery of my Word. It is part of a tradition that goes all the way back to when I first appeared to my disciples after my resurrection. It is part of a tradition whereby the Living Master, Jesus Christ, delivers the Living Word to those who dare to be his living disciples.

Choose life. Choose the Living Word of Christ over the word of an orthodox doctrine filled with dead men's bones.

The scriptures are incomplete

I desire you to realize and accept that the written scriptures you have today leave much to be desired. Many things have been subtracted from them for political reasons, not the least of which is the teaching on reincarnation. Other things have been added to them, once again for political reasons. Furthermore, many things have been lost to honest mistakes in translations and transcriptions.

I am not thereby saying that the current scriptures do not have value. They do indeed have value, and they do indeed contain keys that some lifestreams have used to discover my inner teachings. Yet for most people the current scriptures simply cannot serve as a stepping stone to the discovery of my inner teachings. Therefore, I want you to know that I, Jesus Christ, do not want you to confine your studies to the current scriptures. I want you to open your mind and heart and seek truth wherever it can be found. Do not limit God's ability to bring truth into this world. Do not limit God's ability to bring truth into your heart and mind, even through an unexpected source.

Do not forget to entertain strangers, for thereby some have entertained angels in disguise. The truth of God often appears in disguise. Do not reject the truth simply because you do not like its outer appearance. Those who want the truth of God must look beyond all outer appearances to the inner truth that transcends this world.

The law and the prophets

I would like to explain the true meaning behind the statement that I came to fulfill the law and the prophets. I am aware that some Christians have used this statement to reason that the fulfillment of the tradition of the prophets, meaning the delivery of the Word of God through an individual human being, came to an end with my ministry. I can understand why people would draw this conclusion, and I do not condemn anyone for believing this idea. Yet I must tell you that the idea is incorrect.

When I referred to the "law and the prophets," I referred to a specific period, a specific spiritual cycle, in earth's history. That spiritual cycle began at the time of Abraham.

The spiritual teaching that served as a guiding rod for that cycle was the Law of Moses. This law was given with the hope that, by applying the law, people would raise their consciousness. At the end of the spiritual cycle, people would be ready to receive a higher law. Therefore, the fulfillment of the cycle that I referred to as the "law and the prophets" was the bringing forth of the higher law that I did indeed bring forth in the Sermon on the Mount and other teachings. In other words, by fulfilling the law and the prophets, I initiated the next 2,000 year cycle. This did not mean that I came to bring an end to the delivery of the living Word of God.

The delivery of the living Word of God has been happening for as long as there have been people on this planet. As long as people are willing to raise their consciousness so that they can be the open door for the delivery of that Word, the delivery of the living Word of God will continue indefinitely. I had no intention whatsoever of putting a stop to the delivery of the Living Word. I think the proof should be the very fact that I continued to appear to my disciples after my resurrection.

I hope these words will not fall on deaf ears and that my followers, those who claim to be Christians, will open their minds and hearts to the living Word of God as it is being delivered today and will be delivered in the future.

As I said to Saul on the road to Damascus, I now say to you: "Stop kicking against the pricks."

16 | IS GOD AN ANGRY AND JUDGMENTAL GOD?

One of the greatest problems on earth today is that so many people have come to accept a false image of God. There are many false images, but the one that concerns me the most is the idea that God is an angry and judgmental God who is ready to punish even the slightest transgression of his law.

I have gone to great length to explain to you the Law of Cause and Effect, including reincarnation and karma. If you will contemplate my explanation with an open heart, you will realize that God does not consciously or actively punish people's sins.

The reality of the situation is that because God gave people free will, God had to provide a safety mechanism so that a lifestream would not become lost by misusing that free will. It was God's original intention that all lifestreams would express their individuality and use their free will in a way that did not violate the laws that God used to create this universe. Obviously, if you live in this universe and violate the laws upon which the universe is based, you will inevitably self-destruct.

It is important for you to understand that God's law does not limit your creative expression. For example, look at the situation on planet earth. You have been given a beautiful planet that is perfectly capable of sustaining a large number of people. Yet we now see a pollution of the environment which ultimately could destroy that environment and therefore prevent you from expressing any kind of creativity and freedom. Likewise, human beings have developed nuclear weapons and a large-scale nuclear war could destroy the environment and limit your creative expression. Obviously, pollution and nuclear war is not in accordance with God's law. It is perfectly possible for human beings to live on planet earth without destroying their environment. It is perfectly possible for them to do so in such a way that they still have plenty of room for creative expression.

It is not God's intention to limit your creativity, and his law is not a restriction of your freedom. If you knew God's law, you would naturally choose to express your creativity in such a way that it would not destroy yourself. The problem is, of course, that because people have fallen into the death consciousness and are dominated by the ego, they no longer know God's law. This was not what God intended, yet because God gave you free will, God could do nothing to stop you.

What could God possibly have done with a group of lifestreams who fell into a lower state of consciousness and forgot their divine origin? Well, God could have destroyed these lifestreams, and that is precisely what an angry and judgmental God would have done. The very fact that you are alive demonstrates that your God is not an angry and judgmental God. Your God is a God of mercy and compassion, and therefore He has given people a second chance. In fact, He has given people many second chances.

God does not punish you

My point here is that God does not punish you for your mistakes. When God gave you free will, He simply set up a safety mechanism so that if you misuse your free will, you will not automatically and immediately self-destruct. God created an impersonal law which returns all energy to you with the same qualification that it had when you sent out that energy. Therefore, you will reap as you have sown.

Obviously, if all of your current conditions are the consequences of your own actions, and if all of your actions, past or present, are the results of choices you make with your free will then it simply does not make sense to say that the current conditions on planet earth are the result of God's punishment.

These conditions were not created by God and they are not what God wants for his children. The current conditions on this planet were created by human beings. I freely admit that most people created these conditions out of ignorance. In fact, people have to a large degree been tricked into creating the current misery on earth. They have been tricked into creating this misery by a small group, a power elite, of souls who deliberately and willfully rebelled against God's law.

Nevertheless, the somber fact is that human beings are punishing themselves and they continue to punish themselves because they continue to allow themselves to remain ignorant of God's law. God has sent many prophets, spiritual teachers and messengers in an attempt to make people change their ways.

Yet up until this point, God's message has been ignored by so many people that God cannot bring major changes to planet earth. God must simply wait until more people reach beyond the death consciousness and begin to put on their personal Christhood.

Every human being has the potential to stop this downward spiral and to reach for the Christ consciousness. I will admit that this potential has not been common knowledge. Nevertheless, it is not my intent with this book to lament what might have been. It is my intent to demonstrate to you what can be, both now and in the future.

If you don't like what you see in your personal life, take responsibility for your situation and recreate yourself in the image and likeness of God. If you don't like what you see on this planet, take responsibility for that situation and re-create the earth in the image and likeness of the Kingdom of God.

I am Jesus Christ, and I am part of a team of spiritual beings who have pledged their lives to helping human beings rise out of their current misery. We want to see God's kingdom and the abundant life manifest on earth. We have immense power, and we stand ready to help you at any moment. Yet we must respect our Father's Law of Free Will. If you choose to remain in ignorance, if you choose not to take responsibility for your own life and for the planet as a whole then we must simply wait until you make a better decision.

I have come to tell you that it is time to make that decision. If even a small number of people would make the decision to pursue the path of individual Christhood, we of the ascended masters could immediately bring dramatic change to this planet. We are ready and waiting; we simply need your call. I will later teach you how to make that call.

Make peace with God

I have personally walked the earth, and I know what it is like to be under the intense weight of humankind's karma. Yet I now reside in Heaven, and therefore I know the incredible difference between the state of consciousness found in Heaven and the state of consciousness that currently dominates earth. I also know that God wants every human being to rise to the state of consciousness that we have in Heaven, namely the Christ consciousness. However, to attain this state of consciousness, you must heal your relationship to God. How can you possibly inherit God's kingdom and attain Christ consciousness as long as you fear or resent God? If you are willing to start healing your relationship to God, if you want to overcome the idea that God is an angry and judgmental God then you need to raise your consciousness above the level of the human ego and the death consciousness. If you will make an effort to do so, I promise you that it is possible for you to experience the peace, the joy and the love that exists in Heaven.

If you are willing to begin this process of healing, I suggest that you start reading the teachings on my website (*www.ask-realjesus.com*) and some of the many inspirational books found in bookstores and libraries. Some of these books describe near-death experiences where people left the physical body behind and traveled into the spiritual realms. Such books can be a great inspiration, if you read them with an open heart.

There are also many other spiritual and religious books, from every major religion or from no particular religion, that describe spiritual and mystical experiences that will give you a glimpse of the state of consciousness we have here in Heaven.

In Heaven you find none of the turmoil that you experience on earth. You find peace. You find love, and that love is different from the love most people experience on earth. God's love is truly unconditional. I know that as long as a person is enveloped in the death consciousness, he or she simply cannot fathom the concept of unconditional love. Yet when you start walking the path of personal Christhood, you will, sooner or later, experience a glimpse of God's unconditional love.

You must understand that we of the ascended masters desire nothing more than to have you experience and accept the unconditional love that we feel for you. You might recall that the scriptures contain the concept of the perfect love which casts out all fear. The perfect love that is referred to is the unconditional love of God. Were you to experience even a glimpse of that unconditional love, your life would be permanently transformed.

I am not thereby saying that you would instantaneously be turned into a perfect human being. I am saying that you would realize that there is an alternative to the state of consciousness that you experience on earth. This experience would give you the motivation and the drive to pursue your personal Christhood with all the diligence and fervor of your heart. Once you have experienced God's unconditional love, you simply will not allow any human condition, be it inside or outside your own psyche, to stand in the way of your inner walk towards Christ consciousness.

Christ consciousness is the mediator between Heaven and earth. It is the mediator between the state of consciousness experienced by the spiritual beings here in Heaven and the level of consciousness experienced by human beings who are lost in the relativity of the death consciousness. My greatest desire is that I could give you the experience of God's unconditional love and help you truly accept that the creator of this universe has an infinite love for you personally. So many people believe that they are not worthy of God's love. So many people are afraid to approach God because they have allowed themselves to believe that unless they live up to a standard defined by some religious authority, they will be rejected by God. The simple fact is that your lifestream will never be rejected by God. God wants you, his son or daughter, to inherit the fullness of his kingdom of unconditional love.

Reaching for God

However, you must understand that the flesh and blood of the death consciousness cannot inherit the kingdom of Heaven. You cannot experience God's love through the death consciousness. The problem is that because people have not been taught about individual Christhood so many sincere and well-meaning people attempt to approach God from the level of the death consciousness. When you approach God from that state of consciousness, God does not realize that He is being approached because his eyes cannot behold the iniquity of the death consciousness. Therefore, people feel rejected by God.

Let me tell you a parable that explains the situation. Imagine that you are trying to reach a person who lives in New York City. You have a telephone and a telephone book. If you have ever seen a New York telephone book, you know that it contains millions of numbers. You don't know the name of the person you are trying to reach, and therefore you have no way of finding his telephone number. Yet you know that if you do not dial the right number, you will not reach that person.

What can you do? You can begin from the beginning and dial every number in the book. Yet if you do so, you will inevitably experience many failed attempts, and it might take you a long time to get through to the right person. The simple fact is that most religious people are trying to reach God without having his telephone number. Therefore, they do not get through and they feel discouraged and rejected.

I am here to tell you that it is not difficult to find God's telephone number. To find it, you simply need to reach for the Christ consciousness. I have already told you that if you are reading this book, you have manifested a certain level of Christ consciousness. Therefore, you already have the potential to experience that state of consciousness. You can experience God's unconditional and very personal love for you. I will later give you a more systematic process for experiencing Christ consciousness. In the meantime, please contemplate the concept of unconditional love.

The God of the Bible

I am aware that some Christians will think that the ideas I am expressing here contradict the image of God given in the Bible. Therefore, I would like you to participate in a little thought experiment. I would like you to imagine what it would be like if you were a spiritual teacher residing up here in the spiritual world. You are now looking at humankind and the question you need to consider is how you could possibly help people rise to a higher level of consciousness.

It is not difficult to see that some people are in a very low or dense state of consciousness. They have become so enveloped in the relativity of the death consciousness that they literally believe they have the right to do anything they want to other people. They also believe they can get away with doing anything they want.

From your vantage point as a spiritual being, you clearly see that because of the Law of Cause and Effect, these people are on the fast track to destroying themselves. They are simply creating a mountain of karma, and it is only a matter of time before an avalanche will slide down that mountain and bury them. Yet these people are so entrenched in their state of consciousness that it is impossible to reach them with any kind of spiritual message.

What could you possibly do to reach such people? How could you possibly shake them out of their current state of consciousness and make them realize that unless they change their ways, they will inevitably destroy themselves? I am sure you realize that the only way to reach such people is with a very stern and direct message.

Some people have literally descended to such a low state of consciousness that the only way to shake them out of that state of consciousness is by fear. These people will not change their ways unless they fear the consequences of their actions. In other words, some people will change only out of the fear of punishment.

When you come to this understanding, you realize the dilemma in which we of the ascended masters find ourselves. We do not want to be feared by people. Yet we do not want to see our brothers and sisters destroy themselves. If the only thing that can motivate people to change their ways is fear then what are we to do?

We of the ascended masters are quite serious about saving people and bringing every lifestream back home. We will go to great length to wake up a soul and make that person realize that it must change its ways. If a soul can be awakened only through fear then we will take on the appearance of an angry God.

If the soul needs to be motivated by punishment then we will seek to make people see the threat of such punishment. Because the Law of Cause and Effect makes people punish themselves, this threat is very real. It is essential for you to understand that what you see in the Bible is not the highest spiritual teaching that God desires to bring to this planet.

What you see in both the Old and the New Testament is a measured response that is designed to work with the state of consciousness that people had at the time the teaching was released. I have already told you about progressive revelation. The Law of Moses was given to people in a very low state of consciousness. Therefore, they needed a very stern message.

Obviously, my Sermon on the Mount was a more gentle message. Yet it was still very direct. It has always been the hope of the ascended masters that humankind will grow to a level of consciousness where they can receive the true teachings of God, namely the teachings about God's unconditional love.

This does not mean that the Bible is outdated. Even today, many people are still in the state of consciousness that was addressed in the Law of Moses. Yet today many people are ready for the higher teachings of love. If you are reading this book, you should count yourself among them.

It was my original hope that people would use my teachings to walk the path of personal Christhood. As a critical mass of people walked that path and attained some measure of Christhood, it would be possible for me to release the highest teachings on God's love.

I believe that we are now approaching the time when these teachings must come forth. If a critical mass of people will heed my directions in this book and reach for their personal Christhood then it will not be long before I can deliver the true teachings on God's unconditional love.

No need for guilt

I want you to understand that God created you in his image and likeness. God gave you free will and God gave you the right to experiment with that free will. God realized that it was inevitable that some of his sons and daughters would use their free will to violate his laws. Obviously, God does not want you to make choices that are self-destructive.

Yet God is not angry at you for making such choices, and God does not condemn you for making such choices. Therefore, God does not want to make you feel guilty or condemned for having made such choices. God has no desire to see you live an entire lifetime, or even many lifetimes, with the feeling that you are a miserable sinner who is unworthy to approach God.

God does not want you to feel bad for having made a mistake. God wants you to feel free to admit that you have made a mistake, to accept God's forgiveness and to stop making further mistakes.

The problem on planet earth today is that so many people have accepted the idea that they are miserable sinners, and therefore they dare not even approach God and ask for forgiveness. As a result, they continue to make choices that are based on the death consciousness, and therefore they continue to build a wall between themselves and God's forgiveness and love. This is not what God desires to see happen. God wants all of his son and daughters to step out of the negative spiral whereby they remove themselves further and further from his kingdom.

I am aware that some people will misuse the idea of God's forgiveness. The kind of people who bought indulgences and then sinned with a clean conscience are simply not ready for the teaching that God's forgiveness is infinite. Yet I trust that few of these people will ever read this book. Therefore, I desire to release to you the teaching that God's mercy and forgiveness is indeed infinite. Furthermore, God's forgiveness is instantaneous.

God simply wants you to abandon the relative consciousness that causes you to violate God's laws. Because of free will, you must make a choice to let go of that state of consciousness. However, at the very moment you make that choice, all of your transgressions, all of your mistakes, all of your sins are instantaneously forgiven.

God simply wants you to come home, and you cannot come home as long as you feel like a miserable sinner who is unworthy to approach God. Therefore, God wants you to overcome that feeling so that you can feel worthy to enter his kingdom. God wants you to feel that you are welcome and will be accepted by Him. Your acceptance into God's kingdom does not depend on the acts that you have or have not committed. Your acceptance into God's kingdom depends on only one thing, namely your state of consciousness.

To enter God's kingdom, you must abandon the death consciousness and unite with the Christ mind. The very process of putting off the old state of consciousness and putting on the new state of consciousness is enough to qualify you for God's forgiveness. Therefore, after you make the decision to pursue personal Christhood, you must make a conscious effort to let go of the belief that you are a miserable sinner who is unworthy to enter God's kingdom.

16 | Is God an Angry and Judgmental God?

The Law of Karma

God created you in his image and likeness. Therefore, from the very beginning you were worthy to inherit God's kingdom. From the very beginning, you were worthy to receive God's unconditional love. Nothing you could possibly do will make you unworthy of receiving God's unconditional love. If it could, God's love would not be unconditional.

I want you to contemplate these ideas until you begin to accept that you are indeed worthy of approaching God and that you can, by putting on the full measure of your personal Christhood, become worthy to enter God's kingdom.

However, I must also tell you that God's forgiveness does not remove your personal karma. To fully escape the downward pull of planet earth, you must balance your personal karma. What I am trying to help you see here is that when you commit a wrong act, two things happen:

- You create a certain amount of personal karma. You can think of this as incurring a debt to life. This karma is misqualified energy. Because the energy was misqualified in the material universe, you create a certain gravitational pull that keeps your soul tied to the material universe. That is why you must continue to reincarnate until you balance your personal karma. In other words, as long as you have unbalanced karma in the material world, you are not free to ascend to the spiritual world.

- You create a distance between you and God. That distance exists only in your mind, but it originated when you first decided to turn away from God. Every wrong act you commit only reinforces the wall that you have built between yourself and God. In order to return to God's kingdom, you must tear down this psychological barrier. You can do so only by accepting God's forgiveness and thereby rebuilding your sense of being a son or daughter who is worthy to enter your Father's kingdom. As long as you maintain the slightest sense of unworthiness, you cannot make the free-will decision to step through the gate that leads to God's kingdom.

All wrong acts are the results of a certain state of consciousness, a certain state of ignorance. At the moment you forsake that state of consciousness, your mistake is forgiven by God. You should allow yourself to feel and accept God's forgiveness because it will be of great encouragement to you as you walk the path to Christhood. Yet at the same time you must not forget that God's forgiveness does not remove the karma you made through your wrong actions. That karma must be balanced before you are free of those actions.

I want you to remember what I said earlier about karma as a debt to life. When you earnestly walk the path of personal Christhood, you will lay up treasures in Heaven that will make it far easier for you to balance your karma from the past. In other words, if you become a spiritual millionaire, it will be easy to pay back your debts to life. In the last part of this book, I will tell you about a spiritual technique that will also be of great assistance in the balancing of your personal karma.

For now, I want you to contemplate the concepts of forgiveness and unconditional love. I want you to realize and accept that you are indeed worthy to inherit your Father's kingdom. You see, because God's love is unconditional, you do not have to do anything to earn God's love. You earned that love the moment God created your lifestream. Therefore, you simply have to accept God's love.

If you are not experiencing God's unconditional love, it is not because God is hiding that love from you. It is because you are hiding from God's love. Simply stop rejecting God's love. It is indeed the Father's good pleasure to give you his love.

17 | THE QUESTION OF EVIL

The concept of evil has caused much confusion, not only among Christians, but also among spiritually interested people all over the world. The main reason behind all this confusion is the widespread denial of the importance of free will.

If you consider my previous remarks about a power elite, you will see that a power elite seeking absolute control over the people will do anything they can to spread false beliefs, through religion or science, stating that free will either does not exist or is not important. What this power elite is trying to do is to make you deny your God-given potential to manifest Christhood on earth.

If you deny the existence of free will then it becomes exceedingly difficult to explain the obvious fact that there is evil on this planet. If you are a scientific materialist, you have virtually no explanation for evil so most of these people tend to ignore it. I might add here that ignoring a cancerous tumor is not the best way to deal with it.

If you are a religious person then you end up having to come up with a series of contrived arguments that somehow seek to deal with the problem that if human beings do not have free will then God must have created evil. For most people, the idea that God has created evil just doesn't sound right. It doesn't sound right because it isn't right.

The reality of the matter is that God has not created evil. Contrary to what some religions teach, evil is not the polar opposite of God. God is a completely self-contained being and God has no opposite. I have earlier told you that when God starts creating the world of form, God creates two polarities, as illustrated in the Tai-Chi. Nevertheless, evil does not form the polar opposite of God, and it does not even form the polar opposite of good.

The polarities of the Tai-Chi are not mutually exclusive. They are complementary and through their interaction they bring forth a new aspect of the world of form. That aspect will be in harmony with God's law, and therefore it will be sustainable. It will not self-destruct.

The essence of evil is that it is not in accordance with God's law. Therefore, evil does not form a creative polarity with good. Evil cannot create anything; it can only destroy. Nothing that is influenced by evil is sustainable because it violates God's laws. Therefore, anything affected by evil will be temporary, and it will eventually self-destruct.

Evil as the result of choice

Why is there evil in the world? The presence of evil is the result of a free-will choice, or rather numerous free-will choices. The original free-will choice that brought evil to this planet was not made by human beings. It was made by the leader of a band of beings in a previous sphere, and his name was Lucifer. Lucifer made the choice that he was not willing to follow one of God's commands. Lucifer made this choice because of pride. He wanted to be the most important being in his sphere and when he was not shown this favoritism, Lucifer rebelled.

17 | The Question of Evil

According to the traditional Christian cosmology, there is only the material world and heaven. Yet the deeper reality is that the world of form has been created as a series of spheres. Each sphere starts out at a certain level of vibration, and the inhabitants, the co-creators, of that sphere will then gradually raise their sphere until it goes through the ascension phase and becomes a permanent part of what human beings see as the spiritual realm. As one sphere ascends, a new unascended sphere is created.

The point is that the material world in which you live is simply the latest part of this creative process, it is the latest unascended sphere. Lucifer's rebellion did not happen in this sphere; it happened in a previous sphere. It happened as that sphere was ready to ascend, which meant that all beings in the sphere had to give up the positions and power they had attained. Lucifer was not willing to give up his power – as I demonstrated by going through the crucifixion – and thus he could not ascend with his sphere. Instead, he and many of the beings who were loyal to him, fell into the next sphere that was created.

Some of them have continued to fall until they are now in this latest unascended sphere, and this explains two important things. It explains why they have become so blinded by their pride that they think they have the wisdom and the right to tell the Creator how the universe should function. And it explains why these fallen beings – as demonstrated by some world leaders today and the leaders who had me executed – have absolutely no respect for human beings. These fallen beings consider all inhabitants of this sphere to be far below them, and thus they have no respect for the lifestreams among which they embody. [For further teachings on how the world of form was created as a series of spheres, see *The Power of Self*.]

In the material universe, the energies are so dense that it is not immediately obvious that everything in this universe is created from God's light. Therefore, this universe can serve as a temporary home for those beings who have stepped outside of God's law and therefore no longer see themselves as God's offspring.

If you wonder whether there is any support for this idea, study an old biblical text called the Book of Enoch. This book describes the process whereby fallen angels were cast out of Heaven – in reality, an unascended sphere as no being can fall in heaven – and took on human bodies. The text implies that these fallen angels have continued to appear in human bodies. The Book of Enoch was later taken out of the orthodox Bible, and one might wonder why.

The origin of evil

My basic point is that the origin of evil was a free-will choice made by a group of very powerful beings who chose to rebel against God. They have since formed what I have called the power elite. Many of these souls have so far demonstrated an absolute commitment to stick with their original decision to rebel against God. Therefore, they have attempted to turn planet earth into a world where God does not exist. In other words, they want to shut God out of this world in an attempt to prove that they can exist without God. They also want to set themselves up as surrogate or false gods on earth. They believe that their end can justify absolutely any conceivable means. These souls will do anything to gain and maintain control over the people of earth.

Unfortunately, maintaining such control is not very difficult. The fallen beings have a powerful weapon in their quest for control, namely the relativity of the death consciousness.

Any human being in the grips of the death consciousness is an easy target for the manipulators of this earth. If everything is relative then everything can be defined by some authority here on earth, including right and wrong, truth and error. The fallen beings have created numerous philosophies in an attempt to spread such relative ideas and make them appear as absolute truths.

You must understand that the power elite will do anything to prevent you from discovering the truth of God. For example, for the past 2,000 years they have attempted to use the mainstream Christian churches to prevent the spreading of knowledge. For centuries, the Catholic Church was a very efficient mind control machine, as the burning of books and the Inquisition clearly demonstrate.

Today, the power elite is facing the problem that technology has made it easier than ever to disseminate information. They are attempting to cope with this by actually flooding the market with false information of every conceivable type. That is why you see so many books or websites that promote the most incredible theories (including a number of books that contain false theories about me and my true teachings). The hope of the power elite is that you will be overwhelmed by all of this information so that you will either close your mind (and refuse to consider any new ideas) or become so confused that you no longer know what to believe (and therefore end up doubting everything).

The only way to escape this subtle manipulation is to reach beyond the death consciousness and put on personal Christhood. The essence of personal Christhood is discernment, the ability to discern what is of God and what is not of God. Therefore, a Christed being is the ultimate threat to the fallen beings who consider planet earth their territory. They will do anything to prevent a Christed being from walking the earth.

They will do anything to prevent a large number of Christed beings from walking the earth. Therefore, they will do anything to prevent people from discovering and accepting the path of personal Christhood.

Be wise as serpents

When I appeared 2,000 years ago, I told my followers to be wise as serpents and harmless as doves. You must be wise as serpents so that you can see through the lies and the manipulations that pollute every aspect of life on this planet. You must be wise as serpents so that you can avoid being pulled into the downward spiral that the serpents have created on earth. You must understand that the souls of these serpents are in a state of consciousness that is dominated by the ultimate denial. They are denying God, they are denying themselves (their divine selves) and they are denying themselves as individualizations of God. Therefore, they live in a state of consciousness that is the ultimate spiritual blindness. They do not recognize the Law of Cause and Effect, the Law of Karma. They do not recognize that they have created a downward spiral which will inevitably lead to their own destruction.

The serpents have descended into such a low state of consciousness that even a cosmic being like myself finds it virtually impossible to reach them. You will recall that after my crucifixion I descended to hell and spent three days preaching to the souls who were trapped there. Hell is more than anything a state of consciousness. I was sent to these souls in an attempt to appeal to those who had confined themselves to this level of consciousness. I must tell you frankly that I had little success in terms of reaching these souls.

Yet I will tell you that it is not a hopeless calling. As recorded in the Bible, many beings fell with Lucifer. Many of them have since made a better decision and have started to climb back to our Father's kingdom. Some of them have indeed made it all the way home. Yet I must also tell you that those who remain are very difficult to reach. Therefore, I do not advise you to spend your time and energy in an attempt to help those who are not willing to help themselves.

Instead, I advise you to become wise to the ways of the serpents so that you can avoid being pulled into their negative spiral. The idea of coming apart and being a separate and chosen people is based on the parable of the tares that are sown among the wheat. As long as the two are mixed together, God cannot pull out the tares without pulling out the wheat.

Yet if the wheat, meaning those who dare to recognize themselves as sons and daughters of God, will separate themselves out from those in the death consciousness then God can indeed remove some of these souls from planet earth. God can send them to a different place where they can receive yet another opportunity to make the choice to start the journey home.

How do you become a member of God's separate and chosen people? I have already told you what it takes to be chosen. You must choose to answer the call to manifest personal Christhood. You must choose to accept God's calling.

Coming apart means more than anything else the coming apart in consciousness. You must make a determined effort to rise above the death consciousness on a personal level. You must also make an effort to see through the lies and the manipulations that are spread over this planet by those who are seeking to ensnare you and drag you into their own self-created hell on earth. By reaching for Christ consciousness, you can quickly become wise to the ways of the serpents. At the same time, you can fulfill the second part of my command, namely to be harmless as doves.

Be harmless as doves

When you attain a certain measure of Christ consciousness, you clearly discern what is of God and what is not of God. Therefore, you can leave behind that which is not of God.

We have now come to a crucial point which has confused many sincere Christians (and many other religious people) throughout the ages. The question is: "How can you remove evil from this planet?"

Many people start life as not being particularly religious. Then, they experience a conversion or awakening, and afterwards they are filled with a great (sometimes all-consuming) religious fervor or zeal. This zeal springs from a true desire to do God's will and to help bring God's kingdom to earth. Yet if this zeal is not tempered by the harmlessness of the dove, it all too easily becomes perverted by the subtle logic of the serpents themselves. You see, the modus operandi of the fallen angels who rebelled against God is that the end can justify the means. This is a completely false concept that has nothing whatsoever to do with God.

In Heaven, the end can never justify the means. Yet many religious people become so attached to the idea of fighting evil that they suddenly become willing to violate God's law in order to bring his kingdom to earth. These religious people look at the many horrendous things that are happening on planet earth, and they somehow reason that if only they can remove the evil then God's kingdom will automatically appear. This is the false reasoning that springs from the death consciousness.

You see, my beloved hearts, you simply cannot remove evil from planet earth. To understand why, go into a room at night and turn off the light. You are now in a dark room. I want you to consider how you could possibly remove the darkness from that room? Could you put the darkness into bags and throw it out the window? Obviously, this would not work and the reason is that darkness has no substance and no reality whatsoever. Darkness is the absence of light. Bring light, and the darkness disappears.

When you look at human history, you see that more atrocities have been committed in the name of religion than as the result of any other single cause. I must tell you that all of these atrocities were against the will and the intention of God. There is no such thing as a holy war. God loves religious fervor, but God does not want that fervor to be turned into fanaticism.

All battles, whether they resulted in bloodshed or were fought with other weapons, that were fought by religious people in an attempt to remove this or that darkness from planet earth have done nothing to bring about God's kingdom. Yes, I realize this is a very radical statement that will offend many people.

Nevertheless, I must tell you the truth. The simple fact is that if you fight evil, you are attempting to remove the darkness. I realize that to many people on earth, evil can seem very real. Yet it only seems real because you look at it through the filter of the death consciousness.

Bring the light

If you truly desire to bring God's kingdom to earth then you must focus your attention on bringing the light of the Christ consciousness. You must not allow yourself to be caught in the trap of attempting to remove evil. Simply focus on bringing light, and that light will eventually consume evil.

Our God is a consuming fire. Yet because of free will, God can consume the darkness on earth only when some of the people on earth allow themselves to become the open door for

God's consuming fire. To become the open door for God's fire, you must put on personal Christhood.

Let me make it clear that I am not hereby saying that I want my followers to ignore everything that is wrong on this planet. Obviously, I want my followers to speak out against anything that is not of God. However, you cannot speak out against what is not of God until you have attained a certain measure of Christ consciousness and thereby achieved the inner discernment that tells you what is of God and what is not of God.

My point here is that too many religious people allow themselves to think that they can actually do God's work while they are still trapped by the death consciousness. As a result, these people all too often select a scapegoat and decide that another group of people is the enemy. Such people reason that the main problem on earth is another group of people. Therefore, it becomes their religious duty to force these people to change their ways. If these people refuse to change, they must be eliminated. This is precisely the line of reasoning that caused Adolf Hitler to kill six million people in concentration camps. It is precisely this line of reasoning that caused a group of people to fly airplanes into the World Trade Center and the Pentagon. It is precisely this line of reasoning that has caused more bloodshed than any other single factor seen on planet earth.

When you attain Christ consciousness, you attain the wisdom and discernment to see through the lies of the serpents. Yet at the same time you also attain a total commitment to the will and the perfection of God. Thereby, you become non-attached to the things of this world.

This non-attachment is what I called the harmlessness of doves. When you are non-attached to the things of this world, you clearly see the folly of the idea that the end can justify the means. You clearly realize that the only way to bring God's kingdom to earth is through God's own law. Seeking to bring

God's kingdom through means that are against God's law simply will not work.

The most basic Law of God is the law of love. I preached that law when I appeared on earth. Every aspect of my teaching is permeated by the law of love. Why do you think I told you to do unto others as you would have them do unto you? Why do you think I told you to love your neighbor as yourself? Why do you think every other true religion on planet earth preaches that very same message?

It is because love is the very essence of God's Being. God is love. God is unconditional love.

The only way to bring God's kingdom to earth is through unconditional love. Hatred and fanaticism simply will not do the trick. To bring God's kingdom, you must embody God's love. There is no other way. The many other ways that people follow are the ways that seem right to humans (who are caught in the death consciousness), yet the end thereof is the way of death—the way of those who deny God and their own Divinity.

Bring the kingdom

I want you to be an instrument for bringing God's kingdom to earth. However, to be such an instrument you must overcome the death consciousness and its tendency to see other people as enemies. You must treat everyone with love.

There is nothing wrong with using your Christ discernment, as long as you are certain that it is Christ discernment, to expose an idea or belief that is not of God. I very much want my followers to be the open door through which the truth of God can be brought to the people of earth. I want my followers to bring truth to this planet and thereby expose the many subtle lies of the serpents in your midst.

Yet in bringing truth, you do not have to fight lies and you do not have to fight other people. You simply bring the truth, and then you leave it up to other people to make their free-will decisions as to how they will respond to that truth.

My point here is that the ultimate law of this universe is free will. If you love your neighbor as yourself, you will not violate your neighbor's free will. You will give people the truth as you see it, but you will be completely non-attached to their responses. You will allow your neighbor to make his or her own choices.

This is what God has done for you, and you must do the same for everyone else. What I am saying here is that you cannot bring God's kingdom to earth by violating the free will of another human being. If God's kingdom is to appear on earth, it must appear as the result of choices made by human beings. I am not thereby saying that every human being on earth needs to reach Christ consciousness and make the conscious choice to bring in God's kingdom. God's kingdom can indeed be brought to earth through a relatively small number of human beings who reach a certain measure of personal Christhood. Nevertheless, the very key to bringing God's kingdom to earth is free will. If you want to help bring that kingdom to earth then you must begin by developing an uncompromising respect for the free will of your brothers and sisters.

The serpents on earth have absolutely no respect for the free will of another human being. That is why those who consider themselves to be the servants of God must develop an uncompromising respect for the free will of another.

Free will is a very interesting concept. I earlier said that a teacher cannot learn a lesson for the student. Likewise, no human being can make choices for another. Yes, you can force or manipulate someone into doing what you want them to do. But you cannot force them into doing so as the result of a free choice. You cannot force any human being to make a free choice (if you did, it would not be free).

You can manipulate people into thinking that they only have certain options. Most people make choices based on incorrect or incomplete information about their options. Yet if you do so, you are preventing them from making a free choice. Making a choice is a process that takes place inside the psyche of the individual.

Yet most people on earth are not in a state of consciousness that allows them to make free choices. They are so enveloped in the death consciousness that all of the options they see are affected by the relativity of the death consciousness. To make a truly free choice, the lifestream must be able to see beyond the death consciousness. That higher vision can come about only through the Christ consciousness.

If you feel a desire to help bring truth to earth, start by making a very determined effort to attain personal Christhood. By doing so, you can give people an opportunity to choose between the truth of God and the lies of the death consciousness. Truth is not simply a matter of making a true statement. Truth is a matter of vibration—more about this later.

Turn the other cheek

Despite the manipulation happening on earth, every human being can choose to reach for something higher. No matter how far a person has descended into the levels of the death consciousness, the consciousness of hell, a lifestream can at any moment make the choice to reach for something higher. Not even the most clever and forceful fallen angels can take that potential away from the lifestream.

The potential to make a better choice is truly the hope for this world. If you consider yourself to be one of my true followers then you must respect everyone's free will. You must also hold the vision that a person could, of its own free-will choosing, elect to reach for something higher. You must make it your life's goal to inspire people to make that choice without attempting to force them in any way. I want you to offer everyone you meet a cup of cold water in Christ's name. And then I want you to leave it up to them whether they choose to drink.

I have a very good reason for making this request. You see, if you seek to force someone to drink then you will make personal karma by doing so. If you leave the choice up to them, you have done what is required of you, and therefore you will make positive karma for yourself. If they reject the truth then they will make negative karma, but that truly is none of your concern. Why do you think I told people to turn the other cheek? It is impossible to understand this command without understanding the Law of Karma.

You see, if someone harms you, that person inevitably makes karma. This is simply a Law of God. Unfortunately, most people who are harmed by another react with anger and they often seek revenge. In manifesting this negative reaction, they make personal karma. Thereby, you might start a negative karmic spiral with the other person, and such negative spirals have led to family feuds or even wars between nations. Because of the Law of Karma, you have absolutely no need to seek revenge. Vengeance is mine says the Lord, I will repay. Through the Law of Karma, God has made sure that no human being could ever escape the consequences of his or her actions.

If someone harms you, that person has already made karma. Simply leave it up to God to return that karma to the person. God is perfectly capable of handling that side of the equation. What should be your concern is to make sure that you do not react in such a way that you create karma for yourself. The only way to avoid making personal karma as the result of someone harming you is to remain completely non-attached. By remaining harmless as a dove, by responding with love and forgiveness, you will avoid making karma. Thereby, you will avoid entering a negative spiral that will pull you down.

The downward pull

I must tell you that for thousands of years the serpents in this world have attempted to pull all other people into their self-created downward spiral. They have done so by harming the innocent and thereby seeking to make the innocent sons and daughters of God respond with anger or other negative feelings. Because so many people were caught in the death consciousness, it has been easy for the serpents to make people respond negatively. Therefore, most people are today so heavily involved with these karmic spirals that they simply cannot free themselves to pursue the path of personal Christhood.

When I come to such souls at inner levels to offer them my path, they are so attached to their feelings of anger, resentment or revenge that they simply cannot let go and follow me. When I say: "Leave your nets and follow me," they have no idea what I mean.

If you consider yourself one of my true followers, I want you to carefully contemplate these ideas. I need you to extricate yourself from all entanglement with the serpents of this world, with their institutions of power and with their self-created hell on earth. I need you to stop fighting for causes that are not of God. I need you to achieve the discernment that allows you to see the just causes for which you need to "fight." Do not allow yourself to be pulled into a battle in which neither side is fighting for a just cause.

First of all, I need you to extricate yourself from the consciousness of anger and revenge. Let go of your attachments to this or that injustice. Why do you think I told people to forgive seventy times seven? The reason is that forgiveness, total and unconditional forgiveness, is the very key to your personal freedom. If you will consider how I and my brothers and sisters in Heaven treat each other, I am sure you will realize that we do not hold grudges. Spiritual beings are not above making mistakes. However, in Heaven forgiveness of one's mistakes is instantaneous.

What I am telling you is that you simply cannot enter the kingdom of Heaven until you have forgiven everyone, including God and yourself. Forgiveness is the key to personal freedom. If you have not forgiven another then you are maintaining a karmic tie to that person. If that other person happens to be a fallen being who is absolutely determined to go to hell then that person will pull you down. Why on earth would you want to maintain a karmic tie to someone who is hell-bent on going to hell?

Do you see that it is in your own best interest to quickly remove all such ties? Do you see that the very key to removing such ties is to practice total and unconditional forgiveness?

Why is there still evil in the world?

Let me return to my original question of why there is evil in the world. I have now told you how evil originated. Let me expand my question as follows: "Why is there still evil in the world?"

The foremost reason there is still evil on earth is that those who consider themselves to be spiritual and religious people have not made the choice to practice complete and unconditional forgiveness towards everyone.

If people were to start practicing such unconditional forgiveness, they would immediately begin to come apart and be a separate and chosen people. The good and sincere lifestreams on earth would separate themselves from those souls who are deliberately and intentionally working against God's purposes. If that separation were to happen, God could and would remove the serpents from the earth.

Let me give you a mental image of how this works. Planet earth, as you know it today, is very far away from God's original intention and design. This planet has become a crossroads, a kind of spiritual melting pot, and God has allowed many different types of souls to embody on this planet. The reason this was allowed was that the original inhabitants of this planet had descended into a very low state of consciousness.

When you look at planet earth today, you see a wide variety of souls that have come from many different backgrounds and are manifesting many different levels of consciousness. I do not like the idea that people are comparing themselves to others and judging who is better than who. I have already told you that in Heaven there are no favorite sons. Therefore, I do not want you to misuse what I am now telling you. I do not want you to point the finger at any other human being.

The simple fact is that people on earth are at many different levels of consciousness. Therefore, you can put people on a scale depending on their level of consciousness. At the top of this scale you find those who have achieved the highest degree of personal Christhood. At the bottom of this scale you find those who have descended into a state of consciousness that is dominated by absolute denial of themselves as sons and daughters of God. There is a wide range between those at the top and those at the bottom of the scale. The majority of the people on earth fit somewhere in between the two extremes.

You must understand that there are levels of consciousness both above and below what is currently manifest on earth. In other words, there are indeed lower levels of consciousness than what you see on earth (I know this might seem impossible, but my Father's house has many mansions). We of the ascended masters clearly see that most people on earth are in a very difficult situation. Because of their ignorance, which is due largely to the manipulation by a small power elite, they have very limited opportunities for spiritual growth. We of the ascended masters clearly see that humankind is being pulled down by the lowest ten percent of the souls that are embodied on earth.

We also realize that the only way to effectively change this equation is that the lowest ten percent of souls must be removed from this planet. These souls have had a very long time to embody on this planet. So far, they have not chosen to change their ways and walk the spiritual path. Given the fact that they have been here for so long, it is unlikely that they will do so any time soon. It it far more likely that they will drag the rest of humanity down with them. Therefore, it is our desire to see these souls be removed to another world in which almost everyone is at that same low level of consciousness.

However, the key to bringing about this change is the top ten percent of the lifestreams that currently embody on planet earth. The simple fact is that these lifestreams must choose to raise their level of consciousness. You might recall that I said to my Father in Heaven: "If I be lifted up, I will draw all men unto me." The simple fact is that all people on earth are interconnected in consciousness. If one person raises his or her consciousness, it will pull everybody else up.

Of course, people will be raised up only if they choose to follow the magnetic pull that calls them to come up higher. If they choose to go against that pull, they will not be raised up. Yet if a sufficient number of people on earth reached a certain level of Christhood then those who refuse to be lifted up in consciousness simply can no longer embody on this planet. By their refusal to come up higher in consciousness, they will effectively condemn themselves from this planet, and they will descend to another world according to their state of consciousness. This is exactly what happened when souls descended from a previous sphere.

My point is that all people who consider themselves to be spiritual or religious people must make a determined effort to raise their level of consciousness. As I have said many times, people must decide to walk the path to personal Christhood. However, I hope you can now see that the essential key to walking the path of personal Christhood is to practice complete and unconditional forgiveness towards every part of life.

Forgive your neighbor. Forgive yourself. Forgive your God. For-give, meaning "for-go" or give away, the consciousness of anger, resentment and revenge. Simply let go of that state of consciousness and allow God's unconditional love to take it away from you as if it never even existed. Our God is a consuming fire of love. Allow that fire to consume everything in your consciousness that stands between you and your personal Christhood.

Simply leave your nets of karmic entanglements and follow me, the Living Christ. Withhold nothing from me, and I will withhold nothing from you.

18 | JESUS AND MODERN CHRISTIANITY

This is a topic that all sincere Christians, and many spiritually-minded people who do not consider themselves to be Christians, should be considering. And then they should seek the answer inside their own hearts where I can give it to them directly. However, I will give you some general ideas that will give you a feel for what I, Jesus Christ, think about the religion that claims to be representing me on earth.

First of all, I want to say that modern Christianity is so diversified that it is almost impossible to make any statement without putting forth a sweeping generalization that will inevitably be unjust to some people. I clearly recognize that there are millions of people who are sincerely and devoutly following my teachings to the best of their ability, given the fragmented and distorted versions of my teachings that have been made available to them.

My original vision

Yet I must tell you that the Christianity I see on earth today is far away from my original vision and intention. Fortunately, I am a cosmic being and I am centered in the peace of God.

Otherwise, I would literally weep at the thought of what might have been. Had my true, inner teachings been made available to the people of earth, this planet would already have entered a golden age of peace, prosperity and progress. I came with a vision of such a golden age, and I still hold that vision for earth. Yet I must tell you that before such a golden age could possibly manifest on earth, before my Father's kingdom could possibly descend into physical manifestation, many changes are needed.

I would like to see those who claim to be my followers, those who claim to be Christians, be the very first to sincerely consider and pursue these changes. Yet from a realistic viewpoint, I think this desire is extremely unlikely to be fulfilled. The sad fact is that many Christians have closed their minds so firmly that they are not likely to be receptive to my inner teachings.

Some people have allowed their minds to become so firmly enveloped in false ideas and doctrines that when I speak to them in their own hearts, they explain away my words or even consider them to be the works of the devil. The sad fact is that even I, Jesus Christ, have few options in terms of turning modern Christianity into the movement that I desire it to be. I think you already realize some of my concerns about Christianity. The chief concern being, of course, that the path of individual Christhood has been almost completely removed. Yet let us try to step back from the incredible diversity of the thousands of churches and sects that claim to represent me so that we can look at the forest instead of being blinded by the trees.

A horizontal movement

The true problem with modern Christianity is that it has become what I would call a horizontal movement. I earlier gave you an example of how the scriptures contain a few hints about reincarnation. I also told you how some theologians have gone into a very contrived line of reasoning in order to explain these passages without mentioning reincarnation.

If you look at modern Christianity, you can find literally thousands of examples of this kind of contrived, horizontal reasoning. It is completely amazing to me how some people will go into the most intricate and artificial arguments in order to prove the point that they have already decided must be right. Why are they going through this effort to prove that their idea is right when it would require less effort, albeit a different kind of effort, to receive the Living Truth directly from me?

We have now come to a crucial point in these discourses. I will now explain to you what is the very essence of the problem on planet earth. That problem springs from the key characteristic of the death consciousness.

The very essence of the death consciousness is that it does not want to know reality. It does not want to know truth. The death consciousness does not look at evidence and then use that evidence to reason about what might be the truth. The human ego uses the death consciousness to create an image, an idol, and it decides that this must be the truth, this must be reality, this must be God. Then, it looks for evidence that will support the image that it has already decided must be true. It blatantly ignores, denies or explains away any evidence that does not support its chosen idea.

When you look at modern Christianity, you will see this tendency at work. In all fairness, this is not unique to Christianity. You can see this tendency at work in every aspect of life on this planet. Yet it was my original hope that the very church that claims to represent me would not fall prey to this tendency of the death consciousness. When a soul identifies with the death consciousness, the person makes a decision about what is true. The ego creates an image, an idol, of what it wants to be true. After a person has accepted that false image, the person refuses to accept any evidence that does not support the image. Therefore, the person sees only evidence that supports the image, and this becomes a self-fulfilling prophecy. The person becomes spiritually blind.

The money changers

This is the very reason I repeatedly rebuked the authorities of the Jewish religion. This is why I overturned the tables of the money changers who had turned my Father's house into a place of business and exploitation. These religious authorities had gone away from the tradition of the prophets. The idea of a prophet is that one human being raises his or her consciousness to such a level that God can speak to the people through that person. Therefore, God has a way to communicate with people who have descended into the death consciousness. God can bring a higher truth, and if people choose to accept that truth, they have a lifeline that allows them to climb to a higher state of consciousness.

The Jewish religion had abandoned the tradition of the prophets. Therefore, the religious authorities no longer had access to the living Word of God, and they were left to interpret the Word of God that was delivered in the past. That is precisely why the Pharisees and the Sadducees spent countless hours in pointless arguments about this or that point of the law instead of reaching for the Living Word and delivering it to the people.

I clearly saw the fallacy and the danger of this development, and that is why I said that I came to fulfill the law and the prophets. How did I intend to do this?

18 | Jesus and Modern Christianity

By establishing a direct line of progressive revelation through which I could speak the living Word of God even after I left physical embodiment. I intended to speak that Living Word directly through those of my followers who had walked the path of individual Christhood and who had attained a level of Christhood that allowed them to serve as my mouthpiece or my messenger.

If that tradition, which I truly established in the early years of the Christian movement, had been kept alive, modern Christianity would have had an alternative to the horizontal, relative squabbles about the interpretation of scripture. Bluntly speaking, who needs scripture when the living Word of God is flowing in their midst? Who needs to interpret scripture when they can obtain a higher understanding directly from the source of knowledge, the Christ consciousness?

I have already said that the death consciousness has an infinite ability to create relative arguments about this or that idea. Therefore, as long as Christians keep arguing from the relativity of the death consciousness about this or that point in scripture, they will remain stuck in their present state of division and conflict.

What is the alternative? The alternative to the horizontal reasoning process of the death consciousness is the vertical process of reaching for the Christ mind. As long as you are following the horizontal way of the death consciousness (the way that seems right to the human ego), you can keep searching forever without finding the truth of God.

Yet at any moment the simple act of reaching for the higher way of the Christ consciousness will allow you to go beyond the consciousness of argumentation and confusion. Instead of the uncertainty and doubt of the death consciousness, you can achieve the certainty and inner knowing of the Christ mind.

The Living Church

When I came to earth, I came to bring forth the true Living Church. The Living Church must be based on the Living Word. The Living Word can be delivered only through the Christ consciousness. The Christ consciousness can manifest in this world only through individuals who put on personal Christhood.

I did not intend to become known as the only person to ever walk the earth in the fullness of Christ consciousness. I am a spiritual teacher. The only way for any teacher to be successful is to duplicate himself by raising his students to the same level of consciousness as the teacher. I am the teacher of Christ consciousness, and it was my intention to duplicate myself and to have numerous other people walk the earth in the fullness of their individual Christhood.

If no one follows my example then I have failed as a teacher. When you begin the process of attaining personal Christhood, you begin to see beyond all of the outer divisions that spring from the death consciousness. You see unity behind diversity.

The Living Church that I came to bring was meant to be based on Christhood, a state of consciousness that would allow people to escape the divisions and conflicts found on earth. Thereby, my followers could come into unity as the one Body of God on earth.

I never intended my teachings to be the source of conflict and division. I never wanted my followers, or those who claim to be my followers, to sit in their different churches and think up relative arguments about this or that point in the scriptures that were delivered in the past. Why would I want my followers to argue about scripture when they could receive the Living Word directly from me?

I do not want my followers to be divided. I do not want Christianity to be split into numerous churches and sects that are competing with each other or even warring with each other. Today, there are thousands of churches who claim to represent me, and many of them claim to be the only true church of Jesus Christ.

The one, true church

In reality, there need be only one church of Jesus Christ and that is the Living Church, the Inner Church, the path to personal Christhood. I do not thereby mean that I want to see the emergence of one totalitarian Christian church which will eradicate all other churches. I have no problem with the existence of different churches.

My teachings are vast. My teachings have many different aspects, and each aspect is designed to appeal to a particular group of people. Therefore, I have no problem with different groups of people, organized into different churches, who perceive themselves as following a particular aspect of my teaching. For example, one church might emphasize grace while another might emphasize works.

Yet the only way this division could possibly work is if all churches, and the members and leaders of those churches, see themselves as being part of one movement, namely the Living Church based on the Living Word. I am a spiritual teacher; I am not a totalitarian dictator. My Father in Heaven is not a totalitarian dictator. Heaven has infinite variety and there is room for much variety on earth. Yet in Heaven everyone realizes that the infinite variety originated from the ultimate unity of God.

God has no need to see the formation of one church on earth. I have no need to see the formation of one Christian church. I have a need to see that all of the people who call themselves Christians and who consider themselves to be my followers, will learn to look beyond the outer divisions and differences and begin to walk the path to individual Christhood. I want my true followers to see themselves as part of the one body, the undivided body, of God on earth.

The entire purpose of my coming to this planet was to clear the way for my Father's kingdom to descend into full physical manifestation. That is why I said: "I have come that all might have life, and that they might have it more abundantly." God's kingdom is the abundant life.

God's kingdom on earth

God's desire for this planet is to remove the current imperfection and suffering and to establish his kingdom on earth. God desires to see planet earth manifest the perfection that is already manifest in the spiritual world. In other words, God wants the earth to be his kingdom here below as Heaven is his kingdom Above. As Above, so below. That is why I said: "Be ye therefore perfect, even as your Father which is in Heaven is perfect."

My original desire for the Christian movement was to see it become a forerunner for bringing God's kingdom into physical manifestation. Therefore, I desire my followers to be the Christed ones below as I, and my spiritual brothers and sisters, are the Christed ones Above. I desire my followers to be part of the universal brother/sisterhood of light and to walk the earth as representatives of the cosmic Christ. This is the vision I held for early Christianity. I still hold that vision for anyone who dares to follow my true teachings. Yet as I have told you numerous times in this book, the true key to bringing about that goal is the free-will decisions made by those on earth.

I am Jesus Christ. I am a cosmic being with such power that you would scarcely be able to fathom my power. Yet I cannot use my powers on this earth unless I am authorized to do so by those in embodiment. I need those who are willing to be my hands and feet. I need those who are willing to be the Body of God on earth.

However, to become a member of the Body of God, you must overcome the death consciousness and its tendency to create divisions and conflicts where no divisions and conflicts exist. I can accept that different groups of Christians emphasize different aspects of my teachings. Yet I cannot accept that these groups see themselves as being in conflict with other groups of Christians or with other groups of religious people.

I desire to see you make a sincere effort to leave behind the death consciousness that causes you to see a conflict between yourself and what you conceive to be other people. Those other people are not your enemies. Behind the outer facade, they are your spiritual brothers and sisters. They are my spiritual brothers and sisters.

That is why I said: "If you have done it unto the least of these my little ones, you have done it unto me." That is why I told you to love your neighbor as yourself and to love others as I have loved you and still love you.

No amount of theological arguments could possibly bring God's kingdom into manifestation on earth. Yet even a small amount of hearts united in love can become the open door for that kingdom to descend into this dark world.

My flame of unconditional love

I am Jesus Christ, and I come to this planet with the flame of unconditional love. I have loved you unconditionally, and I still love you unconditionally.

Please set aside time to go deep inside your heart and allow yourself to feel my unconditional love for you. Allow that unconditional love to transform you and raise you out of the relativity and conditionality of the death consciousness. Accept that transformation, and as you feel that transformation reach a critical level, allow the inner transformation to be expressed in your outer actions. Allow my unconditional love for you to fill your heart and then spill over into your thoughts, feelings, words and actions. Then, dare to express that unconditional love towards everyone whom you meet. Allow your heart to become the cup that runneth over with God's unconditional love.

The key to bringing God's kingdom to earth is to create unity between Heaven and earth. To create unity, we must overcome division. The only way to overcome division is to embrace God's unconditional love.

As long as there are conditions in your love, there can be no unity between you and your God. When you accept that God's love is unconditional, all outer divisions fade away. They are simply consumed by the all-consuming fire of unconditional, divine love. I am that unconditional love, and I am offering that unconditional love to you. Will you accept my love?

PART 3

PERSONAL CHRISTHOOD

19 | HOW TO ATTAIN CHRISTHOOD

My beloved hearts, this book has one purpose, and one purpose only. My purpose is to awaken those who are ready to walk the path of personal Christhood. I have said that millions of lifestreams are ready for my true teachings and for the path of Christhood. I will not tell you how many millions we are talking about, but I will tell you that it is a very large number of people.

How do you know if you belong to those who are ready to walk with me on the path to personal Christhood? If you are reading these words then you are one of my own, and you are ready (at inner levels of your lifestream) for my true path.

The first two sections of this book are designed to act as a filter to separate those who are not yet ready for my true path. This is not to in any way condemn the people who are not ready. However, if a person is not ready, that person simply needs to move on and leave this book behind. I am a practical spiritual teacher, and I know from experience that you simply cannot reach everyone. What does it take to be ready for my true teachings? It takes an open mind and an open heart.

The filter

If people have not yet opened their hearts and minds to my true teachings, the first part of this book would have presented them with one or several ideas that such people are not ready to accept. Their human egos would have come up with some kind of reasoning why a particular idea simply could not have come from the real Jesus Christ. Therefore, they would have had the perfect excuse for rejecting the entire book. I have seen people do this very thing millions of times over the past 2,000 years. They will find some little thing to criticize, and then they will use that one detail as an excuse for rejecting me, my teachings or my messenger. I have especially seen this among those who hold positions in the mainstream churches that claim to represent me on earth.

When I personally appeared on earth, I was rejected by almost everyone who held a position of power in the Jewish religion. Since then, I have attempted to appear at inner levels to those who held positions in the Church that they claim represents me. In too many cases, I have been rejected. Because so many people were not able to hear me when I spoke to them in their hearts, I have attempted to send outer messengers. I have worked with those of great courage, those who were not afraid to speak out against authority. So often my messengers have been rejected, treated with contempt or even killed.

Therefore, this book is not designed to appeal to those who are in positions of authority and who are reluctant to give up those positions. This book is designed for those who, for the past 2,000 years, have been willing to let the seed of my inner teachings grow within their lifestreams.

If you were not ready, you simply could not have read what I have said in the first parts of this book. Therefore, I hope that

19 | How to Attain Christhood

you will accept with your outer mind that you are indeed one of my own. I hope you will accept that I, your Jesus, am now calling you to take up the path of personal Christhood.

I am Jesus Christ, and I am telling you frankly that I have need of you. I need you to be the open door through which I can bring the Light of Christ into this darkened world. I am no longer in physical embodiment, and therefore I cannot act directly in this world. I can act only through those in embodiment who make the choice to allow me to enter their consciousness. Yet I can enter your consciousness only through the open door which no human can shut—the door of individual Christhood.

If you are ready and willing, let us move on to consider how you can start walking the path of personal Christhood right now. I am aware that, because of the cult of idolatry that has been built around me, the thought of attaining personal Christhood can seem overwhelming, perhaps frightening. Once again, I must remind you that what one human being has done, other human beings can do. In the rest of this book, I will describe a very practical path that anyone who is willing can follow. I think you will see that walking the path to Christhood is well within your reach.

In the following sections I will outline a series of practical steps that will allow you to successfully attain personal Christhood. I will also give you some of the inner teachings that I was not allowed to release publicly 2,000 years ago because people were not ready for those teachings.

I will give you the steps that will empower you to climb the ladder of life and to achieve the very goal that I came to demonstrate 2,000 years ago. I will show you how to understand and accept the truth in my statement: "They that believe on me, the works that I do, they shall do also." Let us be up and doing. Let us be about our Father's business.

20 | GOING WITHIN

In the following sections I will present a set of tools that will help you walk the path of personal Christhood. For practical reasons, I have to present these tools in a certain order, but that order does not represent a progression or a value judgment. Each tool that I present is as important as any other tool. I want you to use all of them because they truly supplement each other.

Developing listening grace

Any positive change in your life must begin with an increased awareness and understanding. If you look at history, you will see that any progress experienced by humankind originated with one individual who raised his or her consciousness and brought forth a higher understanding of a particular aspect of life.

In many cases, this higher understanding did not come from the outer, analytical mind. It came from what one might call the inner or higher mind, and it came through the process that is commonly known as intuition. Even some of the greatest scientists used intuition to make their most significant discoveries. Certainly, all true spiritual leaders used intuition as the basis for their teachings.

To begin the path of personal Christhood, you must make a conscious and determined effort to improve your intuition. It is quite possible that you are already very familiar with the intuitive process and that you have developed an ability to attain intuitive insights. After all, only such intuitive insights could have prompted you to read, and continue to read, this book. The flesh and blood of the death consciousness could not have revealed to you the Christ Light that is in this book.

If you feel that you might benefit from making a conscious effort to further develop your intuition, I encourage you to use some of the many books that are available. There are numerous self-help books that can help you gain a greater understanding of the intuitive process. Many of these books also contain practical tools for increasing your intuition. I will later present you with one such tool.

I need you to understand that the current scientific view of intuition is incomplete. In reality, intuition is truly a lower version of Christ consciousness. I have told you about the relativity of the death consciousness. When you are caught in the death consciousness, you can argue for or against any idea without coming up with a definitive answer as to the validity of that idea. However, through your intuition you can find a definitive answer. You might not be able to produce a rational argument for why the idea is valid; you simply know it is true. Intuition can be described as the ability to know that an idea is true without necessarily being able to argue why it is true.

If you will think about this, you might realize a profound truth. The truth of God is above and beyond the relativity of the death consciousness. Therefore, it is simply not possible to come up with a relative or outer argument, an argument that the human ego can fathom and accept, for the truth of God.

This explains why so many people have failed to fathom the truth of God. This is especially true of many modern scientists who have allowed themselves to believe that unless you can come up with a factual, rational, logical or intellectual line of reasoning then an idea simply cannot be valid.

To know the truth of God, you must realize that this truth cannot be explained in the relative terms that the death consciousness can understand. The truth of God can be known only by reaching beyond the relativity of the death consciousness. When you do reach beyond that relativity and grasp an idea that comes directly from God then you will often be unable to provide an outer line of reasoning to support your idea. You simply know what you know, and that knowledge is beyond the relativity of the ego and outer mind. It is a truth that passeth understanding.

Sharpen your intuition

It is essential that you make an effort to develop and refine your intuition. However, as you begin to gain more familiarity with the intuitive process, you also need to take that process to a higher level. The true purpose of intuition is to develop attunement with the spiritual world. Through this attunement, you can commune with spiritual beings in that higher world, such as myself. However, you can also commune with a higher part of your own mind, a part that is often referred to in spiritual literature as the "higher self." I would like to call this part of your mind the "Christ Self."

I have already told you that you are an individualization of God. In the Bible, the name of God is given as "I AM THAT I AM." One might say that God, in the ultimate sense, is a pure state of consciousness or awareness, a state of consciousness that simply recognizes that "I am."

When God created you, this pure state of consciousness was individualized for you. Therefore, God created a spiritual self which I prefer to call the "I AM Presence." It is this spiritual self which gives you the sense that "I am" (I exist, I am alive, I am conscious).

People who have already learned to use their intuition will be able to feel that just as you have an I AM Presence in the spiritual realm, there is also a part of your lower being that is pure awareness. Many spiritual people have had an experience of such a pure form of awareness where you experience that you are conscious without having any thoughts or feelings. You are an empty space of "I AM-ness" without the usual sense of being this or that. This pure awareness, this conscious self or "Conscious You," is created as an extension of your I AM Presence. The Conscious You has the ability to travel into the various levels of the world of form, and it can even travel into the material universe and take on a human body. I have earlier told you about the symbol of the Tai-Chi. Your I AM Presence is the masculine polarity of the totality of your being, and the Conscious You is the feminine polarity of your being.

Your I AM Presence is a very high state of consciousness, and it cannot descend into the world of form. Therefore, when the Conscious You does descend, it must maintain a thread of contact from its current level of consciousness back to the I AM Presence. This thread of contact is made possible through the universal Christ consciousness. However, that universal Christ consciousness is individualized for you as your Christ Self.

I have told you that the universal Christ consciousness is the open door which no human can shut. It is the light which lights every human that comes into the world. Your personal Christ Self is the open door which you cannot shut. Your Christ Self is what allows the Conscious You to maintain contact to your spiritual self and the spiritual world. Therefore, it is through your Christ Self that you can know the truth of God.

The process of developing personal Christhood is a process whereby the Conscious You gradually puts off the old identity of the human ego and puts on the new identity of the Christ mind. It is a process whereby the Conscious You can develop a new sense of identity as a spiritual or Christed being who is not separated from God or from the spiritual self.

My point is that you must not be satisfied by merely developing good intuition. You must go beyond what the world currently recognizes as intuition and strive for the complete union (the comm-union) between the Conscious You and your Christ Self. It is only through this union, this alchemical marriage, between the Conscious You and your Christ Self that you can put on the fullness of your personal Christhood.

Balance

I am aware that at this point in your life the goal of attaining full Christhood might seem a bit far off. In reality, it is not, but I will give you a deeper understanding of how to know truth. You can greatly increase the process of coming to know the truth of God by realizing that the key to knowing truth is to strive for balance.

To explain the need for balance, let me remind you, once again, that to the human ego everything is relative. The serpents in your midst, those who are seeking to manipulate the people of earth, have used the relativity of the death consciousness to create division and conflict among God's people. The primary tool used by the serpents is a tactic often referred to as "divide and conquer." You might recall the statement: "A house divided against itself cannot stand." The true meaning is that a person divided against itself by the relativity of the death consciousness cannot recognize the truth of God, and therefore it cannot achieve Christ consciousness.

The tactic that has been used so efficiently by the serpents in this world is to use the relativity of the death consciousness to create two extremes that are, or seem to be, in opposition to each other. The purpose is to make you think that truth must be found in one of these extremes. In reality, both extremes spring from the relativity of the death consciousness, and therefore truth is found in none of them.

By looking at history, you will see how this tactic has been used in many ways. For example, there is the conflict between communism and capitalism. Many people allowed themselves to be drawn into this conflict, and they thought the struggle between capitalism and communism was a struggle between good and evil. In reality, the struggle between capitalism and communism is simply a struggle between two kinds of totalitarianism, two forms of centralized control of the economy.

In a communist system, the state owns or controls the means of production. In a capitalist system, privately held companies are fighting to attain a monopoly. If you take capitalism to its ultimate extreme, one company would own all means of production. However, this can happen only if that company influences (merges with) the government, and thereby the ultimate outcome of a capitalist system is a form of state control that is already present in the communist system. What I am telling you here is that capitalism and communism are simply two different ways of attaining centralized control of the economy.

The middle way between these two extremes is a form of economy called "free enterprise" or the "free market economy" (unfortunately many people believe the lie that free enterprise is the same as capitalism). The very basis of the free enterprise economy in unrestricted competition. In a free enterprise economy, it is not possible to create a monopoly. As long as competition remains free, a company can gain a monopoly only on a temporary basis. It is inevitable that some other company will start producing the same goods at a lower price, and thereby the monopoly is broken.

It is not my intention here to go into a detailed analysis of economic forces. I am simply trying to point out how the relativity of the death consciousness can be used to create two extremes that seem to be in direct opposition to each other. In reality, both of the two extremes serve to further the cause of the serpents who are trying to manipulate and control the people.

Obviously, this has many ramifications. However, in this context, I want to make sure that you understand the need to avoid being pulled into this age-old battle between two extremes. Do not allow yourself to be drawn into fighting the war between the Gog and the Magog (the false gods of this world), neither of which represent the true God in Heaven.

Avoid the relative extremes

To discover the truth of God, you must avoid being pulled into the extremes of this world. You must avoid being drawn into "black-and-white thinking." When you think in terms of black and white (relative good and evil), you tend to develop a simplistic view of reality. It is so easy to think that a particular group of people is the enemy and that you can solve all problems by eliminating that enemy. This black-and-white thinking can so easily pull you into extremism and fanaticism, and these states of mind can never lead you to discover the truth of God.

The truth of God is not relative; it is not black and white. This does not mean that the truth of God is gray because gray is simply a muddled mixture of black and white. The truth of

God is above and beyond all the colorings and the divisions that spring from the relativity of the death consciousness. The truth of God is what my beloved Brother of Light, Gautama Buddha, called the "Middle Way." The Buddha was the first to bring the teaching of the Middle Way to this planet. If you feel the need to understand this concept, I recommend that you study his teachings.

However, you will find elements of these teachings in my own words because I too studied Buddhism, and I followed and practiced the Middle Way. If you study my sayings, you will notice that many of them are the type of sayings that in Zen Buddhism are referred to as "koans." Koans are sayings that are designed to shock and surprise people out of their normal state of consciousness and make them look at life from a new angle. Many of my sayings are designed to shock you out of the relativity of the death consciousness and to help you look beyond that relativity and reach for a higher understanding. These sayings are meant to open the way for an intuitive insight from the Christ mind that cuts through the density of the death consciousness like a bolt of lightning. As one example, think about the situation of the woman caught in adultery.

An angry mob was ready to stone this woman. Yet I was able to pacify them by making one simple statement: "Let him, who is without sin amongst you, cast the first stone." Allow your intuition, allow your Christ Self and allow me to give you these flashes of insight that will suddenly transform your consciousness and help you see that which you could never see through the relativity of the death consciousness.

Listen for answers

Let me give you the essential key to developing intuition. Intuition is a form of communication through which your higher mind and your spiritual teachers attempt to communicate with your conscious mind and give you an insight that will help you rise to the next step on your personal path. The key to receiving this insight is to avoid thinking, analyzing or judging with the outer mind. To avoid this form of thinking, you must strive for balance and avoid having your mind polarized towards any of the relative extremes.

The key to improving your intuition is to simply listen. You must develop a state of mind in which you are constantly directing attention towards your Christ Self and listening for the word of truth. You must develop a state of mind that I call "listening grace." The key to developing this state of mind is to listen with an open mind, a mind that is free from prejudice and judgment. I earlier said that the death consciousness creates an idol of reality and then seeks to force reality to conform to its preconceived image. To truly listen, you must look beyond the idols created by the death consciousness.

That is why I said: "Unless you become as little children, you cannot enter the Kingdom of God." The true meaning is that unless you develop the open and trusting mind of a child, the mind that is free from prejudice and judgment, you will not be able to hear the truth of God that is spoken to you only in the stillness of your heart. Dare to look beyond the many relative idols found in this world.

Dare to listen for the truth of God that is beyond all relativity. In Him, in the mind of God, is no variance or turning. In Him is only the Living Truth; the Living Word.

Clearing your mind of false ideas

I have already told you that for the past 2,000 years numerous things have been taken away from and added to my true teachings. I must admit that I am continually amazed at people's ability to construct and actually believe the most incredible theories and ideas. I can tell you that there are so many false ideas about me, about Christianity, about God, about religion and about spirituality floating around on this planet that I can understand those who refuse to deal with any kind of spiritual topics. I can also understand those who cling to the religion in which they were brought up and refuse to consider new ideas.

However, I have already told you that this is part of the plan of the serpents in your midst. These serpents know that they cannot block the tide forever. It is inevitable that more and more people will begin to open their minds to new ideas in the field of spirituality and religion. Therefore, the serpents are attempting to throw out so many confusing and outrageous ideas that people will either be misled, confused or overwhelmed.

Do not concern yourself with the many false ideas that are out there. Focus on developing your intuition, and I can promise you that through that intuition you will achieve the discernment that will allow you to know what is of God and what is not of God. However, you can greatly enhance this process by making a conscious effort to purge your mind of the false ideas that have already entered your consciousness. I must tell you that most people on this planet have been exposed to such false beliefs. Therefore, it is safe to assume that you could benefit from doing a bit of spiritual housecleaning. To achieve maximum spiritual growth, you must be willing to let go of false ideas. You must be willing to realize the falsity of such ideas even if it causes you to have to change beliefs with which you have grown comfortable. When I said: "I come not to bring peace, but a sword," I was referring to this very process. It is a fact that human beings tend to be creatures of habit. Therefore, they are often reluctant to reconsider or let go of ideas with which they have become familiar.

A perfect example of this is my beloved Paul. He was brought up in the orthodox Jewish religion, and he believed some of the false ideas promoted by that religion. Because of his acceptance of these false ideas, he had reasoned that Jesus Christ and his followers were not of the true faith. He was very attached to these ideas, and he was very reluctant to change his ways and reconsider his core beliefs. To turn Paul around, I had to make use of the drastic measure of appearing to him in a vision so powerful that Paul, given the fact that he was prepared at inner levels, could not deny it or explain it away.

It is my sincere hope that you will be far more open than Paul. I hope you will be willing to reconsider some of your most dearly held beliefs and to be God-taught. I am not thereby saying that you have to abandon all of your current beliefs or that you have to abandon your false beliefs all at once.

I do not desire to throw you into an identity crisis. However, I do desire to see you engage in a process whereby you gradually re-evaluate your current beliefs and use your inner discernment to determine whether you need to expand, change or even abandon some of those beliefs. I am not telling you to follow any outer source in this matter, not even this book. I am telling you to follow the inner source of your own intuition and the insights you receive from your Christ Self.

Study to show thyself approved unto God

What can you do to speed up the process whereby you learn to see through and let go of false or incomplete beliefs? Simply engage in a process of studying spiritual teachings.

Obviously, I would like you to start with this book and some of the other books and websites we have brought forth through this messenger. Do not simply read this book one time and think you are done with it. To fully absorb the teachings

I am giving in this book, you need to read it several times and to carefully digest it. Then, use the understanding I have given you in this book to gain a new perspective on other spiritual teachings.

I think that if you would truly absorb my teachings in this book and then read the New Testament, you would gain much new inspiration from the scriptures. There are also many other Christian texts that can serve as inspiration. Study some of the Christian mystics, especially some of the Gnostics, such as Origen of Alexandria who was truly one of my own. Study some of the texts that have been discovered within this century, such as the Nag Hammadi Library, the Dead Sea scrolls and many other apocryphal texts that are not part of the official Bible. I especially recommend the Gospel of Thomas which contains many of my direct sayings.

Many people will want to stay within the context of Christianity itself, and this is acceptable as long as you follow your inner direction. However, I also know that many people are prepared to look at spiritual teachings from other sources. There are many spiritual teachings on this planet that can serve as a great inspiration for you. The texts of the major world religions can be a great help. So can many texts that have been brought forth even in this century.

I have told you that I am part of a team of spiritual teachers who have been working with humankind for a very long time. Throughout the ages, we of the ascended masters have attempted to bring forth a progressive revelation of the spiritual mysteries. We have done this through many different people who were willing to raise their consciousness and serve as the open door for bringing forth a particular spiritual teaching.

In the last century, this process has been greatly accelerated and the reason is that we are now at the end of one age and the beginning of the next. The past 2,000 year period has been what many people call the "Age of Pisces." I was the spiritual hierarch for that age. Planet earth is now entering the next 2,000 year cycle, namely the "Age of Aquarius." Because of this change, there is a great opportunity for spiritual growth. In the last century, millions of people have opened their minds to new spiritual ideas. God has responded to this openness in many different ways. There are many, many sources of spiritual teachings that are truly sponsored by the ascended masters. There are also many false teachings, produced by the serpents in an attempt to confuse and confound. If you will work on developing intuition, you will have the discernment to know the difference.

I am aware that some orthodox Christians look upon any new movement or teaching as a New Age cult. Because you are reading this book, I am sure you will not be unduly concerned by these labels. The fact is that if I walked the earth today and did the things I did 2,000 years ago, these very same orthodox Christians would label me, Jesus Christ, as a very dangerous New Age cult leader.

Therefore, let not the judgments of other people prevent you from discovering and reading the spiritual teachings that we of the ascended masters have given to you. I am not thereby saying that you should study all of the teachings available. I am not saying that you should join any particular organization. Simply let your intuition guide you and show you what to study.

21 | HEALING YOURSELF

We have now come to a topic that I consider to be extremely important, but which many religious and spiritual people ignore. I have already told you that your lifestream has been on this planet for a very long time. One glance at history should demonstrate that you have most likely been involved with one or more wars or other atrocities. It should be obvious that such traumatic experiences can cause your soul to become wounded and bruised. Therefore, it should be easy to see that you have a need to heal your soul.

The word "soul" comes from the Greek word "psyche." Psyche and soul are interchangeable terms. In the terminology that we of the ascended masters use today, the soul is a vehicle that the Conscious You creates in order to interact with the physical body. Your soul does follow you over many lifetimes, but in the end, you can ascend only by giving up the soul, by letting the soul – the sense of identity based on the soul vehicle – die so you can be reborn into a new identity based on the Christ mind. As I told Nicodemus, only the being that descended from heaven can ascend back to heaven. That being is what I have called the Conscious You, the pure aspect of your lower being. If your soul has been severely wounded, it can be difficult for you to stop identifying with the soul, and thus you cannot give up the soul, give up the ghosts that make up the soul. [For further teachings on the soul, see the book *The Power of Self*.]

I have told you that the essence of the path to personal Christhood is that you must put off the old human, the sense of identity based on the death consciousness, and put on the new human, namely a sense of identity based on the Christ Self and your God-given individuality. The biggest obstacle to this process is that people tend to become very attached to certain aspects of their lower sense of identity, the soul. The cause of this attachment is the emotional wounds that your soul has received in the past.

Your emotional wounds can cause you to become attached to elements of your false sense of identity or to certain false ideas. In many cases, a traumatic experience from the past caused you to accept a false belief about yourself, about God or about some aspect of life. The traumatic experience also caused your soul to experience intense emotional pain. The pain generated a pool of negative energy, and this energy is stored in the soul (in your personal energy field).

If you have not healed your soul, the emotional energy is still there. Therefore, any attempt to reconsider the false belief will inevitably open up the old wound and cause your conscious mind to reconnect with the negative energy. As a result, you will re-experience the emotional pain. Many people are afraid of reconsidering a false idea because they do not want to deal with the pain. However, it is a brutal fact of life that in order to free yourself from your false beliefs, you must be willing to open the Pandora's box of your past.

Many people are afraid to open this box and look into their own psyche. In fact, I see many people who use religion or spirituality as an excuse for not dealing with the wounds of the psyche. These people focus their attention on the outer aspect of religion or they focus on practicing a spiritual technique. They reason that if only they follow all of the outer rules, go to church every Sunday or practice some spiritual technique then they can somehow avoid having to deal with the pain in the psyche.

I am very happy to see the numerous self-improvement techniques that are available today. Not all of them are beneficial, and not all of them were inspired by the ascended masters. Yet many of them do come from us, and we have released them to assist you on your path. However, I must tell you that a spiritual technique cannot replace the need for psychological healing. You cannot simply pray, meditate or sit in a Yoga posture and assume that this will automatically heal your psychology.

Why a spiritual technique cannot heal you

Let me explain why a spiritual technique cannot heal your psychology for you. The human experience is produced by the choices you make by exercising your God-given free will. When you experience a traumatic situation, there are two aspects of that situation. One aspect is the outer situation, for example what another human being does to you. Another aspect is the inner situation, namely how you choose to respond to that situation.

I want you to understand that I am in no way saying that it is right to harm another human being. If someone harms you, that person will inevitably make karma. However, it is a brutal fact that the cause of a psychological wound is not the other person's actions. What causes the wound is your inner reaction to those actions.

Human beings react very differently to similar situations. One person might think that a situation is no big deal, and that person simply moves on without being emotionally scarred by the situation. Another person can use the same situation to build a negative self image that can stay in the soul for lifetimes.

The causes of your psychological wounds are the decisions you made concerning how you responded to traumatic or painful situations. Therefore, the essential key to healing your wounds is that you must consciously go back to the original choice and make a better decision. For example, a child who is sexually, physically or emotionally abused often builds a negative self image dominated by guilt and a sense of unworthiness. No amount of prayer, meditation or yoga exercises will remove that negative self-image (as we will see in the next section, a spiritual exercise might remove the negative energy created in the original situation). To remove the false image, you must replace the original decision (or decisions) with a new and better decision based on the understanding that you are a spiritual being created in the image and likeness of God.

There are many techniques on the market today that can assist you to go into the depths of your psyche and free yourself from the negative gravitational pull of your past. I can assure you that if some of these techniques had been available 2,000 years ago, I would have had all of my disciples go into some form of therapy or psychological healing.

I consider it absolutely vital that you make a conscious and determined effort to heal the wounds in your psychology. These wounds form a dead weight that will greatly hinder you as you attempt to climb the path of Christhood. Why drag along this heavy weight when you can remove it by applying a suitable method of psychological healing?

The healing of your psychology is an extremely important topic, and I simply do not have space to cover all of its facets in this book. However, we of the ascended masters have provided several other books that outline the practical steps to healing your psychology. One final thought. I earlier told you that by turning the other cheek you will avoid making personal karma from a situation.

However, this also has an inner aspect. If you can turn the other cheek and react with total forgiveness then you will avoid creating an emotional scar in your soul. You can simply let go of the situation and move on as if it never happened. As you grow in Christhood and heal your psychology, you will attain the ability to respond with love, forgiveness, harmony and peace to any situation that life throws at you. The ability to have full control over your inner reactions to outer situations is the very key to personal freedom. It is also the key to spiritual freedom.

Transforming negative energy

I have told you that you live in a universe in which everything is energy. Therefore, everything you do is done with energy. If you commit a wrong act, that act has the following consequences:

- An energy impulse is sent out into the universe, and it will be returned to you in the form of personal karma.

- You generate negative energy that is stored in your personal energy field, and it can have unpleasant effects on your thoughts and feelings.

I have also told you that I have personally carried humankind's karma for these past 2,000 years. My dispensation for doing this is coming to an end, and therefore humankind's karma is now descending upon this planet. This descent of karma can have negative effects for your personal life and for the planet as a whole. Therefore, any serious spiritual seeker needs to consider the question of how he or she can transform negative energy. You can greatly accelerate your spiritual growth by finding a spiritual technique that allows you to raise the vibration of negative energy into its original purity as spiritual energy. How could you possibly do this?

Science tells us that energy exists in the form of waves that have different frequencies, amplitudes and wavelengths. When two energy waves meet, the interaction of the two waves creates what scientists call an interference pattern. This pattern can change the vibrational properties of both waves. To make a long story short, if a wave of high-frequency energy meets a wave of low-frequency energy, the resulting interaction can raise the vibration of the low-frequency energy. The potential of transforming low-frequency energy into spiritual energy is the foundation for all spiritual growth.

You have heard it said that not one jot and tittle of the law shall pass away until all be fulfilled. When you chose to descend into the material universe and cut yourself off from your spiritual teacher, the Law of Cause and Effect became your teacher. According to this law, you are ultimately accountable for what you do with God's energy. This accountability goes all the way back to your first embodiment in the material universe.

You have had thousands of embodiments on this planet, and therefore you could potentially have created a very large pool of negative energy. God requires that before you can ascend into the spiritual world, you must transform that negative energy back into its original purity. There are many ways to transform negative energy, such as prayer, fasting, good works or various spiritual techniques and practices.

You can also balance or neutralize negative energy by experiencing the effects of the return of that energy or karma. This can manifest as negative events in your life, such as disease or accidents. Obviously, this is the hard way to balance your karma.

It is far better to balance the karma before it actually manifests as a physical event. This is quite possible, and from the beginning of time God has provided the opportunity to balance negative energy without experiencing physical effects of that karma. One might say that every spiritual technique known to humankind was originally designed to help you invoke spiritual energy, spiritual light, that can serve to transform the negative energy that you have generated.

Obviously, these ideas are another example of what was removed from my true teachings. In fact, hardly any orthodox religion contains these ideas. Nevertheless, I strongly encourage you to realize the validity and the value of these teachings.

I can assure you that you live in a time when there is a great need for the transformation of negative energy. The personal aspect of this is that you must transform your personal karma. In fact, if you are serious about attaining Christhood, you need to make a determined effort to apply a spiritual technique for transforming negative energy.

The planetary aspect is that the returning karma of humankind could have a number of negative effects for society and for the planet. These potential effects have been described through a number of prophecies delivered from various sources. I want you to understand that prophecy is not set in stone. Prophecy is given as a warning of what might come to pass if people do not change their ways. Therefore, there is a potential to turn back prophecy, and the key to doing so is to transform the negative energy before it actually manifests as physical events.

A special dispensation

Our God is a God of mercy, and your heavenly parents are not blind to the current predicament on planet earth. Therefore, they have decided to provide a way out. I already told you that all spiritual techniques are designed to help you invoke spiritual energy and thereby transform negative energy. However, I must tell you that the spiritual techniques practiced by most people simply are not powerful enough to transform the amount of personal and planetary karma that is being returned in these years. Once again, there is a way out.

I earlier told you that my father, the beloved Saint Joseph, is today an ascended being, an ascended master. His name is Saint Germain, and he has been appointed as the spiritual hierarch for the Age of Aquarius. I can assure you that I have the utmost respect and admiration for my Brother of Light, Saint Germain. I am extremely gratified that he has been appointed as the spiritual leader for the next 2,000 years.

When Saint Germain was appointed to be my successor, he clearly realized the predicament of humankind's returning karma, as I have described it to you. Therefore, Saint Germain saw the need to release a spiritual technique that was more efficient than anything previously released on this planet. This was not a straightforward matter because people have shown a great willingness to misuse any spiritual technique given to them. As people have been willing to misuse atomic energy, they have also been willing to misuse spiritual energy.

Therefore, Saint Germain had to apply for a cosmic dispensation, and after much deliberation by the spiritual hierarchs above us, that dispensation was granted. Saint Germain was granted permission to publicly release a spiritual technique that for thousands of years has been known only by a small group of advanced lifestreams. In the past, this technique has been known by many names. Saint Germain chose to release this spiritual technique under the name the "Violet Flame." The name refers to the fact that this technique is aimed at invoking a form of spiritual light that vibrates at frequencies just above the material universe (violet light has the highest frequency of visible light).

If you are serious about transforming personal and planetary karma then I cannot see how you can do this without making use of the Violet Flame. This form of spiritual energy is extremely efficient in terms of transforming the negative energy created by human beings. It is more powerful than any other spiritual technique currently found on this planet.

There are many ways to invoke the Violet Flame, including religious rituals, prayers, affirmations and visualizations. However, the most efficient way to invoke this energy is through the spoken word. I highly recommend that you make use of a technique for invoking the Violet Flame, such as the decrees included in the following discourse. You do not have to abandon your membership of any current church or spiritual organization to do this. The invocation of the Violet Flame is a universal spiritual technique that is truly a gift from God. I would like to see it practiced by all who consider themselves to be my followers. The spiritual technique called the Violet Flame is a gift from God to all people on earth.

When I decided to carry the burden of humankind's karma, it was my hope that people would make wise use of this dispensation. I had hoped that by applying my true teachings, people would become spiritual millionaires. Therefore, when their karma had to be returned to them, it would have been easy for them to pay off their debt to life without slowing down their spiritual progress. Unfortunately, as I have already explained, this did not come to pass.

Therefore, humankind is now in a double jeopardy. For the past 2,000 years, people have created more karma, and they are currently dealing with the effects of that karma. At the same time, the karma that I have carried is being returned to them. Obviously, it is not my desire to see people in this predicament. The very best hope I see for turning around this situation is that millions of people will decide to apply Saint Germain's gift of the Violet Flame. If millions of people, be they Christians or non-Christians, will apply this technique, it will be possible to consume the burden of returning karma on both the personal and planetary level.

Therefore, my original intention for carrying humankind's karma could still be fulfilled. The golden age that I envision for planet earth could be manifest during the Age of Aquarius. I hope you will seriously consider applying a technique for invoking the Violet Flame. I do not know what more I could say to recommend the Violet Flame to you.

Come apart in consciousness

Modern science has demonstrated that the entire material universe is made from energy. Science has also demonstrated that energy cannot be created and it cannot be destroyed. These two facts contain an important key to understanding the statement: "Come apart, and be a separate and chosen people." I have already told you that this statement first and foremost means that you must come apart in consciousness. Let me now give you a more detailed explanation.

I am a spiritual being, and I see many things that are hidden to the physical sight of most people. I see many things that are attacking those who are truly striving for spiritual growth. Let me describe these forces to you.

21 | Healing Yourself

First and foremost, you need to learn how to protect yourself from negative energy. I have told you that everything you do is done with God's energy. You are constantly receiving a stream of spiritual energy that flows from your I AM Presence into your energy field. You express that energy through thoughts, feelings and actions. In the process of expressing energy, that energy is qualified according to the contents of your consciousness. In other words, as you express spiritual energy, you change the vibration of that energy. A positive thought, feeling or action will generate energy of a high frequency. A negative thought, feeling or action will generate energy of a low frequency.

Energy cannot be created or destroyed; it can only be transformed into another form of energy. The significance of this fact is that the negative energy generated by human beings will not simply disappear. Some of that negative energy will be sent out into the universe, and it will be returned to you by the Law of Cause and Effect, the Law of Karma. However, some of the negative energy generated by human beings will remain with them.

Even modern science is beginning to realize that there is an energy field surrounding the human body. Science has also begun to realize that there is an energy field surrounding the planet. I will not go into further detail here, but I will tell you that your personal energy field acts as a storehouse for both negative and positive energy. Likewise, the energy field of the planet is a storehouse for both negative and positive energy generated by human beings. I am sure that if you look at human history, you will realize that humankind has generated an enormous amount of negative energy. It should not be difficult to imagine that the energy field of planet earth is literally a cesspool of negative energy.

You live in that cesspool of energy. You can look at your personal energy field as one drop in the planetary ocean of energy. The question now becomes how your personal energy field, and thereby your thoughts and emotions, is affected by the energy in the planetary energy field?

I must tell you that there is currently so much negative energy stored in the energy field of this planet that unless you make a very determined effort to free yourself from the negative gravitational pull of this energy, you will inevitably be pulled down. Millions of people on this planet are so overpowered by the planetary energy field that they literally are unable to maintain the integrity of their personality and individuality. In other words, their minds and emotions have been swallowed up by what one might call a mass mind or mass consciousness. These people are like sheep who blindly follow the currents that flow through the ocean of the mass consciousness.

Obviously, I do not want my followers to be part of this mass mind. How could you possibly walk the path of individual Christhood if your mind is overpowered by some mass consciousness that cancels out your individuality? Therefore, you must come apart from this mass consciousness and establish a hallowed sphere around your personal energy field. Doing so is not difficult when you have the right tools, and I will give you those tools.

Defend your light

You must learn how to defend yourself from evil spirits. I am aware that many Christians, and many spiritually interested people who are part of the so-called New Age movement, are reluctant to consider the topic of evil spirits. This reluctance is based on a defense mechanism that is built into the human psyche. The simple fact is that the human psyche does not want to recognize a danger from which it thinks it cannot defend itself. Yet if you read the scriptures you will see that I often cast out evil spirits. Therefore, you cannot afford to ignore the topic of evil spirits.

Let me make haste to tell you that there is indeed an effective defense against all evil spirits. When medical science first discovered bacteria, many people refused to accept the existence of bacteria. They did not want to accept that there could be some microscopic organism, an organism which they could not see, that could attack their bodies. Yet as soon as you recognize the existence of a hidden danger, you can begin to look for ways to defend yourself against that danger. On the other hand, if you remain willfully ignorant, you cannot find such a defense. There are three types of spirits that you need to know:

- **Malicious spirits.** A malicious spirit (also called a demon) is a spirit that has rebelled against God and therefore has cut itself off from God. I have stated that you can remain alive only because you are receiving a constant stream of spiritual energy from Above. If a being continues to rebel against God for a long period of time, that being will gradually diminish the flow of spiritual energy, and eventually that flow is completely cut off. Due to a mechanism which I will not here describe in detail, such a being (or spirit) can continue to exist, but it can do so only by stealing spiritual energy from those who are still receiving energy from Above. In other words, a malicious spirit is a spirit who can survive only by stealing spiritual energy from human beings. Such spirits will seek to steal this energy through many different means, but one of the most frequently used is to manipulate human beings into engaging in negative thoughts, feelings or actions. You must understand that such spirits exist. You must understand that they can continue to exist only by stealing spiritual energy from human beings. You must understand that they will do absolutely anything to force or fool you into misusing or misqualifying God's pure energy.

- **Disembodied souls.** A human body is only a temporary abode for the Conscious You and the soul. When the human body dies, you leave the body behind and travel into one of the lower levels of the spiritual world. Usually, a being resides in this realm for some time and goes through a process of healing and learning. Unfortunately, some people become very attached to the life they live in this world. When the body dies, the person cannot get itself to leave the body and the life behind. Therefore, instead of going into the realms of light, as described by so many people who have had a near-death experience, the soul remains stuck in the material world. It is possible that such a discarnate soul can attach itself to you and seek to gain entrance into your energy field and consciousness. The soul might not necessarily do this out of evil intent, and the soul is simply trying to fill some kind of need that it was not able to fill while in a physical body. While such a soul might not have evil intent, seeking to influence you is nevertheless a violation of your free will and a violation of the Law of God. You must never allow such a soul entry into your consciousness.

- **Entities/spirits.** Everything is made from energy, but energy is simply a manifestation of God's consciousness. Therefore, energy is truly a form of consciousness (which some scientists have already realized). If you concentrate negative energy to a sufficient intensity, that energy can develop a certain rudimentary form of awareness. This does not mean that the energy has individuality or self-awareness. However, it does mean that the energy has a certain form of survival instinct and a drive to multiply itself. Therefore, a concentrated cloud of negative energy can become what I call an "entity" or "spirit." You can think of this as a floating cloud of negative energy, but it is a cloud with a certain state of consciousness and an intent to multiply itself by stealing energy from human beings.

Invoke spiritual light

I am aware that most people would rather not think about such topics, yet being forewarned is being forearmed. I can tell you that evil spirits, disembodied souls or entities are a major factor in any type of addiction known to human beings. It becomes much easier to defend yourself from falling into the trap of addiction (or to escape this trap) when you know what you are up against.

To see how you can defend yourself from these forces, you only need to understand that everything is made from God's energy. The material universe is made from energy of a much lower vibration than the energies found in the spiritual world. Therefore, there is a very simple way to defend yourself against evil spirits or negative energies. Your defense is to invoke high-frequency spiritual energy from Above. That energy can literally create a shield around your mind and energy field which no lower energies can penetrate. It can also fill your energy field so that there is no room for evil spirits to enter.

When I cast out evil spirits, I gave the teaching that if the house (meaning the person's energy field) was left empty, the evil spirit might return and bring other spirits with it. To avoid this, you must never leave your house empty. Therefore, make an effort to fill your energy field with high-frequency spiritual energy. Many religious rituals are designed to fill your mind with God's light, and I will later teach you other ways to invoke light. In fact, if you will let us, I or your Christ self will enter and fill your energy field so that no imperfect spirits can enter.

I need you to recognize that you are living in a sea of negative energy. In that sea are sharks in the form of demons, disembodied souls and entities or spirits. I am sure this will not cause you to be unduly frightened. You know that there are sharks in the ocean, yet that does not keep you from going for a swim. You simply take the necessary precautions to avoid being attacked by a shark. In other words, I do not want you to be paralyzed by fear so that you do not dare to engage in the process of life. I simply want you to be aware of the dangers so that you can take the necessary precautions and protect yourself from these dangers.

In a later section, I will give you the necessary tools to build an effective spiritual defense. However, any positive change in your life begins with increased awareness and understanding. You need to increase your awareness of negative energy so that you can recognize places, people or situations that have a concentration of such energy. Thereby, you can begin to make wise choices and avoid rushing in where angels fear to tread.

Surrender

The tools I have described so far have all been active tools that empower you to do something about specific aspects of your situation. I will now give you a tool that might seem to be passive, and that some may think is less powerful. Yet in reality, it is the most powerful tool of all. This tool is the act of surrender, the act of letting go of all that is unreal.

You might recall that the Archangel Gabriel appeared to my beloved mother to announce that she would give birth to the Christ child. You must understand that giving birth to a child at that particular time in her life was not a simple matter. For example, the fact that she was unmarried would inevitably pose certain complications. Yet my mother did not reject the Messenger of God. She simply said: "Be it unto me according to thy will."

Had it not been for this act of surrender by my blessed mother, the Christ might not have been born on this planet. You must understand that before the Christ can be born in you, you too must come to a point where you are willing to surrender your all to God.

What exactly is it that you must surrender? I have told you many times that you are created in the image and likeness of God. Therefore, you are already a son or daughter of God. Presently, your outer mind cannot accept that divine identity. Therefore, your true identity as a spiritual being is covered up by an image or idol. This image can be likened to a jigsaw puzzle with many pieces. The path to personal Christhood is a process whereby you systematically remove the pieces of the jigsaw puzzle that are covering up your true identity. Therefore, it is these pieces that you must surrender, one by one:

- You must surrender every aspect of the death consciousness.

- You must surrender relativity and horizontal reasoning.

- You must surrender all prejudice.

- You must surrender all judgment.

- You must surrender all fear.

- You must surrender all anger.

- You must surrender all guilt, all sense of unworthiness.

- You must surrender the very idea that you are a sinner.

- You must surrender all false beliefs with which you have become comfortable.

- You must surrender all attachment to the things of this world.

- You must surrender all human or relative desires.

- You must surrender all wounds and scars in your psychology.

- You must surrender the original decision to turn away from God, and you must surrender the human ego which sprang from that decision.

- You must surrender all false sense of identity as a mortal, limited human being.

- You must surrender the human or egoic will which is always out of sync with the divine will.

- You must surrender all sense of separation from God and your spiritual self.

- You must surrender the belief that you are the doer and accept that God is the only doer in your life.

- You must surrender all pride so that you can fully understand and accept the truth in the statement: "I of my own self (the egoic mind) can do nothing; it is the Father (the spiritual self) within me who is doing the work."

- You must surrender everything that stands between you and the acceptance of your true identity as a spiritual being with the potential to walk the earth as a Christed being.

Be it unto to me according to your will

When I appear to announce that you are ready for the birth of the Christ in you, you must be able and willing to simply say: "Be it unto me according to thy will." You must be able to make that statement out of your own free will and with a peace of mind that comes from a complete resolution of all that stands between you and your God.

All of the other tools I have given you are designed to help you reach a state of mind wherein you have made peace with God and peace with me. God has given you free will. God desires to see you come home to his kingdom, but God wants you to come home as the result of your own free-will choosing. God has no desire to force you. I have no desire to force you. Both your Father and I want to see you resolve all that causes you to turn away from God or feel that you are not worthy of coming home to God.

As long as you have any trace of resentment, fear, pride, anger, unworthiness or any other negative emotions towards

God, you will not be able to make the choice to fully accept your true identity. Therefore, you cannot put on the fullness of your individual Christhood.

Surrender is not something that can be forced. Therefore, do not try to force yourself into surrendering. Instead, I am asking you to use the other tools I have given you and resolve the issues in your psyche that prevent you from being at peace with God. As you begin to resolve some of the wounds and blocks in your psychology, you will begin to feel a greater sense of inner peace. You will begin to realize that you are making peace with God. As you become aware of this process, I am asking you to deeply and sincerely consider the concept of surrender.

Do not seek to force yourself to surrender. Seek to resolve the issues in your soul that are preventing you from accepting who you truly are. If you will go through the effort of resolving the issues that separate you from your true identity, you will find that the act of surrender will begin to happen spontaneously.

Suddenly, you will feel as if a knot in your psyche has been undone. As a result of this resolution, a heavy burden will be lifted from you, and when you are no longer weighed down by that burden, you will begin to feel the unconditional love that God has for you.

As you begin to experience, absorb and accept God's unconditional love, you will realize that all sense of separation and all sense of unworthiness is completely unreal. Therefore, the act of surrendering that which is unreal will not seem like a loss. When you begin to experience God's unconditional love, you realize that you are not giving up anything by surrendering the human imperfections. Instead, the act of surrender is the master key to immortal life.

Choose life. Choose to surrender all that is less than eternal life. Surrender all that is unreal, and you shall have all that is real.

Holding the immaculate concept

I will now give you another tool which at first might seem passive, but which is extremely powerful. Because of the cult of idolatry built around my person, many people think I was born in the fullness of my personal Christhood. I did indeed have great attainment before that last embodiment, but I had not put on the fullness of my Christhood. I followed the very same path that you are following, and I did not manifest my full Christhood until I appeared at the wedding in Canaan.

During this entire process, my blessed mother used a very powerful spiritual tool to help me. My mother knew of my potential before my birth, and she always held the vision of what I would become. She held the immaculate concept of my Christhood.

You will recall that when I was at the wedding in Canaan, it was my mother who gently prodded me to turn the water into wine and thereby perform the miracle that would mark the point of no return for my Galilean mission. You will also recall that I resisted her prodding. I was hesitant to begin my mission because I knew that as soon as I started it, there would be no way of turning back. As she had done so many times before, my blessed mother held the immaculate concept for me, and by doing so she gave me the inner strength to cross the line and begin my mission.

I have told you that I want to see God's kingdom manifest on earth. I have also told you that this can come to pass only as a result of free-will choices made by those in embodiment. The most important thing you can do to help bring about God's kingdom is to practice the spiritual technique of holding the immaculate concept.

You must visualize God's kingdom as being already manifest on earth. When you hold the immaculate concept, you are not engaging in wishful thinking. Some people will think that visualizing God's kingdom when there is so much darkness on earth is simply denial or daydreaming. However, this is a very superficial viewpoint.

I have told you that without God was not anything made that was made. The consequence is that everything in the entire universe is made from God's substance and energy. Obviously, many of the things happening on planet earth are not in accordance with God's vision and God's perfection. Nevertheless, everything that is occurring on this planet is done with God's energy. Therefore, no matter what the outer appearances might be, the inner reality is that all conditions on earth have the potential to be transformed into the original purity of God's perfection.

Seeing perfection

Why are there imperfect manifestations on earth today? Because human beings have used their creative potential to focus their attention on imperfect forms and images. Therefore, the spiritual energy streaming through their minds has been qualified according to this imperfect vision. The imperfect conditions found on planet earth today can continue to exist only because people continue to allow their spiritual energy to flow into these imperfect images and visions. What is the only possible way to change this situation? It is that people take their conscious attention away from human imperfections and focus it firmly on the perfection of God.

I earlier used the image of a film projector and movie screen. The current conditions on earth are simply images that are projected unto the screen of life. The light that projects these images is the spiritual energy that flows through the minds of all human beings. However, the images themselves are the product of the film strip through which the light passes on the way to the screen. That film strip represents the contents, the images and beliefs of the consciousness of human beings. The only way to change the images that appear on the screen of life is to change what is on the film strip in people's minds. Therefore, the only way to bring God's kingdom to earth is that a large number of people decide to hold the immaculate concept and focus their attention on God's perfection.

I want you to seriously contemplate that holding the immaculate concept is an extremely powerful spiritual technique. I want you to do the following:

• Hold the immaculate concept for yourself and your personal Christhood.

• Hold the immaculate concept for all of your brothers and sisters on the path.

• Hold the immaculate concept even for those who seem to be your enemies.

• Hold the immaculate concept for your local community.

• Hold the immaculate concept for your nation.

- Hold the immaculate concept for your planet.

About prophecy

You might be aware that there are numerous prophecies that predict various negative events for the near and distant future. I will tell you that there are many false prophesies in the world, but I can assure you that there also many true prophecies. Once again, prophecy is not set in stone. Prophecy is a warning from God, and the purpose is to tell people what will come to pass if they do not change their ways.

I am not here to discount prophecy, but I desire to give you a new view of prophecy and the potential for changes in the earth. I have already told you that I desire to see the manifestation of a new age of peace, prosperity and progress. The spiritual hierarch for the Age of Aquarius, my beloved Saint Germain, also desires to bring forth such a golden age. However, before we can bring in this new age, many changes are needed. Therefore, I can tell you that there is a real potential for many dramatic changes on this planet. In fact, if you read the newspapers or listen to the news, you might realize that such changes are already taking place.

However, I do not want any of my followers to be afraid of such changes. What is actually happening is that planet earth, the earth mother, is giving birth to a child, a Christ child, in the form of a golden age. If you were to witness a women in the process of giving birth and if you did not know anything about childbirth, you might see this as a terrible event that inflicts great pain and suffering upon the woman. Obviously, giving birth is painful, yet most women are not overly troubled by this pain. They know it is only a temporary phenomenon, and it is simply a necessary step in the process of bringing forth a beautiful child. Likewise, changes in the earth are simply birth pains as Mother earth gives birth to a new age.

I want you to realize that the best way to help bring about this new age is to let go of all fear and concern about the future. The best thing you can do for me is to hold the immaculate concept for earth. No matter what happens in the outer world, I want you to focus your inner vision on God's kingdom being manifest on this planet. If you will use your inner attunement, I will give you the vision of God's kingdom on earth. If you will seek the inner vision, that vision will help you attain a state of inner peace.

The most important thing you can do for me in the coming decades is to maintain inner peace and to focus your attention on the immaculate concept for yourself, your brothers and sisters and the planet as a whole. The forces of this world will attack you and attempt to make you take your attention away from God's perfection and focus it on human imperfection. Do not fall prey to this temptation. Maintain your inner peace and practice the spiritual technique of holding the immaculate concept.

Today, planet earth is a reflection of the inner vision of human beings. Tomorrow, the earth will be a reflection of the inner vision of human beings. Let those who have ears, hear my words. You can help create a better future for this planet. Focus your attention on me. I will give you inner peace.

My peace I give unto you.
My peace I leave with you.
Walk in my peace always.

22 | TECHNIQUES FOR ATTAINING CHRISTHOOD

In this discourse I will give you a set of practical tools for attaining the goals outlined in the previous discourse.

Consecrate your life to Christ

To assist you in holding the immaculate concept, use the following affirmations and give them silently or aloud.

Give each affirmation at least 3 times, or give an affirmation until you feel inner peace. As often as is practical, say:

> **I consecrate my life to Christ-victory, and I see only Christ-perfection.**

Before getting out of bed, say:

> **I consecrate this day to Christ-victory, and I see only Christ-perfection.**

Before beginning any activity, say:

> **I consecrate** *[give a brief description of the activity]* **to Christ-victory, and I see only Christ-perfection.**

You can also say:

> **I consecrate** *[my family, household, community, nation or world]* **to Christ-victory, and I see only Christ-perfection.**

The Seal of the Lord

I have said that you must come apart from the mass consciousness that is currently dragging humankind down into what is truly a self-created hell on earth. This has an inner and outer aspect. The outer aspect is that you need to refrain from activities that serve to bind you to that mass mind or that drag you down into a state of consciousness where you have no chance of manifesting Christhood. I will not tell you what you should do or what you should not do, and I will later explain why.

The inner aspect of coming apart from the mass consciousness is that you must seal yourself from the energies of the mass consciousness. This requires some effort on your part because you need to build and maintain a shield of high-frequency spiritual energy that surrounds your personal energy field and thereby your mind. You need to invoke spiritual energy to transform the negative energy already stored in your field. You also need to fill your energy field with spiritual energy and keep it filled.

I am aware that many Christians believe that you should say a prayer only once and that you should refrain from rote repetition. However, we are not here talking about prayer. We are talking about invoking spiritual energy to build a shield of high-frequency energy around your energy field. This simply cannot be done by saying a prayer once. After you invoke a shield of spiritual energy, that shield will be bombarded by the lower energies of this world. These energies will be transformed by the energies in the shield, but this will cause the shield to gradually break down. Therefore, you must invoke spiritual energy daily or even several times a day.

To fully seal yourself from the mass consciousness, you need to build a personal relationship to my beloved Brother of Light, the Archangel Michael. Archangel Michael is assigned by God as the protector of your faith. Obviously, protecting your faith involves sealing you from the mass consciousness that will drag you down into a state of mind dominated by fear, doubt, questions with no answers, hopelessness and despair.

I can assure you that Archangel Michael is an infinitely powerful spiritual being, and he has an absolute dedication to his assignment and to your growth. However, as everyone else in the spiritual world, Archangel Michael is bound to respect the Law of Free Will. I have already explained to you that you are ultimately responsible for what you do with God's energy. What you have created in ignorance, you must uncreate with understanding. Therefore, you cannot simply assume that God will take all of your negative energy or karma away from you as the result of one prayer. If God did so, God would deprive you of the learning experience and the sense of victory.

Likewise, you cannot simply pray for Archangel Michael to seal you from the mass consciousness and expect that one prayer will be enough. You must make an effort to invoke the spiritual energy of Archangel Michael and build a wall of that energy around your energy field. I will give you affirmations and a decree that will allow you to invoke spiritual protection from Archangel Michael. To reap the full effect of the following affirmations, you must speak them aloud, and you must give them with power and authority. Why must you say the affirmations out loud? Because when God created the world, God said: "Let there be Light." In other words, God used the power of the spoken word to create the world. A thought holds power, but the spoken word releases that power in the material world. To make maximum spiritual progress, you must learn to use the power of the spoken word. It is your birthright.

To give these affirmations, you must start by making an invocation. I suggest the following:

> **In the name of the Living God, in the name of Jesus Christ, I call to the heart of Archangel Michael to protect me from all imperfect energies, all forces of evil, all forces of anti-Christ and all forces of anti-peace.**

(Here you can make a personal request to Archangel Michael to protect you from specific dangers that you perceive.) After you make the invocation, repeat one or all of the following affirmations 3, 9, 33 or 144 times:

> **I accept the electronic Presence of Archangel Michael around me, and I fully accept that I am sealed from all imperfect energies.**

> **I consciously accept and know that with God all things are possible. Therefore, I accept that Archangel Michael seals me from all imperfect energies.**

I accept and affirm that Archangel Michael cuts me free from all imperfect energies, all forces of evil, all forces of anti-Christ and all forces of anti-peace.

In the name of Jesus Christ, I call forth the full flaming Presence of Archangel Michael to consume all imperfect energies, all forces of evil, all forces of anti-Christ and all forces of anti-peace that are attacking my lifestream. I accept this protection, and I know that I am sealed from all that is less than Christ-perfection.

To further seal you from the energies of this world, I offer you a special gift from my heart. I am willing to place the Seal of the Lord upon you and thereby seal you as one of my own. However, the law requires that you affirm this by using your free will. Therefore, I request that you repeat the following affirmation on a daily basis:

In the name of Jesus Christ,
I accept that the Seal of the Lord is upon me now.
I accept that the Seal of the Lord is upon me now.
I accept that the Seal of the Lord is upon me now.

After you complete a set of affirmations, I request that you seal the energies by giving the following statement:

In the name of Jesus Christ, I accept it done this hour in full power. Nevertheless Father, not my will, but thine be done. Amen.

To gain the full effect of these affirmations, you must repeat them daily. I am not going to tell you how much time you should spend on this because it truly is an individual matter. I know that many people feel burdened by negative energy. In fact, everyone should be able to quickly develop a sensitivity that will allow them to feel when they are being attacked by imperfect energies.

Whenever you feel such an attack, repeat the affirmations in this book until you feel that the negative energies are no longer affecting you. If you know that you have been attacked by negative energies over a long period of time, make a very determined effort to use these affirmations to seal yourself from such negative energies. This might require a great effort for a period of time until you feel that you have broken through to a new level of consciousness. You need to be sensitive to your individual situation, and in one of the following sections I will give you a tool for attaining this sensitivity.

22 | Techniques for Attaining Christhood

A decree matrix

For those who are serious about spiritual protection and the transformation of negative energy, I will suggest a powerful daily matrix. By giving a certain matrix on a daily basis, you build a momentum that increases the power of your decrees. You will then feel how the light flows from your I AM Presence through your Christ self and then through your mind. The following matrix is a good general guideline. However, be alert to your individual situation. If you are going through a difficult situation, give each decree more times than suggested here. If you are busy for a time, give the decrees less times rather than doing nothing at all. Be careful not to set an unrealistic goal. Many people make a decision to give too many decrees, and then they find it difficult to keep it up on a daily basis. Do not let this become a cause of stress. Remember the story about the tortoise and the hare, and set a goal you can keep every day.

My suggestion is to spend time each morning and each evening to give the decrees. In the morning, give the I AM Sealed decree once then the decree to Archangel Michael 9 times and the decree to Saint Germain 9 times. In the evening, give the I AM Sealed decree once then the decree to Astrea 9 times and the decree to Saint Germain 9 times. Do this for a three-month period to asses the effect this has on you. If you find that it has a positive effect then continue or use some of the other tools we have given. [NOTE: To find more tools for invoking spiritual light and for instructions on how to use them, see the website: *www.transcendencetoolbox.com*.]

I AM Sealed in a Sphere of Light

Instructions: Give the following decree one or three times. Visualize that you are sealed in a sphere of bright, white light. Visualize an intense violet light inside the sphere.

> In the name of Jesus Christ, I accept the flaming presence of my Christ self and I AM Presence all around me, as a perfect sphere of Christ Light, Christ Power, Christ Truth and Christ Love. I am sealed from all energies less than Christ perfection.
>
> I surrender all that is less than Christ perfection in my consciousness, and when the prince of this world comes, he has nothing in me. Therefore, the forces of this world have no power to separate me from my Christ self, my I AM Presence and my God.
>
> I surrender all sense of separation from God and the sense of being the doer. I accept that my I AM Presence is the true doer in my life, and that my Presence works hitherto and I work.
>
> I am an invincible surge of the Violet Flame of Freedom to fill me and to consume all imperfections in my consciousness, being and world. I am purified and made whole by the power of the Holy Spirit, and therefore I am spiritually reborn this day. I accept the alchemical union of my conscious self with my Christ self, now and forever.

By the power of my Christ self, I am set free to see that everything is God. I am free to be all I am in God, and therefore I affirm that I am here below all that I am Above.

I hereby go forth radiating the Love and Truth of Christ to all whom I meet, and I hold the immaculate concept for myself, for all life and for planet earth,

I am the Lord's and the fullness thereof.
All people are the Lord's and the fullness thereof.
The earth is the Lord's and the fullness thereof.

It is done this hour by the full power of the Living Christ within me. Therefore, it is finished. Amen.

Decree to Archangel Michael

Instructions: This decree is especially powerful for invoking the Presence of Archangel Michael and his protection. Give it at least 9 times every morning. Give the following preamble once.

In the name I AM THAT I AM, Jesus Christ, I call to my I AM Presence to flow through the I Will Be Presence that I AM and give these decrees with full power. I call to beloved Archangel Michael and Faith to shield me in your wings of electric blue light, and shatter and consume all imperfect energies and dark forces, including…

Instructions: Make a short call to direct the energies for a specific purpose. Then give the following decree nine times or more.

1. Michael Archangel, in your flame so blue,
there is no more night, there is only you.
In oneness with you, I am filled with your light,
what glorious wonder, revealed to my sight.

**Michael Archangel, your Faith is so strong,
Michael Archangel, oh sweep me along.
Michael Archangel, I'm singing your song,
Michael Archangel, with you I belong.**

2. Michael Archangel, protection you give,
within your blue shield, I ever shall live.
Sealed from all creatures, roaming the night,
I remain in your sphere, of electric blue light.

Michael Archangel, your Faith is so strong,
Michael Archangel, oh sweep me along.
Michael Archangel, I'm singing your song,
Michael Archangel, with you I belong.

3. Michael Archangel, what power you bring,
as millions of angels, praises will sing.
Consuming the demons, of doubt and of fear,
I know that your Presence, will always be near.

Michael Archangel, your Faith is so strong,
Michael Archangel, oh sweep me along.
Michael Archangel, I'm singing your song,
Michael Archangel, with you I belong.

4. Michael Archangel, God's will is your love,
you bring to us all, God's light from Above.
God's will is to see, all life taking flight,
transcendence of self, our most sacred right.

Michael Archangel, your Faith is so strong,
Michael Archangel, oh sweep me along.
Michael Archangel, I'm singing your song,
Michael Archangel, with you I belong.

With angels I soar,
as I reach for MORE.
The angels so real,
their love all will heal.
The angels bring peace,
all conflicts will cease.
With angels of light,
we soar to new height.

The rustling sound of angel wings,
what joy as even matter sings,
what joy as every atom rings,
in harmony with angel wings.

Instructions: Give the following sealing once.

In the name of the Divine Mother, I fully accept that the power of these calls is used to set free the Ma-ter light, so it can outpicture the perfect vision of Christ for my own life, for all people and for the planet. In the name I AM THAT I AM, it is done! Amen.

Decree to Elohim Astrea

The Bible uses the word "Elohim" as one of the names of God. In Hebrew Elohim is a plural word, meaning there is more than one Elohim. In reality, the earth was created by seven Elohim that each represents certain God qualities or spiritual rays. The Elohim named Astrea represents the purity of God and this decree is the most effective way to cut yourself free from the death consciousness and any demons, discarnate souls or spirits that have entered or attached themselves to your soul vehicle.

Give the following preamble once:

> In the name I AM THAT I AM, Jesus Christ, I call to my I Will Be Presence to flow through my being and give these decrees with full power. I call to beloved Mighty Astrea and Purity to cut me free from all imperfect energies and all ties to any dark forces or conditions not of the Light, including…

[Make personal calls]

1. Beloved Astrea, your heart is so true,
your Circle and Sword of white and blue,
cut all life free from dramas unwise,
on wings of Purity our planet will rise.

**Beloved Astrea, in God Purity,
accelerate all of my life energy,
raising my mind into true unity
with the Masters of love in Infinity.**

2. Beloved Astrea, from Purity's Ray,
send forth deliverance to all life today,
acceleration to Purity, I AM now free
from all that is less than love's Purity.

**Beloved Astrea, in oneness with you,
your circle and sword of electric blue,
with Purity's Light cutting right through,
raising within me all that is true.**

3. Beloved Astrea, accelerate us all,
as for your deliverance I fervently call,
set all life free from vision impure
beyond fear and doubt, I AM rising for sure.

**Beloved Astrea, I AM willing to see,
all of the lies that keep me unfree,
I AM rising beyond every impurity,
with Purity's Light forever in me.**

4. Beloved Astrea, accelerate life
beyond all duality's struggle and strife,
consume all division between God and man,
accelerate fulfillment of God's perfect plan.

**Beloved Astrea, I lovingly call,
break down separation's invisible wall,
I surrender all lies causing the fall,
forever affirming the oneness of All.**

Accelerate into Purity, I AM real,
Accelerate into Purity, all life heal,
Accelerate into Purity, I AM MORE,
Accelerate into Purity, all will soar.

Accelerate into Purity! (3X)
Beloved Elohim Astrea.

Accelerate into Purity! (3X)
Beloved Gabriel and Hope.

Accelerate into Purity! (3X)
Beloved Serapis Bey.

Accelerate into Purity! (3X)
Beloved I AM.

Sealing: In the name of the Divine Mother, I fully accept that the power of these calls is used to set free the Ma-ter light, so it can outpicture the perfect vision of Christ for my own life, for all people and for the planet. In the name I AM THAT I AM, it is done! Amen.

Decree to Saint Germain

Instructions: Give the following preamble once:

In the name I AM THAT I AM, Jesus Christ, I call to my I AM Presence to flow through the I Will Be Presence that I AM and give these decrees with full power. I call to beloved Saint Germain and Portia, the other Chohans and the Maha Chohan to release flood tides of light, to consume all blocks and attachments that prevent me from becoming one with the eternal flow of the seventh ray of creative freedom and ever-transcending oneness, including… *[Make personal calls]*

1. Saint Germain, your alchemy,
with violet fire now sets me free.
Saint Germain, I ever grow,
in freedom's overpowering flow.

**O Holy Spirit, flow through me,
I am the open door for thee.
O mighty rushing stream of Light,
transcendence is my sacred right.**

2. Saint Germain, your mastery,
of violet flame geometry.
Saint Germain, in you I see,
the formulas that set me free.

**O Holy Spirit, flow through me,
I am the open door for thee.
O mighty rushing stream of Light,
transcendence is my sacred right.**

3. Saint Germain, in Liberty,
I feel the love you have for me.
Saint Germain, I do adore,
the violet flame that makes all more.

**O Holy Spirit, flow through me,
I am the open door for thee.
O mighty rushing stream of Light,
transcendence is my sacred right.**

4. Saint Germain, in unity,
I will transcend duality.
Saint Germain, my self so pure,
your violet chemistry so sure.

**O Holy Spirit, flow through me,
I am the open door for thee.
O mighty rushing stream of Light,
transcendence is my sacred right.**

5. Saint Germain, reality,
in violet light I am carefree.
Saint Germain, my aura seal,
your violet flame my chakras heal.

**O Holy Spirit, flow through me,
I am the open door for thee.
O mighty rushing stream of Light,
transcendence is my sacred right.**

6. Saint Germain, your chemistry,
with violet fire set atoms free.

Saint Germain, from lead to gold,
transforming vision I behold.

**O Holy Spirit, flow through me,
I am the open door for thee.
O mighty rushing stream of Light,
transcendence is my sacred right.**

7. Saint Germain, transcendency,
as I am always one with thee.
Saint Germain, from soul I'm free,
I so delight in being me.

**O Holy Spirit, flow through me,
I am the open door for thee.
O mighty rushing stream of Light,
transcendence is my sacred right.**

8. Saint Germain, nobility,
the key to sacred alchemy.
Saint Germain, you balance all,
the seven rays upon my call.

**O Holy Spirit, flow through me,
I am the open door for thee.
O mighty rushing stream of Light,
transcendence is my sacred right.**

Sealing: In the name of the Divine Mother, I fully accept that the power of these calls is used to set free the Ma-ter light, so it can outpicture the perfect vision of Christ for my own life, for all people and for the planet. In the name I AM THAT I AM, it is done! Amen.

Attunement with the Christ within

I am fully aware that this book cannot answer all of your questions. Obviously, this book is written for a large number of people, and therefore I cannot give you answers about specific aspects of your personal situation. However, I do not intend to leave you comfortless. I have already told you that you have the capacity to commune directly with me and with your Christ Self. Establishing this communion might take some time and effort. Yet if you will use the following exercise, the process will be much easier.

The following exercise is a visualization designed to help you receive personal answers to any questions you might have. Before you perform this exercise, I strongly recommend that you use our decrees to seal yourself from the energies of the mass consciousness. You must understand that there are many forces in this world that will seek to prevent you from getting true answers. If these forces cannot prevent you from attempting direct communion with me, they will seek to give you false ideas and answers.

You must also realize that there are forces inside your own mind (the enemy within or the human ego) that will try to interfere with this communion. These forces will seek to give you the answers that they want you to have. It is a general human tendency that people hear what they want to hear. You must be aware of this tendency so that you can gradually build the discernment that allows you to see through imperfect answers and know the answers that come directly from me. The following exercise will be of great help in building your discernment and communion. However, using the aforementioned decrees will greatly increase the accuracy of the answers you are able to receive.

Go into a quiet room where you can remain undisturbed for some time (at least 10–15 minutes). Seat yourself in a comfortable chair so that you are not disturbed by discomfort in your physical body. Spend 5–10 minutes sealing yourself from imperfect energies, for example by giving the decree matrix in the previous section. Then, go into the following visualization:

- Visualize the angels of Archangel Michael surrounding your personal energy field. There are four angels, one on each side. These angels are 12 ft. tall and they carry swords that burn with a bright blue flame. They are fierce and able to protect you from any forces in this world. Now turn your attention to your personal Christ Self which is located right above your head. Give the following affirmation:

In the name of Jesus Christ, I invoke a wall of brilliant white light around my body, mind and energy field. I accept that this energy seals me from the energies of this world. I now invoke the Violet Flame to burn inside the wall of light and to consume all imperfect energies in my own being.

- Allow yourself a few moments to feel that you are completely sealed from the energies of this world.

- When you feel at peace, focus your attention at the center of your chest at the height of your physical heart. Visualize that a spiritual flame burns inside your chest. This spiritual flame does not require fuel to burn. It is the unfed flame.

- Focus your attention on this flame and allow your attention to enter the flame itself. Behind the flame, you see a doorway. Enter that doorway. As you go through the doorway, you move into a tunnel. As you move forward, you see the proverbial light at the end of the tunnel.

- Keep moving forward until you emerge from the tunnel and walk into the light.

- You now see that you have entered an exquisitely beautiful garden. The garden is surrounded by tall hedges. It has beautiful flower beds and walkways. In the center of the garden is a fountain that gently whispers. All over the garden, birds are singing cheerfully.

- As you walk into this garden, you feel that the cares of the world are simply falling away from you. The further you move into the garden, the more light and peaceful you feel.

- Simply keep walking and allow yourself to feel how the peace and tranquility of the garden absorbs all of your worries and cares. When you feel uplifted and at peace, take a moment to look around.

- As you look around, you see two seats carved from stone. Sit down in one seat and make yourself comfortable. Then, focus your attention on your heart and close your eyes. Allow yourself to feel that you are completely at peace in this beautiful garden. In fact, you somehow feel that this is home.

- Now imagine that you open your eyes and look at the seat in front of you. To your surprise, you notice that someone is now sitting in that seat. When you look closer, you realize that it is indeed I, your Jesus, who is sitting before you. Allow yourself to get comfortable in my Presence.

- Now focus your attention on my heart and allow yourself to feel that my heart radiates an unconditional love for you. Give yourself a few moments to accept that I love you unconditionally.

- Then, allow yourself to absorb my unconditional love for you and feel how it consumes everything that is imperfect and unreal. This is indeed the perfect love which casts out all fear and all other imperfect emotions.

- While you are seated in front of me and fully absorbed in my love, allow yourself to think back to your situation on earth. Do not allow yourself to be disturbed by any aspect of that situation. Simply bring your situation to your conscious awareness for a moment. Then, look at me again and in your mind formulate a question. Do not ask me what to do about your situation because you must use your free will to choose what to do. Ask me to show you a greater understanding of the situation so that you will know the right solution or answer.

- After you formulate the question, send it to me.

- Then close your eyes and focus your attention on my love. Allow yourself to be so absorbed in that love that you forget all the cares of the world.

- After some time of being absorbed in my love, your attention might naturally drift back to the question. Simply focus your attention on my heart and listen for an answer. If you do not receive an immediate answer, be not disturbed. Simply focus on my unconditional love and allow yourself to be absorbed in that love for as long as you like.

- When you feel you have absorbed what you can, when you feel that your heart has become the cup that runneth over with my love then visualize that you quietly leave the beautiful garden and walk back through the tunnel.

- You are now seated in the chair in your room. Give yourself a few moments to return back to your normal state of consciousness. Perhaps give another round of affirmations, especially the affirmations that I will give you in the next section, to seal the experience.

In your patience possess your soul

In the beginning, you might not get an immediate answer from this exercise. It might take some time before the answer reaches your conscious mind. Simply be alert and try to set aside a few moments every day to listen from within. After some time, be it hours, days or even weeks, the answer will come to you.

Repeat this exercise as often as you like. If you truly want answers about a specific situation, repeat the exercise daily for 33 days or until you have received sufficient inner direction. I recommend that you always have a notebook and pen next to you as you perform this exercise. After the visualization, take a few moments to write down any thoughts or insights that come to you. If you will make this part of the exercise, you will be amazed at the directions you will receive.

The purpose of this exercise is to help you attune your consciousness to me and to your personal Christ Self. After having performed this exercise for a while, you might feel that you can attain this attunement even during your daily activities. This is good. I desire you to have constant, at-will communion with me.

However, even when you begin to feel this communion, do not forget the exercise I have given you. Once in a while set aside time to go into my beautiful garden and commune with me. Forget me not.

Going to night school

I want you to know that many ascended masters maintain spiritual retreats above the earth. These retreats are not physical locations; they are located in the spiritual realm. The retreats serve as spiritual learning centers, and you can can travel to such centers in your "energy body" while your physical body is asleep. Your conscious self can then receive instructions that you often remember upon awakening or during the day.

I can assure you that you have already traveled to such centers (or you would not have been open to reading this book.) However, you can increase the frequency of these visits by silently making the following invocation before going to sleep:

> **In the name of the Living God, I call to the angels of Jesus Christ to escort my energy body to the spiritual retreat that Jesus wants me to attend. I call to the angels of Archangel Michael to protect my soul and my physical body and to help me return safely to my body. I pray to**

my beloved Christ Self to help me remember the instructions I receive and to help me use them wisely. I accept it done this hour with full power. Amen.

Christhood affirmations – Neophyte

In the following sections I will give you a very special gift from my heart. This gift has never before been released on this planet. My gift is a set of affirmations that are specifically designed to help you attain personal Christhood.

To use these affirmations, you must realize that the path to personal Christhood has several stages. Therefore, my presentation will be divided into several parts, and each part will address one of the stages of Christhood.

When you first discover the path of Christhood, you might have many questions or reservations concerning that path. You might find it difficult to fully accept that you are a son or daughter of God and that you have the potential to manifest personal Christhood. As long as you have an open mind, these questions and reservations are acceptable at this level of the path. However, because of such questions and reservations, you are what Saint Paul called a "babe in Christ."

Therefore, the main focus of your efforts should be to resolve all questions and reservations that stand between you and your progress on the path. You must strive for inner attunement, discernment and you must surrender all that stands between you and your God. The following affirmations are designed to help you accomplish this goal. You can give some or all of these affirmations. I recommend that you give each affirmation at least 3 times, or in multiples of 3. If you feel that one affirmation has special meaning to you then give that affirmation more often. A very powerful exercise is to give an affirmation 144 times.

Before giving any of the affirmations in the following section, give this invocation:

> In the name of the Living God, in the name of Jesus Christ, in the name of my own Christ Self, I call to the heart of my beloved Jesus Christ and I declare: Beloved Jesus, I am willing to be God-taught. I am willing to let go of all that is unreal. I am willing to walk with you to a higher understanding of the truth of God. Beloved Jesus, show me the way and give me the understanding that will empower me to walk in the Way of Light. Therefore, I affirm:
>
> Oh Jesus, I invite you into my temple, and I ask to be filled with your unconditional love.
>
> I accept the unconditional love of Jesus Christ, and I accept that I am worthy of that love.
>
> I accept and affirm that the Presence of Jesus Christ is with me always.
>
> I accept my freedom from all imperfections and pain of the past. Jesus delivers me now, and I am made whole.
> Oh Jesus, I accept that you are setting me free from all imperfect beliefs.
>
> Oh Jesus, I accept that you are delivering me

from all imperfect energies.

Oh Jesus, I accept that you are sealing me from all attacks by the forces of anti-Christ and anti-peace.

Oh Jesus, I am willing to walk the path of personal Christhood. Show me the way.

Oh Jesus, I accept your Sword of Truth, and I ask you to cleave the real from the unreal that I might see your Living Truth.

Oh Jesus, I accept that you are consuming my human ego, and I surrender it all to you.
[Instead of human ego, you can be more specific. For example, you can insert fear and doubt or anger.]

Oh Jesus, deliver me from all imperfections.

Oh Jesus, deliver me from all attachments to the things of this world.

I lovingly surrender all imperfections and attachments, and I know that Jesus delivers me now.

The things of this world mean nothing to me. I will follow you, Jesus Christ.
Jesus, set me free from all that is unreal, all that is unholy, all that is anti-Christ and all that is anti-peace. I accept that Jesus delivers me now.

I accept that the Living Truth and the Living Word of Christ is manifest in my being and world now.

Oh Jesus, be it unto me according to your will.

I accept and affirm that I am a true disciple of Jesus Christ. I surrender all attachments to the things of this world, and I follow Jesus always.

I accept that the Peace of Christ consumes all that is anti-peace in my being and world.
I fully accept the Peace of Christ that is beyond all understanding.

I fully surrender all imperfections, and I fully accept my Christhood now.

After you complete a set of affirmations, seal the energies by giving the following statement:

In the name of Jesus Christ, I accept it done this hour in full power. Nevertheless Father, not my will, but thine be done. Amen.

Christhood affirmations – Intermediate

At this level of the path, you have fully accepted that the path of personal Christhood is real. You have also accepted that you are worthy of walking that path. You might not be able to fully accept that you are a son or daughter of God or that you

22 | Techniques for Attaining Christhood

are a Christed being. However, you do accept your potential to become a Christed being.

You must focus on building a new sense of identity as a spiritual being. As you build this new identity, you must contemplate and begin to accept that you are indeed worthy of being a sister or brother of Jesus Christ. You might recall the situation recorded in Scripture where I am teaching a group of people. A disciple tells me that my mother and my brothers have come to see me. I make a gesture towards the crowd and say: "These are my brothers and sisters."

The significance of this statement is that being a brother or sister of Christ is not a matter of birth. It is a matter of choice. When you choose to accept your divine identity, you choose to become a brother or sister of Christ. Therefore, you must affirm that you are a brother or sister of Jesus Christ.

At this level of the path, you must also seek to acquire a vision of the Kingdom of God. You must take your attention off all of the imperfections found in this world. Then, you must focus your attention on the perfection of God and see only Christ-victory and Christ-perfection in your personal situation and in the world around you.

I am not asking you to disconnect yourself from reality. Remember that I want you to become wise as serpents and harmless as doves. Therefore, I do not want you to be blind to the problems of this world. However, I want you to avoid giving these problems power through your attention. You must focus most of your attention on the perfection of God's kingdom. You must visualize and affirm the manifestation of God's kingdom in your personal life and in the world around you.

Some of the following affirmations contain the words "brother/sister." Obviously, if you are male, say only "brother," and it you are female, say only "sister." Before giving the following affirmations, give this invocation:

> In the name of the Living God, in the name of Jesus Christ, in the name of my Christ Self, I invoke the manifestation of the electronic Presence of Jesus Christ in my personal forcefield. Beloved Jesus, I invite you into my being, and I affirm that I am your brother/sister. Therefore, I say:
>
> I accept that I am the brother/sister of Jesus Christ, and I know that Jesus protects me from all evil.
>
> I consciously accept and affirm that I am the brother/sister of Jesus Christ.
>
> Oh Jesus, I accept that I am your brother/sister.
>
> I consciously know and affirm that I have absolute faith in my brother Jesus Christ. Oh Jesus, I do trust you fully.
>
> Oh Jesus, I accept that I am your brother/sister, and I surrender all sense of separation from you. I fully accept that I am the brother/sister of Jesus Christ, and I lovingly surrender all lesser sense of identity.
>
> I am the brother/sister of Jesus Christ, and I am the Kingdom of God manifest where I am.

> **Oh God, I gratefully accept your kingdom and your abundant life manifest in my world.**
>
> **In the name of Jesus Christ, I accept the abundant life manifest now.**
>
> **I am the Kingdom of God manifest where I am.**

After you complete a set of affirmations, seal the energies by giving the following statement:

> **In the name of Jesus Christ, I accept it done this hour in full power. Nevertheless Father, not my will, but thine be done. Amen.**

Christhood affirmations – Advanced

At this level of the path, you have fully accepted that you are a spiritual being and that you are a brother or sister of Christ. However, you must now go beyond this sense of identity. You must overcome all sense of distance between you and your personal Christ Self. You must not only be a member of Christ's family, you must attain union with Christ.

The first step towards this union is to go through the initiation that I referred to as the "marriage of the lamb." This is the alchemical marriage whereby your conscious self is married to your personal Christ Self. The Conscious You literally becomes the bride of Christ. At this level of the path, you must let go of all sense of separation from Christ, all sense of distance between you and Christ. You are not simply related to or affiliated with Christ. You are not simply a person with the potential to put on Christhood. You are Christ.

Before you give any of the following affirmations, give this invocation:

> In the name of the Living God, in the name of Jesus Christ, in the name of my Christ Self, I call directly to the heart of God and I say: My Father-Mother in Heaven, I accept and affirm that I am your son/daughter. I accept and affirm our oneness, and in that oneness I say:
>
> I accept that I am the bride of Christ, and I know that Jesus protects me from all evil.
>
> Oh Jesus, I accept and affirm that I am your bride, and I surrender all sense of separation from you.
>
> I fully accept that I am the bride of Christ, and I lovingly surrender all lesser sense of identity.
>
> I am the bride of Christ, and I am the Kingdom of God manifest where I am.
>
> I accept and affirm that I am the bride of Christ. I am the bride of Christ, and I accept my wholeness now.
>
> I am the Living Christ where I am.
>
> I am the Christ: here, now and forever.

After you complete a set of affirmations, seal the energies by giving the following statement:

In the name of Jesus Christ, I accept it done this hour in full power. Nevertheless Father, not my will, but thine be done. Amen.

The I am affirmations

As you attain this level of oneness with Christ, you earn the right to use the affirmations that I gave during my mission. You will notice that I gave a number of affirmations beginning with the words "I am." I want you to feel free to use any of these affirmations, such as:

I am the Way, the Truth and the Life.

I am the open door, which no human can shut.

I am the Light of the world.

I am come that all might have life and that they might have it more abundantly.

I and my Father are one.

Use the following affirmation to resurrect Christ-perfection in specific situations. For example, you can say: I am the Resurrection and The life of my financial situation, I am the Resurrection and the Life of my health or I am the Resurrection and the Life of my nation or the world.

I am the Resurrection and the Life.

Becoming my twin

When you have achieved union with Christ through the alchemical marriage, you have the option of going through another initiation. I encourage you to study the Gospel of Thomas, which was discovered at Nag Hammadi in 1945. Some of my other disciples referred to Thomas as my twin.

Obviously, this does not mean that Thomas was born as my physical twin. It means that Thomas had attained a level of union with me so that he could act as my twin in this world. Even after my resurrection and ascension, I could speak and act through Thomas because we were truly spiritual twins. Therefore, Thomas was the Christ below as I am the Christ Above.

I am Jesus Christ, and I desire to bring many changes to this dark planet. Because of the Law of Free Will, I can bring these changes only through those in physical embodiment who elect to be my mouthpieces, my hands and feet.

If you so desire, you have the potential to become my twin. You have the potential to be the Christ below as I am the Christ Above. Through this extraordinary union, you and I can be as Above, so below. You can be the Christ below as I am the Christ here Above. When you feel that you are ready for this initiation, use the following affirmations:

As Above in Jesus, so below in me.

I and Jesus are one.

I accept and affirm that I walk the earth as the twin of Jesus Christ.

I am the twin of Jesus Christ.

NOTE: Many more affirmations and decrees can be found on *www.transcendencetoolbox.com.*

23 | THE SECOND COMING OF CHRIST

I am fully aware that millions of sincere and devout Christians are looking forward to an event that they describe as the second coming of Christ. There are many different theories and beliefs about this second coming and what it might be like. However, most of them describe an event in which I will appear physically and remove all darkness and imperfections from this planet. I will appear as the King, and I will bring God's kingdom to earth.

I am Jesus Christ, and I must tell you the truth about this matter. I very much desire to see the second coming of Christ as a physical reality of this planet. I very much desire to see my Father's kingdom manifest on earth. However, I must tell you frankly that the event envisioned by most Christians simply will not come to pass. Allow me to explain why.

Let us begin by considering the historical fact that shortly before the year 1000 AD many Christians believed that the second coming of Christ was imminent. People believed that I would appear physically and roll up the world as a scroll. It is an undeniable fact that these expectations were not fulfilled. Likewise, shortly before the year 2000 many Christians expected the second coming of Christ as the inauguration of the new millennium. This did not come to pass.

Based on these observations, I hope you will accept the simple fact that I will not suddenly appear and remove all darkness from this world. There are two good reasons why this event will not come to pass.

The outer reason is the Law of Free Will. I have already told you that humankind has created the current conditions on planet earth. Therefore, these conditions are the sole responsibility of humankind. People must learn that they are responsible for their use and misuse of God's energy. Therefore, God will not simply take away from them that which they have created in violation of his laws.

God has provided a way out so that people can uncreate the darkness they have created in ignorance. However, people must do so consciously and willingly. Planet earth is a schoolroom for lifestreams. If God or I suddenly removed all imperfections created by human beings, how could people possibly learn the lesson of life? When you accept the Law of Free Will, it should not be difficult to see that the second coming of Christ, as envisioned by many Christians, would prevent people from learning the lesson of life.

I am Jesus Christ. I am a spiritual teacher. I want to see people learn the lesson of life. I will go far in my attempts to help people learn that lesson. However, I will not take away people's opportunity to learn the lesson.

The true second coming

Let me now explain the inner reason why the second coming of Christ will not be as envisioned by many Christians. I have already told you that it is the deepest desire of both God and myself to see you and all other human beings walk the path of personal Christhood and eventually put on the fullness of that Christhood. God wants all of his sons and daughters to come home and join the wedding feast in his kingdom. However, you can come home only by putting on the wedding garment of personal Christhood.

My beloved Brother of Light, Gautama Buddha, gave a very profound teaching that relates to this topic. The essence of Buddhism is that human beings have fallen into a lower state of consciousness dominated by maya, or illusion. Because of this illusion, people cannot see the fundamental reality that everything is the Buddha nature.

Therefore, people have built a false sense of identity as mortal beings, and they cannot see themselves as the Buddha incarnate. The essence of Buddhism is that all lifestreams must strive to reach a state of consciousness called "enlightenment." When you reach enlightenment, you realize that everything is the Buddha nature. Therefore, you see and accept that you already are the Buddha.

Many followers of Buddhism subscribe to the belief that the goal of Buddhism is to become the Buddha. This belief is both correct and incorrect at the same time. A human being cannot suddenly shift from a state of consciousness that is dominated by illusion into a state of consciousness of full enlightenment. Therefore, all spiritual teachings on this planet talk about a path. If you are a follower of Buddhism, you are walking a path towards enlightenment. However, you are not walking a path whereby you are becoming the Buddha.

The very concept of becoming something implies a distance between you and what you are becoming. The very essence of Buddhism is that everything already is the Buddha nature. Therefore, you are not in the process of becoming the Buddha. You are in the process of coming to the realization that you already are the Buddha. This is not simply a play on words. It is essential that you realize the difference between being and becoming.

Overcoming separation

How do you come to the realization that you already are the Buddha? You must overcome the sense that you are separated from the Buddha, that you are not yet the Buddha. As long as you think that you have to become the Buddha, as long as you think that you have to become something that you are not, there is a sense of separation and distance between you and Buddhahood. As long as there is this sense of separation or distance, you are not the Buddha.

The consciousness of Buddhahood is a state of consciousness that is higher than the consciousness of Christhood. Yet in this context I desire you to realize that what I have said about Buddhahood equally applies to Christhood.

When I talk to you about the path of personal Christhood, I want you to realize that this is indeed a gradual path whereby you raise your level of consciousness to a higher level. This path cannot be traversed in one giant leap. You must travel this path by taking many small steps. Yet the end goal of the path is that you accept your true identity as a Christed being. In other words, the goal of the path is not that you become the Christ. The goal of the path is that you come to the realization that you already are the Christ and that you were never separated from your Father in Heaven. That sense of separation was simply an illusion; it was maya.

The practical implications of this is that as long as you identify the Christ as being someone or something outside yourself, you cannot fully merge with that Christ. For me as a spiritual teacher this fact presents an interesting dilemma.

23 | The Second Coming of Christ

I am the spiritual teacher who was appointed by God to descend to this planet and demonstrate the path of personal Christhood. I could demonstrate that path only by walking the path and therefore putting on my personal Christhood. When you put on that personal Christhood, you literally overcome all sense of separation between your sense of self and the universal Christ mind. You are an individualization of that Christ mind. You are the Christ in embodiment. That is why I made many statements that began with the words "I am." I am sure you recall some of these statements: "I am the Resurrection and the Life," "I am the Way, the Truth and the Life" and "I and my Father are one."

Can you now see my dilemma? In order to demonstrate the path of personal Christhood, I must be the Christ, I must become one with the universal Christ mind. When I achieve that oneness, everything I do and say reflects that oneness. Therefore, my statements reflect the fact that I am the Christ.

Yet when people hear another person say: "I am the Christ," the relativity of the death consciousness automatically makes these people believe that the person is something which they are not. In a sense, as long as a person is dominated by the death consciousness, that person obviously is not the Christ in embodiment. That person has the potential to be the Christ in embodiment. Yet if the person identifies the Christ as someone else, such as myself, the person might solidify the sense of being separated from Christ. In other words, the very act whereby I demonstrated Christhood can, if misunderstood, prevent people from personally attaining that Christhood.

I came to show people the open door that no human can shut, namely the door of personal Christhood. If people do not understand my true teachings then I become an idol that prevents people from walking through the door that I walked through. I hope you realize that this is the last thing I want to see happen.

A new sense of identity

How do you become the Christ in embodiment? By overcoming all sense of separation or distance between you (your sense of identity) and the universal Christ mind. The problem is that as long as you think that someone outside of you is the Christ (especially if you think that person is the only Christ), then you probably cannot fully accept that you are the Christ. To accept your personal Christhood, you simply cannot identify the Christ as being something or someone outside or apart from you. In unity, there can be no separation or distance.

The point I am making here is that if I appeared on earth in some sort of physical manifestation, that appearance would actually make it more difficult for people to put on their personal Christhood. You might remember that I warned people about false appearances related to my second coming. I told you that if people say that the Christ has appeared here or there, you should not go there. Why did I make that statement? Because as long as you think the Christ is appearing somewhere outside of you, you cannot accept that the Christ is appearing inside of you.

What I am saying here is that the second coming of Christ is indeed a real event which I and my Father are looking forward to with great anticipation. However, the second coming of Christ is not an event whereby the Christ will appear in the form of the individual known as Jesus Christ. The second coming of Christ is an event whereby the universal Christ mind will appear in individualized form through those people who are willing to walk the path of personal Christhood. In other words, the second coming of Christ is an event whereby the Christ appears in you. This idea of the second coming in you is not blasphemy. It is very much part of God's plan.

When I appeared as the sole representative of the universal Christ, the powers that be quickly killed me. I do not want to see that happen again. Therefore, I want thousands of people to put on the fullness of their personal Christhood. When that happens, the powers on this planet simply cannot kill all of them (and therefore are likely to kill none). I also want millions of people to put on a high degree of personal Christhood so that they can bring forth the Living Word that I am. When that happens, the powers that be simply cannot silence all of them.

Therefore, I am asking you to understand that I do not want the first coming of Christ (in me) to become a roadblock that prevents the second coming of Christ (in you).

I am Jesus Christ, and at this moment I am kneeling before your lifestream at inner levels. I am pleading with you to please consider these ideas. Please accept that your personal Christhood is the best hope I have for bringing my Father's kingdom to this planet. Please accept that I desire to see you put on the fullness of your personal Christhood. Please accept that I also desire to see thousands of your brothers and sisters put on the fullness of their Christhood. Please surrender the entire idea that there is only one person who can become the Christ.

In reality, there is no competition between Christed beings. My Father's grace is indeed sufficient for all. When God individualized himself as you, God gave you a portion of his being. However, a portion of infinity is still infinity. Therefore, you do not lose anything by recognizing the Christ in your brothers and sisters. God is all and God is in all.

If you have one part of God's Being, you have access to all of God's Being. Simply accept that you are a part of the allness of God. Then accept that your spiritual brothers and sisters are also part of the allness of God. In fact, all that was ever made is part of the allness of God. You are a part of God's Being. A part of God cannot be apart from God.

24 | WHAT YOU CAN DO FOR JESUS

I am fully aware that many of the ideas in this book can be shocking to people who have grown up in a Christian culture. I am fully aware that many of my readers need to go through a process of inner transformation before they can fully accept the ideas I am bringing forth in this book. Many people need to go through some soul-searching before they can accept their own potential to walk the path of personal Christhood.

I do not want to rush you through this process. I want you to take the necessary time to internalize my ideas and to come to an inner resolution and an inner understanding of what this book means for you and your personal life. However, I must tell you that you will make things far easier for yourself if you will engage in a process of seeking greater understanding.

You must understand that this book was written for a specific purpose, namely to awaken your inner memory of your potential to walk the path of Christhood. I obviously cannot cover all possible topics in this book. Consequently, I am aware that for some people this book might raise many questions.

To answers such questions, I and other ascended masters have brought forth additional books through this messenger. I am also offering you another way to resolve the questions you have as a result of reading this book. I can assure you that if modern technology had been available to me during my mission on earth, I would indeed have made use of it. Therefore, I intend to make use of it today.

I have instructed my messenger to create a website that will give you an opportunity to pose questions directly to me and other ascended masters (*www.ascendedmasteranswers.com*). I will then answer these questions through my messenger.

I also hope you will realize that it truly is not my desire to make you co-dependent on an outer source. What I really want to see is that you attain such inner attunement with your Christ Self and with me that I can give you answers directly in your heart. Therefore, use our books and websites only as tools for expanding your inner attunement with me. Use the exercises I have given in this book for increasing your attunement with me. Make a sincere effort to purge your mind from all incorrect beliefs. Make a sincere effort to heal your psychology.

If you will use the tools I have given you, you can quickly go through a personal transformation and raise yourself into a state of inner peace. This is what I desire to see for you. However, I cannot make it happen for you. You must make it happen through your own choosing.

Your divine plan

I am aware that many of the readers of this book will feel a great inner desire to help me bring God's kingdom to earth. Naturally, this desire will prompt you to take some form of outer action. In other words, I know that many of my true followers will ask: "Jesus, what can I do for you?"

I want to assure you that there is much you can do for me. Before a lifestream comes into embodiment on planet earth, that lifestream meets with its spiritual teachers. In many cases, I am part of this team. The lifestream and its spiritual teachers create a plan for the lifestream's coming embodiment. This plan has the following elements:

- A plan for how you can pay back your personal karma and fulfill your debts to life.

- A plan for how you can bring a unique gift to this planet. This can be a specific idea or quality that only you are capable of expressing. I like to call this your "sacred labor."

What I am telling you here is that your lifestream and your spiritual teachers created a divine plan for this lifetime. Obviously, when a lifestream is born it often loses the conscious memory of this divine plan. Yet most people have some inner sense of what they came to do in this life. And all people have the potential to regain the conscious memory of their divine plan.

You must understand that each lifestream has a unique divine plan. What I want to see for you is that you fulfill your personal divine plan. Therefore, I cannot tell you what you should do to help me bring God's kingdom to earth. This is far too personal and individualized to be expressed in a book like this. Furthermore, I do not want you to receive instructions from any source outside yourself pertaining to your divine plan. It is important that you get inner direction so that your outer consciousness can fully accept and internalize your divine plan.

I am setting you free

How can you find out about your divine plan? Let me make a suggestion. Most people have something that pulls them away from executing their divine plan. This is usually an attachment to the things of this world. It might be a great (but unbalanced) zeal of fighting for a particular outer cause. It can be an attachment to certain people, such as spouses or family members. It can be a sense of unworthiness or other psychological problems. It can be loyalty to a particular outer organization. It can be a fear that unless you follow certain outer rules, you will not be saved.

There are numerous attachments that can pull you into a frame of mind in which you think you have to live your life a certain way or attempt to turn yourself into a certain type of person. Such attachments always spring from the relativity of the death consciousness, and they obscure your inner vision so that you cannot see your divine plan. These attachments are often characterized by a certain feeling of obligation or duty. You feel that you simply have to do something. You feel compelled to do something.

As you walk the path of personal Christhood, you must free yourself from these old, worn-out habits. Therefore, I would like to help you start a new cycle of spiritual growth.

I am Jesus Christ, and I am your Savior and your spiritual teacher. I am right now standing before your lifestream at inner levels, and I am releasing you from all attachments and sense of obligation related to this world. I want you to feel free of any and all attachments you have to the things of this world. I want you to let go of all feelings of "I should," "I must" or "I have to."

I want you to examine yourself to determine which attachments you have. Then, I want you to allow yourself to feel that I, Jesus Christ, am releasing you from these attachments.

I want you to feel completely free from these attachments. I want you to feel that there is nothing you should do and there is nothing you have to do. You are simply free of all of these outer attachments, obligations and responsibilities. You are free of all sense that you have to live your life a certain way or that you have to be a certain type of person. I am Jesus Christ, and I am releasing you from all of this, and I am asking you to accept the freedom that I am giving you. I now want you to set aside time to use the tools I have given you in this book:

- Make an effort to seal yourself from the mass consciousness.

- Make an effort to purge your mind of false beliefs.

- Study this book and other spiritual teachings.

- Diligently use the technique for tuning in to my heart and seeking answers directly from me.

If you will use these tools for a period of time, I can guarantee you that you will begin to gain a new sense of inner direction, a new sense of purpose and a new sense of meaning. You will begin to know, through an inner knowing that is based on the Rock of Christ, what is included in your divine plan.

Strive for balance

I hope you can see the psychological value of going through this exercise. I am aware that many people have great zeal and fervor, and they want to help bring the Kingdom of God to earth. Yet many of these people have allowed their vision to be clouded by the relativity of the death consciousness and by their own self interest. Therefore, they easily become misled into using inappropriate means, unlawful means, in their attempt to bring in the Kingdom of God. As I explained earlier in this book, this is not the acceptable offering.

I am sad to tell you that there are millions of people on this planet, and they are found in every religion, including Christianity, who believe that they are doing God's work. Yet because their motives are influenced by the relativity of the death consciousness, they are in reality pushing God's kingdom further away from this planet.

The way of extremism and fanaticism is not the true way. The true way is the middle way of Christ discernment. It is the way of balance in all things. It is the way of love.

Let me give you an example of what I do not want you to do. The logical consequence of the teachings I am giving in this book is that many Christian churches are promoting false teachings about me and about the true path of Christhood. Therefore, a person with an extremist or zealous attitude might reason that it is his or her holy duty to engage in a battle with mainstream Christianity and to expose its shortcomings.

Let me assure you that I do not want any of my true followers to engage in such a conflict. I do not want to see this book become a weapon in the eternal human power struggle because this would only prejudice people against this book and my true teachings. More importantly, I do not want you to start accusing your brothers and sisters of anything whatsoever. Do not point the finger at anyone. Do not accuse them of anything.

What I want you to do is to internalize the truth of my inner teachings. I want you to focus all of your attention on developing your personal Christhood. My purpose for releasing you of all obligations is to help you set aside all preconceived ideas of what you should or should not do.

In other words, I am not saying that I do not want you to do anything for me. I am saying that I do not want you to act from the relativity of the death consciousness. I want you to make a sincere effort to go within and attain a certain measure of Christhood. Then act based on the insights you get directly from your Christ Self and from me. Do not allow the forces of this world, including the forces in your own psychology, to push you into anything.

What I am asking you to do here is to set aside all preconceived ideas. Go within and seek first the Kingdom of God and his righteousness. The Kingdom of God is the Christ consciousness. His righteousness is the right use of your free will by making choices based on Christ discernment.

Seek first the Christ consciousness, and then all else will be added unto you. Through your personal Christhood, you will get inner direction, and then you will know what to do. Your actions will then be based on the Rock of Christ instead of the shifting sands of the death consciousness. You will no longer act based on some decision by the lower mind. You will act as a natural extension of who you are. Get out of the "I should" consciousness and get into the "I AM" consciousness.

The guiding rod

Let me give you a guiding rod for determining whether your actions spring from the lower or higher consciousness. The death consciousness is characterized by a number of imperfect feelings. People who are extremists or fanatics are always driven by such feelings. Let me describe the most common of these imperfect feelings:

- **Fear.** Many devoutly religious people think they are doing God's work, but their actions are motivated by fear. They might fear God, they might fear punishment, they might fear eternal damnation, they might fear hell or they might fear some kind of prophecy. Therefore, they seek to instill fear in everyone they meet. They think that fear of God somehow brings you closer to God. Not so. Your soul will always seek to run away from what it fears.

- **Anger and Hatred.** Many devoutly religious people think they are doing God's work, but their actions are motivated by anger. The bottom line is that anger is always anger against God and against yourself. However, in most cases anger is expressed as anger towards another group of people. This group of people becomes the scapegoat. People who act based on anger and hatred might think they are doing God's work. Yet in reality they are not for God, they are against someone else. Do not allow yourself to fight against anyone or anything. Fight darkness only by bringing the Light and the Truth of Christ.

- **Pride.** Many devoutly religious people think they are doing God's work, but their actions are motivated by a need for self-aggrandizement. They are not seeking to glorify God, they are seeking to glorify their own egos. This often causes people to feel self-righteous, and they begin to think that they are better or more important than other people. They also tend to think that their religion is superior to any other religion and that other people must be made to see this.

I want you to increase your sensitivity so that you begin to realize that each of these impure feelings have a specific vibration. All feelings are energy, and all energy has a certain frequency. Your inner sense of the heart is fully capable of recognizing the frequencies of imperfect feelings. By becoming consciously aware of this ability, you can instantly know when a person is motivated by an imperfect feeling. By using this sensitivity while looking in the mirror, you can instantly know about your own motives. Be honest with yourself. Be sincere. If you detect an imperfect motive or feeling, use the tools I have given you to set yourself free from that feeling. Surrender it to me, and I will help you become free.

Put on your Christhood

What I am telling you is that the most important thing you can do for me is to put on your personal Christhood. With your outer consciousness attuned to your Christ Self, you will gain a clear inner direction that will show you what you can do for me. You will know how to give people the Living Truth of Christ instead of giving them an outer doctrine or a set of rules.

When your actions and motives are based on the Rock of Christ, everything springs from love. Therefore, I can give you a guiding rod for evaluating the purity of your motives and actions:

- Ask yourself why you feel compelled to engage in a certain activity. Are you motivated by love?

- If you are motivated by love, you will not feel a sense of attachment. You will not feel that this is something you simply have to do. In other words, you will not obsess about the activity, and you will not feel a compulsive need to do something.

- Non-attachment means that you are not attached to the outcome of your actions. In other words, you do not expect that other people will respond a certain way or that God or life will somehow give you something in return.

- When you are non-attached, when you are acting from love, you are not expecting anything in return. You are simply giving the way God gives. Freely you have received, and freely you must give. God lets it rain upon the just and the unjust because God gives his love unconditionally. You must do the same. If you find yourself giving with conditions, if you find that there are strings attached to your gift then you are not fully acting from the Christ consciousness.

- When you are acting as the Christ, you are not giving with the expectancy of a reward. You are giving as a natural expression of who you are. Therefore, the act of giving releases its own reward.

- When your motives are based on love and free from attachment, you find yourself able to act from a state of inner peace. If you find yourself contemplating a new activity, check your inner sense of peace. It is like a barometer, and you can learn to read it. If the barometer is not at peace, reconsider your motives and feelings about the activity. Then, use the tools I have given you to seek inner peace before you act. Do not allow the forces of this world to fool or manipulate you into acting in a state of non-peace.

My peace I give unto you. My peace I leave with you. When your motives are pure and grounded in love, you have ultimate respect for other people's free will. You simply give them the cup of cold water in Christ's name, and you leave them to decide what they will do with it.

You lead people to water, but you do not seek to force or manipulate them into drinking. You do what you know is right, but you are not attached to the outcome of your actions. In Western culture people have traditionally been far too attached to results. As you begin to grow in Christhood, you will realize that the process itself is far more important than the outcome. I am the Way, the Truth and the Life. In the Christ consciousness there are no limitations; there is only continued progress.

Do not become so focused on a specific result that you forget to appreciate and enjoy the journey towards that result. The reason the end cannot justify the means is that what matters to God is not the end, but the means you use to get there. God wants you to come home, but God does not want you to harm yourself or others in the process. Therefore, God wants you to be at peace as you follow your personal path. Do not rush in where angels fear to enter. It is better to pause for a moment and establish inner peace than to rush forward and lose sight of the Kingdom of God.

God is everywhere in his creation. God is present with you at every step of your personal journey. Look for the God who is smiling to you behind many disguises. Once you know what to look for, it is not difficult to see the Living Truth. When you see that truth, the truth will set you free. How can you be free if you have no inner peace?

Inner peace is freedom. Let all of your actions spring from inner peace.

About the Author

Kim Michaels is an accomplished writer and author. He has conducted spiritual conferences and workshops in 14 countries, has counseled hundreds of spiritual students and has done numerous radio shows on spiritual topics. Kim has been on the spiritual path since 1976. He has studied a wide variety of spiritual teachings and practiced many techniques for raising consciousness. Since 2002 he has served as a messenger for Jesus and other ascended masters. He has brought forth extensive teachings about the mystical path, many of them available for free on his websites: *www.askrealjesus.com, www.ascendedmasteranswers.com, www.ascendedmasterlight.com* and *www.transcendencetoolbox.com*. For personal information, visit Kim at *www.KimMichaels.info*.

www.ingramcontent.com/pod-product-compliance
Lightning Source LLC
Chambersburg PA
CBHW050101170426
43198CB00014B/2420